JONATHAN HANCOCK'S
MINDPOWER SYSTEM

Jonathan Hancock won the World Student Memory
Championships two years running before becoming
World Memory Champion in 1994. He is 22 years
old and a graduate of Christ Church, Oxford. He
now works as a freelance broadcaster and lives in
Oxford.

Jonathan Hancock's Mindpower System

A Step-by-Step Guide to Improving Your Memory

Hodder & Stoughton

First published in Great Britain in 1995 by Hodder & Stoughton
A division of Hodder Headline PLC

10 9 8 7 6 5 4 3 2 1

British Library Cataloguing in Publication Data
Hancock, Jonathan
Jonathan Hancock's Mindpower System:
A Step-by-Step Guide to Improving Your Memory
I. Title
153.1

ISBN 0 340 64030 8

Typeset by Hewer Text Composition Services, Edinburgh
Printed and bound in Great Britain by
Cox and Wyman Ltd, Reading.

Hodder and Stoughton
A division of Hodder Headline PLC
338 Euston Road
London NW1 3BH

To my family,

for all the good memories.

CONTENTS

Part Three – MINDPOWER FOR NUMBERS 119

Part Four – MINDPOWER FOR LIFE   181

INTRODUCTION

Shuffle a pack of playing cards for me. If you'll give me a minute to look through them all, I will tell you the order of the cards from memory, forwards or backwards. Name any card, and I'll tell you where it appears in the sequence. Shuffle twenty packs of cards for me, mix them all together into one huge pile if you like, and I'll do the same. I can memorise anything. Give me fifty telephone numbers – I'll recall them faster than you can find them in a directory. Write down a random sequence of ones and noughts – make it a thousand if they'll fit on the page – and I can read them back to you from memory. I can learn names, words, pictures, poems – but ask me if I have a photographic memory, and my answer is an emphatic No. In fact, if by 'photographic' you mean remembering something without even having to think about it, then mine is the most *un*-photographic memory imaginable.

What I have is a memory that I've learnt how to use. It works because I make it work; it's not trickery, not a con, but at the same time it's not some mysterious gift I was born with. I just decided that I was going to start remembering things, to start using my mind and benefiting from its full potential and power.

It was a decision motivated by an ambition. Since childhood I had been fascinated by the *Guinness Book of Records* and the idea of being 'the best in the world'. As a family we had always played a lot of card games, and I also enjoyed learning and performing card tricks, so I became most interested in the record for memorising shuffled packs of cards. I knew I couldn't possibly remember long sequences of cards just like that, but perhaps there was a way of making it easier – some method I could develop to help lodge the order of hundreds of cards in my mind. I started to experiment.

Six months later I was the proud owner of a world record. Even more importantly, I had made a crucial discovery. Faced with information to learn, the memory doesn't work unless you *make* it work. But, if you can get to grips with how your mind works and make a decision to use it, the results are phenomenal. We all have at our disposal a living computer more powerful than anything created in an electronics factory, a miraculous machine capable of making more connections than there are atoms in the universe.

The aim of the *Mindpower System* is to show you how to take it out of its box and start putting it to use.

HOW TO USE THIS BOOK

The book is divided into four parts. As well as containing tips and guidelines for specific areas of memory – telephone numbers, faces, foreign words, etc – each part also works to build up a wider picture. *Mindpower* is not a system which employs just one method; it is the ability to use many different techniques, combining and refining them to suit your own needs.

Part One outlines four basic *Mindpower* rules, the central principles of memory.

Part Two focuses on words, explaining techniques for remembering foreign languages, difficult words in English, essays, quotations, poems and plays.

Part Three is all about numbers; how to remember telephone and credit-card numbers, as well as the numbers in dates and times, and how to make use of numbers to help remember other information.

Part Four demonstrates that *Mindpower* techniques can be combined and adapted to suit any situation. With the basic skills at your fingertips, you need never again forget a name, a face, recipe, speech, appointment, errand . . .

As you read through each part, concentrate on the key areas that are of most use to you. These will help you with your immediate memory needs, but there are also more general techniques to be absorbed and put into practice. You may not need to know many numbers, but even a simple number system can help you to learn names, words or essays. You might think that your days of learning foreign vocabulary are over, but these same techniques can be applied to remembering quotations, scripts, addresses, or tricky spellings in English.

The more techniques you learn, the better prepared you'll be to commit *anything* to memory. Read through the suggestions, practise memorising the examples, and you'll amaze yourself with the power of your own mind. Put your new skills into practice as soon as possible; while your general awareness of *Mindpower* is still growing, the specific benefits will be plain to see.

Of course, this could all be wholly unnecessary. Here's an experiment: printed below is a list of forty words. Give yourself a couple of minutes to learn them all in the order they appear here.

CANDLESTICK, CHEESE, SCISSORS, PARIS, BAS-KET, HOT, COAT, BICYCLE, HORSE, TABLET, TREE, BUTCHER, CADDY, EIGHT, TEA, LIME, RICH, BATH, HOCKEY-STICK, MARCH, GRASS, TANK, SMELL, BISHOP, ASH, DONALD, CREAM, PEAR, RHINO, TRAIN, BOX, LIFT, TAPE, FOREST, MILE, TELE-PHONE, PEPPER, AMSTERDAM, GLOVE, ROAD

When the two minutes have passed, cover up the list and read it back from memory. Each word must be recalled exactly as it is written above, and in the correct order.

There are two levels of success: either you managed the task perfectly, or you didn't. If you fall into the first category, you have my congratulations, and permission to leave at this point. But if you had less than perfect success, then the *Mindpower System* is of use to you.

Even by the end of Part One, I can guarantee you'll be able to remember this or any list, forwards or backwards – and that's only the beginning. All that is required is a desire to start using your mind.

PART ONE

MINDPOWER

Odd as it may seem, our natural tendency is to try to learn things without using our minds at all. How often do you find yourself having to take down a telephone number, address or list of directions with no pen or paper to hand? When it happens, chances are that you try to perform a juggling act with the facts, desperately repeating them to yourself over and over again until you find the pen at the bottom of the drawer and scribble down the information. And how often does somebody try to talk to you while your juggling is in full swing, and in a second the details have vanished . . .

For many people, memory *is* repetition, a parrot-fashion style of repeating information until somehow, when you've gone over it again and again, the facts take hold in your mind. But it is only a very shaky hold – few people can have escaped the panic-filled experience of having the mind 'go blank', every single scrap of information gone completely. In those moments, the reason for memory-loss tends to be as mysterious as the way in which the information was supposedly learnt in the first place!

Try the four questions printed below. The answers involve information that most people will have seen, heard, even used at some point in their lives. What they demonstrate is the tendency to keep facts in our minds for the short-est possible length of time – and the way in which we often remember only those things that necessity forces us to learn.

Question one When sailors or pilots talk about 'port' and 'starboard', which word means the left side and which the right?

If you *are* a sailor or a pilot, then you'll know the answer to this as instinctively as we all remember our own right side from our left. Otherwise, even if you were told the answer now, would you remember it this time next year? Come to that, would you remember it tomorrow? If you're not used to making constant use of your mind, and your life or hobby doesn't make facts like this essential knowledge, then the temptation is to avoid the effort of making real contact with the facts, and they disappear as quickly as the juggled telephone message.

Question two On a map of the London Underground, what colour are the following lines: Circle, Central, Piccadilly, Victoria, Bakerloo?

Again, if you have a real reason for remembering these details then you will almost certainly answer the question correctly. But for the majority of people, information like this is not learned but held, shakily, for a very short length of time.

Question three In their order from the sun, what are the nine planets of the solar system?

Like so many lists, this is the sort of information that you probably learned for a test at school, and then forgot by the following lesson. This experience of testing is what gives many people the idea that memory is repetition – as well as an expectation of being *able* to hold on to information only for very short periods of time.

Question four When do the clocks have to be put forward each year – in autumn, or in spring?

How often do we find we have to be reminded of a fact like this again and again, each time holding on to it briefly, yet never once making the simple, conscious effort to fix it in the memory? If you were to do it properly, once is all it would take.

Just by reading this book you've made a decision to start using your memory, so let me now use these four questions to demonstrate how one, conscious act of memory can last for ever.

Answer one 'Port' refers to the left side of a boat or plane, and 'starboard' refers to the right.

Possibly the simplest way to remember this is to notice that the words 'port' and 'left' both have four letters. But just noticing this fact is too much like the juggling of information criticised earlier. Holding on to the information in this way is not likely to last for long.

Perhaps if you were about to take to the seas for real, though, the process of using this simple technique would help to hold it in your mind for good. Imagination is the key to the *Mindpower System* – so now, why not put to sea in your mind?

Imagine you are standing behind the wheel of a beautiful pleasure-cruiser. Close your eyes for a moment and try to picture the scene as vividly as possible. This boat is the extremely expensive possession of a millionaire friend of yours, so you are slightly nervous at being in control – especially when you notice some sharp rocks protruding from the water just ahead. A crew-member begins calling out directions to you, trying to help you avoid a collision: 'port . . . more to port . . . back to starboard . . .' Desperate to remember which word means right and which left, you notice suddenly that the boat comes equipped with reminders of its own.

On the left hand side of the deck, in very small letters, is written the word LEFT, and underneath, in equally precise lettering, is the word PORT, with each letter of the word made exactly the same size as the one above. The lettering is also a reddish colour, and it occurs to you that the signwriter has used port *wine* – you can even smell it, and there's a half-empty bottle of port by the side.

In contrast, on the right of the deck – you have to turn your head to see it – the word RIGHT has been painted in huge, sprawling letters. As in traffic lights, the opposite colour to red is green – so that is the colour of paint that has been used here for RIGHT, and for the word STARBOARD printed underneath and stretching even further. Dotted around the word are hundreds of bright green stars. Imagine your nervousness and fear turning to confidence now that you can be sure of knowing the crucial information.

In fact, you also now know – properly – that a ship's port light is red, and its starboard one green. Your imagination is able to make very forgettable points much more real and memorable, to add extra reminders – even to let you practise putting the memory to use.

Answer two On the London tube, the Circle line is *yellow*, the Central line *red*, the Piccadilly line *deep blue*, the Victoria line *light blue*, and the Bakerloo line *brown*.

Once again, the key is imagination. Imagine you are standing inside an Underground station; in front of you is a map of the Tube, behind you the track. That's about where reality ends, though . . . because, stretching in a circle around you, is the world's longest banana! Imagine its bright yellow colour, and what it feels like when you try to step over it, but slip and squash part of it with your foot. People have started looking at you, and you begin to blush at being the centre of attention. In fact, when you catch a glimpse of yourself in a mirror, your face is a bright, pulsating red – but only in the centre. Strangely, the edges of your face have remained their normal colour.

Suddenly, you realise that things are happening behind you. Turning round, you see that water has flooded the track, more and more pouring in all the time from a waterfall on the left hand side. The water there, as it falls, catches the light, and looks pale blue compared with the deeply-coloured liquid in the tunnel itself. As if to explain the presence of the waterfall, a railway-worker is busy on a ladder at the side nailing up a sign that says VICTORIA FALLS.

Meanwhile, out of the deep, darker water, an elephant is emerging . . . followed by a clown on stilts . . . and soon a whole circus is performing, splashing about in the water. Crowds of noisy people are gathering on the platform to watch, and several stalls have also been set up to sell food and drinks. One of them is being run by a baker, who opens the door of his oven to reveal his masterpiece: a full-size toilet made entirely from brown bread! Unfortunately he seems to have left it in for just a little too long – the toilet has been singed, and the brown of the bread is nothing compared with the brown clouds of billowing smoke . . .

Perhaps you should have been warned; things start to get a little surreal when the imagination really gets to work! This is a scene you are unlikely to forget in a hurry – especially since imagination has allowed you to be in the middle of it all. And if you can remember this scene, then you can also remember the colours on the Underground map: the CIRCLE of the *yellow* banana; the CENTRAL patch of *red* on your face, when you were also the centre of attention; the (PICCADILLY) circus rising out of the *deep blue* water; the *light blue* colour of VICTORIA Falls; and finally, the *brown* of the BAKER'sLOO!

Answer three In order from the sun, the planets of the solar system are Mercury, Venus, Earth, Mars, Jupiter, Saturn, Uranus, Neptune, Pluto.

It's time for another flight of the imagination. As a memorable starting point, imagine you're sitting on the surface of the sun – and feeling a little warm to say the least! In fact, to find out exactly *how* warm, use the MERCURY thermometer you have with you. You take your own temperature . . . but when you see that the reading has shot right off the scale, you collapse in a heap.

In your moment of need, the perfect character arrives; VENUS, the god of love, descending from the heavens and covered in bright red love-hearts. You're brought back to life and carefully returned to earth; as if to stress this point, Venus sets you down in the muddy EARTH of a flower bed.

At least you *thought* it was mud. To your amazement it turns out to be chocolate; you've landed on top of a huge MARS bar! You can pause a moment to enjoy eating it – imaginary chocolate has no calories . . .

It feels so comfortable lying in your bed of chocolate that you decide to spend the night there. But when you wake in the morning, so much dew has fallen that the whole garden is awash – a huge 'dew pit' (JUPITER!). You need someone to help pull you out. Luckily Satan (SATURN) is there to offer you his assistance. By grasping on to his fork you are hauled to safety, and, as you dry yourself off, he explains that *he* is responsible for all the water – in fact, for *all* the wet weather on the planet. 'You rain on us?' (URANUS), you cry in amazement . . .

All the struggle has worn you out. You'd love to go back to sleep, but this latest piece of disturbing information keeps you awake. Desperate to nod off, you're delighted to hear the sound of sweet, soothing music – a 'nap tune' (NEPTUNE) – and, looking to see where it's coming from, you catch sight of a long parade of Disney characters coming towards you, each playing a musical instrument and led from the front by . . . who else but PLUTO!

Answer four In spring the clocks go forward, in autumn they go back.

As demonstrated above, word-plays are often an invaluable part of memory, and can form the first step in a process of effective learning. The best way to remember something can often be found within the information itself.

Autumn, to an American, is 'Fall' – so clearly the key line to remember here is SPRING FORWARD, FALL BACK! Imagine sitting curled up uncomfortably inside a Swiss clock – perhaps you're filling in for the cuckoo – when suddenly the chimes ring and you spring forward, out into the open air. For a moment you're motionless, but then it's time for the return journey and you feel your stomach drop as you fall back inside the clock.

So which is the left, port or starboard? What colour is the Bakerloo line? Which planet is next out from the sun after Venus? When do the clocks go back? These examples demonstrate the importance of making a conscious decision to use your mind – to learn information in such a way that once really is enough. Rather than being a vague power that sometimes works, but more often fails, a faulty instrument that you just have to put up with, memory turns out to involve a wide range of techniques with, as a constant centre, the ability to control your own mind.

WHY A GOOD MEMORY IS ESSENTIAL

Memory seems to play a strange role in our lives. On one hand, this is an age that discourages us from using our minds: more and more jobs are being taken over by computers, and the most up-to-date information technology is at our disposal, from calculators to word-processors, memory-bank watches to electronic organisers. The temptation is always to neglect the most powerful computer of all, the human mind. Yet, the faster and more complicated the world becomes, the more we as individuals need to stay in control of our lives. Competitiveness has never been greater; our time and energy are constantly being pushed to the limits. If neglect of the mind is increasing, then so too are the opportunities for benefiting from a power that brings with it great advantages – at home, in school and at work.

In everyday situations, it means absorbing shopping lists and telephone numbers, remembering things-to-do, dates and anniversaries, and maintaining a position of organised control. In education, with tests now at primary level and increasing stress placed on (and caused by) examinations and the struggle for qualifications, there has never been greater need for an awareness of the potential of the mind. And in the world of work, no matter what job you do, the sort of confident control created by a powerful memory is vital. Consider how many business deals might have succeeded if the right people had remembered each other a fortnight after a conference. Think how impressive it would be to conduct a lecture or meeting without notes, or to arrange to meet a client without having to search for your diary. So much time is spent today on image-making and creating an impression – yet so little attention is paid to what is potentially the most impressive skill of all.

How ludicrous it would seem if someone owned a car, but kept it trapped inside a garage to seize up and turn to rust. Imagine the owner fiddling with his car from time to time, occasionally finding bits that work – the headlights, say, or the wipers – but staying completely motionless because he expects the car to do the driving for him. 'Either this is going to work, somehow', he thinks, 'or it isn't'. Ludicrous it may seem – yet this is the relationship so many people have with their mind.

Like a car, to develop and enjoy the potential of the mind it isn't necessary to understand exactly *why* it works. Even at the height of the technological age, many of the mind's functions continue to baffle the world's top scientists. What is necessary is a knowledge of how to *use* it, the right buttons to press to achieve the desired results. The *Mindpower System* is a practical guide to learning to drive the mind, showing you how to adapt the key techniques to a range of specific conditions and situations, and proving that practice really can make perfect.

WORKING WITH YOUR MEMORY
The Four Rules of Mindpower

When I made the decision to start developing my memory, I experimented. I realised it was important to discover the sort of information my memory was *able* to absorb, and then use that knowledge to help with the things I found difficult. Now, the whole *Mindpower System* is based on this simple principle of using the way the memory works for your own advantage.

So just what are the natural techniques of the mind, the basic forces controlling memory? My experience tells me that they can be divided into four key rules.

MINDPOWER RULE ONE
You Remember Things That Happen to *You*.

Imagine if you were given seven digits at random, and you looked at them for a few seconds before they were covered up. Now, even after a couple of minutes, which would you find easier to remember: the numbers, or what you did yesterday?

Go back a few days in your mind. It's likely that even the most mundane parts of life seem a lot more memorable than information which has no connection with you or with real life. Certainly, as you go back further and further, the days begin to blur together and some of the detail is lost. But some days, some moments, do remain strong and vivid in the memory, and almost always these are the times when the centre of the action, often the centre of attention, was *you*.

We remember what happened on our birthdays, we recall our holidays, job interviews, competition wins, accidents. The stronger our connection to the events, the more likely we are to remember them, and often that connection is built on a strong emotional response. This can vary greatly, and a few moments' thought about our own most memorable experiences confirms that they often involve some of the following reactions: happiness, fear, embarrassment, excitement, disappointment, pain, sadness, relief. The most embarrassing moments from our early childhood, for example, are likely to be far more memorable now than the breakfast we had last Thursday!

A song from years back is played on the radio. Suddenly, you remember where you were living and what you were doing when that song was being played all the time. Radio-programmers understand this, and choose music that was current when their target audience was experiencing most of its 'key moments' – falling in love, buying the first car, getting married. Television programmes looking back at old news reports regularly inter-twine pictures and contemporary music. And, when we think about some event in world history, we often find it's bound up in the memory with events in our own lives from the same point in time.

It seems that memory works on a foundation of personal experience. So, if we're going to make the mind work to our advantage, this in-built technique needs to be taken into account. To return to the car analogy, it's like the ultimate novice discovering, by trial and error, that his car travels faster and is easier to control in forward gear than in reverse, and then resolving to put this knowledge to use as he learns to drive.

But what good can all of this be when we have to learn dry, lifeless information such as numbers, dates, foreign words or facts? The answer is that, with imagination, information like this can *become* part of our experience. This will be explained in detail later on – but for now, just to prove the point, here's an experiment to try for yourself.

Look at the following five words for a moment, and then cover them up.

DRILL   CARTON   PIPE   PICTURE   SALT

While the words are covered, recite aloud the months of the year, the days of the week, and today's date. This confuses you, rather in the same way as when someone talks to you while you're 'juggling' between remembering the telephone message and struggling to find the pen!

So what were the five words? Possibly you can remember them all – but what is their order in reverse? And would you be able to recall them in an hour? Tomorrow? Next month?

Now try a rather unusual way of learning them, one that you're unlikely to forget in a hurry.

Look at the room around you. You need to choose five places within the room – often the four corners and the middle of the floor are best, but perhaps there are even more distinct areas in this particular room. While you're still seated, number the five areas in your mind in a logical order. If you are using the corners and the middle, possibly the best way is to call the corner nearest the door 'area one', and then to move around the room clockwise, finishing with the centre as 'area five'.

Now, if it's not going to cause too much of a stir, get up from your seat and go to each of the five areas in turn. In the first, as you stand there, imagine drilling into the wall or into an object you can see nearby. When you've finished with the drill, imagine leaving it in area one.

Next, in area two, picture yourself standing inside a huge carton. Imagine climbing out of it, and then filling it with some of the real objects nearby.

As you stand in the third area, visualise yourself taking out a pipe and starting to smoke. Clouds of smoke are staining the ceiling above your head, billowing around the whole of this area of the room.

In area four, take out an imaginary sketch-pad and start drawing a picture of the room as you see it from where you stand. As you leave this area, imagine pinning the finished picture to something nearby.

Finally, standing in area five, imagine noticing a tiny pot of salt on the floor. You pick it up and start tipping out its contents – but, somehow, huge amounts of salt are pouring out, rising up in large piles all around you. You'll have to push your way through them to get back to your chair . . .

When you're seated again, look back around the room. Let your eyes move from area to area in order, and at the same time call out the object you've left in each place. How much easier it is to remember information when you've turned it into your own experience.

You should now be able to remember the list with ease, backwards and forwards. You know which item was number two, say, or number four – and there isn't really any clearing up to be done!

MINDPOWER RULE TWO

You Remember the Things You Can See,
You Forget the Things You Can't.

To a certain extent, this was shown in the experiment above. Words on a page are flat and dry, but if you can turn them into objects and substances that can be seen and touched, maybe even heard, smelled and tasted, then they become much easier to remember. Once again, it comes down to the idea of taking control and of asserting your own role in the memory process. Words or numbers, names or even pictures on a page remain connected *to* the page, until you take hold of them and start to put them under your control.

Even when they still exist purely as words, it's clear that completely abstract bits of information are much harder to remember than things which can be visualised. As an example, read through the following list, made up of various different sorts of information.

BOTTLE, THREE, TOMORROW, GORILLA, MAYBE, CHALK, COUNCIL, CASTLE, SHARPLY, TRAIN, HAMBURGER, FULL

Now, cover over the words, pause for a minute or so, and then see how many of them you can remember, in any order.

Chances are that you remembered GORILLA, HAMBURGER and CASTLE, but that you found TOMORROW, SHARPLY or MAYBE a little harder to recall!

Memory is about taking control, taking hold of information – and if you can't hold on to it, then you have to change it. Apart from seven letters on a page, what is there to hold on to about SHARPLY? At least you can form a picture of CASTLE, and, when you read HAMBURGER, the senses of smell and taste can also help you to connect. But what does SHARPLY look like? Abstract ideas such as this need to be given form.

Often the first step is to play around with the letters on the page. Think of somebody called Lee – maybe you picture a family-member or friend, or perhaps it's a famous person like the actor Lee Majors, martial arts actor Bruce Lee, or gravel-voiced Lee Marvin. Now, form a mental picture of this person covered in sharp objects. Knives are strapped to his legs, he has scissors for hands, and bits of broken glass are glued along his shoulders. Even his head tapers to a sharp point. This is sharp Lee – SHARPLY! – a character you're not likely to forget in a hurry!

As it appears on the page, COUNCIL is a very general word – it doesn't suggest any single image, unlike CHALK or BOTTLE. But why not make use of this vagueness and scope?

Imagine a council chamber, packed to bursting-point with every possible council committee and sub-committee. On a stage in the centre, an emotional counselling session is being carried out by a team of therapists. Council workmen are adding to the pandemonium with their pneumatic drills. The word COUNCIL itself is being printed in huge letters across the ceiling – but the noise below is making the letters crash to the ground, one by one.

Every element of this picture increases the 'visibility' of COUNCIL, and acts as a reinforcement of the memory. As soon as information is placed under the control of the imagination, it's ready to be *made* as memorable as possible.

MINDPOWER RULE THREE

You Remember Unusual Things.

To be unusual means to stand out from a pattern, to refuse to blend in with anything else. When we think about our most memorable personal experiences, the unusual moments are the ones we recall first – these are the things that stick in the mind.

It's time for another experiment and another list. Read through the words below at a reasonable pace, then cover them over and see how many you can remember.

SHOE, BALL, BOX, WALL, COAT, RICE, BAG, DRA-GON, NAIL, APPLE, PEN, HOUSE, SCHWARZENEGGER, KEY, STRING, PLATE

Even if you only remembered three of the words, I'll bet two of them were DRAGON and SCHWARZENEGGER! The rest are common, boring, everyday words, and although they're perfectly visible and concrete, there is nothing about them to stimulate the imagination.

The mind is ready and waiting to absorb information, but it needs something to hold on to. It's like a powerful electro-magnet, able to pull things towards it and to grasp on to them, just as long as they contain sufficient magnetic material. Some things stick on with no problem, but others have to be *made* to. Items made from wood or fabric need to have pieces of metal attached, and the more work you do, the better suited you make the objects the more likely they are to rise up to the magnet and never fall off. Even a substance as un-magnetic as water could fasten on to the magnet – just so long as it was poured and sealed into a metal box.

In the *Mindpower System*, this magnetising process is carried out by the imagination. Imagine going back to some of the items on this list and making them 'magnetic'. Make them unusual; take hold of the plate, cover it in expensive gold-leaf, and then ruin it by scratching your initials in the centre. Look again at the ball; this time, as you watch, see how it's growing bigger and bigger, until finally it bursts and showers you with scraps of rubber. When you looked at the list the first time,

I'll bet you didn't spot Humpty Dumpty sitting on top of that wall . . .

MINDPOWER RULE FOUR

You Remember Things that
Fit into Patterns

Printed below are two lists of numbers. It's not difficult to decide which is the easier to remember.

One 14, 8, 2, 16, 10, 4, 6, 12
Two 2, 4, 6, 8, 10, 12, 14, 16

Here, the same information has been presented in two different ways, but in the second, more memorable list, a pattern has been found. A similar effect can be demonstrated in words. Below are two more lists from which the same comparisons can be drawn.

One JIM WORK I A PLAYED AFTER SQUASH OF GAME AND
Two AFTER WORK JIM AND I PLAYED A GAME OF SQUASH.

When information is patterned, it is connected. In this example, the connections created through language mean that, in the second list, the ten words are no longer ten separate chunks of information. Putting them into a sentence gives the memory a single idea to hold on to, and each individual word is given its 'magnetism' by being connected with the words around it.

Imagine you went to see a film at the local cinema, and the projection equipment went haywire, showing the various reels in entirely the wrong order – first a bit of the third reel, a car-chase, then the very end, the unmasking of the murderer, then part of the introduction . . . You would leave having seen the same film as in any other cinema, but you would probably have great difficulty trying to remember what on earth had happened.

The answer would be to go and see the film again when the machinery had been mended. You would get all the same individual bits of information, but this time they would have a pattern to them, connected together into the logical sequence of a story.

When you listen to a favourite tape or CD, it's often possible to remember exactly which track is about to come next – even to start humming it before it appears. But could you write down the order of songs if you were sitting in silence and the recording was kept firmly in its case? The answer is likely to be No; the memory works best when it can move by connections from one piece of information to the next in sequence.

I can remember the order of thousands of numbers, words or playing-cards, but I can only do so because I've moulded them into a sequence. Just as you remember a story or a film, I give my memory a starting point, and then it moves forward along a connected chain, stopping on each link only for long enough to be led on to the next.

As with all of these rules, an awareness of the memory's natural techniques must be used to change information – to make it 'magnetic', compatible with the mind.

To recap: information must be turned into a form in which it can be *experienced*. It must be made *real*, visible, touchable. Each item must be made *unusual* enough to stand out from the rest. But at the basis of it all must be a *pattern*, a series of connections allowing the memory to continue moving forward along the chain towards infinity.

Memory needs to be made P.U.R.E. – the key elements are Pattern, Unusual, Real and Experience.

At the heart of the *Mindpower System* is the desire to take control, and, as I have hinted at already, the key to that control is imagination.

THE POWER OF IMAGINATION

Imagination has no rules. You have a whole new world at your disposal, a place where there are no laws of gravity, no policemen – nothing to limit or restrict. It's like the world of dreams, except that now your conscious mind is allowed full control. In reality we may not be able to run as fast as a train, or to look down on the world as we fly above it unaided. We may not be allowed to smash up a china-shop or punch the mayor. But in the land of imagination, we can choose to be or do anything we want.

Too often, presented with information to learn, people think they're bound by a rule which says they must remember the material precisely as it's been given to them. They struggle to learn dry, boring, unconnected information and, by doing so, they are fighting against the power of their mind, rather than using it.

Imagination allows us to switch on the electro-magnet of our minds and change information so that it *becomes* magnetic. The process of change takes place easily; if we have an imagination, then we have all the tools and materials we need.

Think of imagination as a studio for making feature films. You are the director with a limitless budget and, since this is just make-believe, anything can happen. All the memory's natural techniques can be combined to turn dry, unpatterned, even meaningless facts into the most dazzling, most exciting, most memorable film ever. As director you are at the very centre, staying true to the first rule of *Mindpower* by taking an active part in everything that happens, and even casting yourself in the leading role.

When we watch a film, we are most likely to remember a story that excites some sort of emotional response in us. So when we *direct* one, there are several key elements that must be injected into the film-making process.

Excitement. The imagination allows you to work to the greatest possible scale, at the fastest speeds if necessary, and to take the biggest risks. As you work your material into a memorable sequence, you can make use of the most dangerous substances – walls of fire, tons of explosives, poisonous gases – and you can perform the most amazing special effects.

Imagine you are a travelling salesman, and you want to work out a way of remembering the particular shops you need to visit in a town. How impressive it would be to be able to go about your business without having to struggle with long, tattered lists. How much more confident you would feel. You know the basic layout of the town well enough from personal experience, so why not take control through imagination?

Close your eyes and imagine walking through the town. *Mindpower* is all about organisation, and this dry run will allow you a chance to work out beforehand the most efficient route and the best use of your time. In your mind, call at each of the shops on your route in turn, and use your newfound creative freedom to leave behind reminders for when you come to visit the town for real.

Centre your imagination on something that actually exists at each place. If the first shop is a butcher's, visualise the meat hanging in the window. Another shop might have a post-box outside, an advertising hoarding or an unusual piece of decoration.

Then spice things up a bit. In your mind, spray paint all over the meat, then set it on fire. Tear down the post-box, and replace it with a model of your own to startle passers-by with bizarre sound-effects. Set off a spectacular fireworks display, using the barber's pole as a holder for the Catherine-wheels . . .

When you have finished, take a mental walk back through the whole route, noting the various reminders. Then, when you come to walk the route for real, you'd only have to notice the meat to remember what you did to it; only have to pass the post-box to recall the strange noises, and to realise that this must be another of the shops to visit.

The success of a story like this points out several more of the key creative elements. The more **Humour** you can inject the better. This is linked with the idea of making things unusual, and the beauty of imagination is that the most bizarre, most surreal things can happen. You may not recall much about your journey to work two weeks ago, but you might just have remembered it if a green elephant had barred your way into the car-park, or you had been caught up in a crowd of geriatric ballet-dancers skipping and jumping down the street to pick up their pensions!

Another element suggested is **violence**. In the lawless world of imagination, you can let go of all your inhibitions and vent all your frustrations. The next experiment demonstrates the violence of a good memory.

Below is a list of twenty household objects. Don't look yet, but over the page is another list of twenty items made up of seventeen from the first list, plus three new ones. Your task

is to learn the first list well enough to be able to spot the three
new items when you eventually turn the page.

List one
VASE, CLOCK, ASHTRAY, CUP, PLATE, WATCH, LAMP,
TABLE, TEAPOT, T.V., CHAIR, TRAY, SHOE, BIN,
RUG, COOKER, RADIO, DOOR, BROOM, LADDER

Now, let all your violent instincts go to work! Taking each
item in turn, imagine inflicting terrible damage to it. Each time,
do something appropriate to the object itself, find some way
of managing the most effective destruction. Drop the vase
from the top of a house, for example. See people in the
street below trying to catch the vase, but hear it smashing
against the pavement, hundreds of broken pieces clattering into
the gutter.

An important part of the *Mindpower System* is the ability to
combine several different ways of remembering information. So,
after ruining each object, imagine what you would have to do to
repair it. The vase is going to need glueing back together, and
it'll be quite a jigsaw-puzzle trying to work out which bit goes
where . . .

Pull out all the springs of the clock, bend the hands out of
shape – and then mend it by making some new springs from
the wire of old coat-hangers, and ringing up the speaking clock
to re-set the time. Saw all the legs off the chair, then fix them
back on with four bits of pink chewing-gum. Go to work on the
ladder with a whirring chain-saw . . .

When you've finished all this destruction and rebuilding, you
have confirmed once and for all your position of freedom and
control. Now study the list below:

List two
TEAPOT, RUG, COOKER, SHELF, RADIO, BOX, DOOR,
SHOE, LADDER, CUPBOARD, VASE, WATCH, LAMP,
ASHTRAY, BIN, PLATE, BROOM, CLOCK, T.V., TABLE.

To find out which three of these items were not in the original
list, simply look at each object in turn and recall whether or not
you imagined destroying it. If you think you did, just confirm it

by remembering how you planned to mend it, and then move on to the next item. Underline any object that you can't remember dealing with earlier – and when you reach the end of the list, the three new items should have been found. Finally, turn back the page to check your answers, and to confirm that you've taken another step towards *Mindpower*!

Learning How to Cheat

In many ways, to develop a powerful memory you have to cheat. When I memorise 1,000 random ones and noughts, or fifteen packs of playing-cards, I start off with the information as it's presented to me and finish by recalling exactly the same information. But in between these two points I haven't been dealing with numbers or playing-cards at all; I have taken control, and changed the material in order to *make* it memorable and to benefit from the mind's natural techniques.

As I have said, the first step in the process of change is to turn abstract information into something that can be held on to and controlled. So much of the material we have to learn is given to us in this abstract form – numbers, names, directions, words on a page. How much easier life would be if every list we were given was presented in a three-dimensional form. A shopping list, for example, would be simpler to remember if replicas of all the items were in front of us; learning details for a geography exam would be less of a chore if we had three-dimensional models of countries and cities. Even when words on a page refer to real places and things, without imagination there is no possibility of proper contact between them and our minds, and we're left with the old, vague practices of repeating the material again and again and juggling it within our most temporary memory.

Imagine you needed to remember the following three pieces of information. The first is a number: 3185; the second is a name: Jack MacDonald; and the third is part of an address: 8 Farthing Street, Oxford. As it's presented here, the information is abstract; by re-reading it a couple of times, you could probably remember it for a few minutes at best. Clearly these details need to be learned so that they can be recalled exactly as they appear above. But what rule says that they have to be *remembered* as they appear above? In between reading and recalling comes cheating.

The number **3185** like all of the information here, is the sort of thing we often have to remember when it's simply not possible to use pen and paper. When you hear the number, it exists in the most abstract form possible – so the first step ought to be to imagine writing it down.

There are many techniques for doing this – especially since the imaginary writing-materials can be chosen from the limitless storehouse of your imagination. Forget about writing on paper; choose something that ties in with your *reason* for remembering the number, something that will allow your creative (and destructive!) instincts to run riot.

Perhaps this is the number of a post-office box you must write to in order to cancel a shipment of books. In that case, imagine the post-office box itself full to bursting with books, and write the number on to the box.

You could visualise yourself taking a nail and scratching the number into the metal, concentrating on the shape of the digits and working out the most memorable way to write them.

You could put eyes on the number eight to make it into a snowman, or perhaps write the number one as a Roman numeral.

If you're having a face-to-face conversation with somebody when the information is given to you, you could even imagine writing the number on that person! Take out your imaginary can of green paint and spray the numbers on to his jacket, or perhaps use an indelible marker to write on his face, again noticing the shape of the numbers as you weave them around his eyes, nose and mouth. By imagining the process of writing the number down, you take the first step towards cheating, giving some substance to otherwise purely abstract information.

But this is only the first step. The number will now be memorable for long enough to find some paper, tell the right person or call a certain telephone number. But if you need to remember it for longer, then you have to bring it even more firmly under your creative control.

The benefit of this first step is that it gives you the time you need. Be honest – how often have you heard a piece of information, and then forgotten it within three seconds! So often we're called to remember things in a hurry, yet the panic of the situation alone is enough to make us forget. This first step gives you the all-important time to consider the best way to go about learning something, allowing you to remember it comfortably – and *permanently*.

Once you have that time, there's so much more that you can do. Why not make the number into a three-dimensional model. Your own control is the key to *Mindpower*, so imagine how *you* would go about constructing it, and consider the most appropriate materials to use.

This might be the serial-number for an order form for dresses – so use imaginary scissors, fabric and a sewing machine to make a nice little number that you can wear!

If it's the number of cakes your bakery needs to make in a year, imagine laying them all out on the shop floor in the pattern of the number, and visualise what your creation would look like from various angles around the room.

A name can also be brought under the power of the imagination. The first step is to split it. In the case of **Jack MacDonald** there are three obvious parts: JACK, MAC and DONALD. It's easy to come up with ways of turning each of them into a visible, touchable object.

JACK becomes a piece of equipment for lifting up a car; MAC becomes a raincoat, and why not make DONALD into a duck! Suddenly, an abstract name has been turned into three very real items, and these can now be joined together to create a single, mental, moving picture.

Imagine the experience of jacking up a bundled raincoat, which seems to be bulging and moving as though there's something inside it. You open it up – and stand back in amazement as Donald Duck jumps out! The more humour, surprise and movement you can inject, the better, and the more bizarre the situation, the more memorable it will be.

Once a scene like this has been created, you can link it with your reason for remembering the name. Perhaps the real Jack MacDonald is your bank manager.

Imagine waiting to be served in your local bank, and watching this strange scene being played out behind the cash-desk. Donald Duck is as tall as you, and suddenly he pulls off a mask to reveal that he is really the bank manager, who ushers you into his office.

Maybe Jack MacDonald is your greengrocer. In this case, imagine him showing you that his scales work like a jack, and demonstrating by lifting up a wriggling, quacking raincoat . . .!

Any information can be brought to life in the imagination. With the address **8 Farthing Street, Oxford**, the trick again is to break it up into pieces. You can make 'eight' into 'ate', allowing you to choose an image linked with eating and food. The 'farthing' could be an old coin, or perhaps a penny-farthing bicycle, and 'street', converted into its abbreviation 'st', becomes a 'saint', complete with dazzling halo. Sometimes you only need to recall one part of a word in order to remember the whole thing, so, for Oxford, simply picture an ox. Imagination has made the abstract material real, and it's now at your disposal.

You have in front of you some food, an old bicycle, a saint and an ox. As a quick image you could picture a woman sitting in a restaurant, eating an old bicycle. She pays for the meal with old coins, too – but before she has a chance to finish eating, a saint descends from heaven and turns her into an ox, using his halo as the ring through her nose!

With more time, this strange scene could be linked with the real address. If it was a friend's house, for example, you might put your friend into the story in the role of the woman, or set the scene in a real location. An important part of the *Mindpower System* is the ability to reinforce information once it's been learned. So, when you finish creating your story, look through it a few times to remind yourself of the key points, and how they relate to the real information. With a little practice you'll have no trouble converting your pictures back to the original material – no matter what amazing things have been happening in the meantime!

Try It Yourself

Printed below are five varied pieces of information, along with 'reasons' for knowing them. Consider each one in turn; practise turning dry facts into living, moving, colourful pictures, and inventing memorable scenes.

When your imagination has brought each of the examples to

life, spend a few minutes going back through the pictures and ideas. Add extra reminders if need be, and practise breaking your images back down into the original material.

When you're ready, pause for five minutes or so, then test yourself from the list. Cover up the left-hand column, and take one 'reason' at a time, recalling the connections, recreating the imaginative scene, and finally retrieving the information. Uncover the left-hand column gradually as you check your success.

FACTS	REASONS
1. 3 Temple Road, Braintree.	Address of Book Club
2. 4008	P.O. box number for a competition
3. Phil Trench	Your new tutor
4. Judy – number 9	Friend's house number
5. 21 High Street	Doctor's surgery

By combining all the techniques I have described to take information under your control, you are staying true to the first three rules of *Mindpower*. Your methods of learning are being adapted to the natural tendencies of the mind.

You're placing yourself in the key position of *control*, creating a *connection* between yourself and the material and *imagining* emotional responses and interactive experiences. Abstract material is being brought to life, and dry, mundane facts made into unusual, bizarre, memorable images.

Everything is ready now for you to capitalise on rule number four, and to create for the mind the patterns and connections it needs.

TELLING STORIES

I remember information by moulding it into a story. I give my memory a starting-point, and off it goes, moving forwards through the connections and allowing me to recall huge amounts of material. As I learn thousands of words, numbers or playing-cards, each item plays its own role in the story, and each individual part of the story takes me on to the next.

Here's an example of the power of storytelling. Are you sitting comfortably . . .?

'A man woke up and climbed out of bed. He'd spent a very restless night, and he ached all over. Something, it seemed, was wrong with the bed, and as he bent down to take a closer look he noticed that the sheets were actually sheet *metal* – no wonder it had been an uncomfortable night! To soothe himself he took a shower; but, to his horror, instead of water pouring out he was covered in thick, sticky oil, colouring him jet black from head to foot.

It was the oil in his eyes that prevented him from seeing the hundreds of ball bearings at the top of the stairs. He tumbled forward, crashing against stair after stair, ball-bearings rolling down all around him. Dazed, he knew that he was going to do himself even more damage if he didn't clean the oil out of his eyes, so he rummaged around in a drawer until he found some rags that he could use. Soon these were blackened and wet, but when he tried to throw them away, he found that the bin-lid wouldn't open; for some reason, the bin was already full, and when he looked inside he saw that it was packed with hundreds of old paint tins.

One of the tins still had a little paint inside, so the man fetched a paint brush to see if he could make use of his find. He dabbed some of the paint on to the wall and it seemed fine, but as he was trying to put the lid back on he dropped the tin and sprayed paint all around the kitchen walls.

At that moment he heard footsteps. His wife was approaching – she would go berserk if she saw the mess! He dashed into the garage, grabbed a bottle of paint-stripper, and was just washing away the last trace of paint when his wife walked into the room.

He sensed immediately that there was something different about her. He thought for a moment – and then it hit him: she was wearing new earrings, which looked as though they were made out of pieces of lead pipe! He decided to take a closer look, and reached out his hand to touch the one on the left – but as he did so it fell off and hit the floor with a loud clang.

It was a good job for him that his soldering kit was handy. It didn't take him long to carry out a repair job, and he even showed some creativity of his own by fixing on to the side of each pipe a brand new screwdriver . . .'

As long as you can recall that it started with a man getting out of bed after a restless night, you shouldn't have too much difficulty remembering the key points of this story. It's made up of a series of incidents, each involving, a particular object or substance, and each incident leads on to the next. If you were to forget one part, you could think forward in the story to a moment you do remember, and then work back to fill in the missing link. In fact, it wouldn't be too hard to list all the major events of the story in reverse.

The story ended with a man fixing on some screwdrivers. He was using a soldering kit, and was mending his wife's lead-pipe earrings. When his wife came into the room he was using paint stripper, hurriedly removing all trace of his experiments with a paint brush. He had started using the paint brush after finding a tin of paint. That had happened when he was trying to throw away some cleaning rags. He was using the rags at the bottom of the stairs, where he'd fallen after tripping on some ball-bearings. He fell because his eyes were blocked with oil – the result of a shower taken to soothe the pains of a night spent on sheet metal.

In other words, you have just memorised a list of ten boring, lifeless items from a D.I.Y. enthusiast's shopping-list:

SHEET METAL, OIL, BALL BEARINGS, CLEANING RAGS, PAINT, PAINT BRUSHES, PAINT STRIPPER, LEAD PIPE, SOLDERING KIT, SCREWDRIVERS.

You know the list forwards and backwards, you can recall what comes before or after each individual item – and, of course, the story doesn't have to end with the screwdrivers. The man might be using one of them (still attached to his wife's earrings!) to mend some SHELVES, when they collapse, showering him with hundreds of TYRES. Suddenly he's surrounded by the tyres in a great cylinder of rubber, but luckily he has a SAW in his pocket and can cut himself free . . .

Stories to Remember

Storytelling is a crucial part of the way memory works, and one of the foundations of the *Mindpower System*. So the next question that must be asked is, what makes some stories more memorable than others?

The importance of special-effects, excitement, violence and

humour has already been seen. But an equally significant element, the staple device of all good story-telling, is the involvement of the senses.

By including as many senses as possible, you take your material further and further away from its abstract state, and increase the connections with *you*.

Imagine you are dealing with a piece of information as dry and dead as the word BOX. You can involve *sight*, the first of the senses, by creating a picture of the box in your mind, taking the crucial first step away from the abstract word on the page.

Your imagination has no limits, and it certainly doesn't have to work within a budget, so why not transport your box to some unusual location. See it standing in the middle of a desert, floating in the sea or sitting inside a crater on the moon. In your mind, take a walk around the box and see how it looks from different angles. At present the box is a boring, uniform shade of brown, so why not consider what you could do to make it more eyecatching. Maybe some fluorescent paint wouldn't come amiss – perhaps even a few neon lights!

The next stage is to involve the sense of *hearing*. An obvious thing to do in this case is to transform your object into a musical box; it makes a dull thud when you kick it, but when the lid is lifted you can hear the most beautiful music. Imagine the effects the sounds have on your emotions. Perhaps it's a very quiet, precise tune played by a clockwork mechanism. On the other hand, since the aim is to make it as memorable as possible, perhaps the sound you hear is the crash of heavy metal!

What does the box feel like to *touch*? How heavy is it? Perhaps you pick it up easily, but put it down straight away when you feel the razor-sharp edges.

Bring your sense of *smell* into play. The box may have no smell of its own, but you can give it one – either a pleasant aroma, or a foul stench. Smell may not be something you've ever considered to be part of the learning process, yet how many times have you caught a smell that took you back to a moment ten, maybe twenty years ago? A smell can spark off memories of your first schoolroom, of the kitchen when you were a child or of some foreign holiday location. In fact, smell has been described as the sense most *closely* linked with recall – so clearly it's only sensible to make full use of one of the strongest natural forces behind memory.

Finally, imagine trying to *taste* the box. Use your teeth to pull off a corner; perhaps you're pleasantly surprised to find that it tastes of your favourite food. On the other hand . . .

The contrast is a powerful one. You begin with BOX, three letters on a page, but finish with an item alive to all five senses. Each time you involve a new sense, you give yourself an extra connection with the material to be learned – and it can be no coincidence that the most memorable stories have always excited as many of the senses as possible. In ages and cultures where stories were passed on by word of mouth, and where information had to be remembered at the first time of hearing, no description was complete unless it excited the audience through all of their senses. Anyone who has read the epic works of Homer and Virgil will remember descriptions of battles, voyages and adventures, because they are *designed* to be memorable.

Metaphorically Speaking . . .

Another characteristic of stories is their tendency to describe things more than once. Great poets and writers have always realised the power of metaphor – of creating a memorable picture to back up and to strengthen a description – and it's interesting to notice the way we do this ourselves in everyday speech.

'He ran out of the room like a bat out of hell'. 'His books are selling like hot cakes'. 'She was as cool as a cucumber'.

We give visible form to our words, repeating the original description, and by doing so we make our ideas many times more memorable.

It's a technique used constantly in the advertising industry. The message being emphasised is almost always the quality or desirability of a particular product – yet rather than simply presenting us with its name or slogan, advertisers try to communicate on a number of different levels.

In a television commercial, the messages are being carried in the style of the music, the tone of the voice-over – even the design of the lettering on the screen. A particular product is surrounded by a range of other images and ideas, and often a specific brand-name only appears at the very end, after the appropriate thought and feelings have been evoked. For example, we can usually tell from the music, scenery and action that what we are being sold is a holiday, a car or a pair of jeans – but if we miss the last few seconds of an advert we're likely to be none the wiser about the particular company or brand.

This technique is a powerful element of the *Mindpower System*. Key moments in a story are most memorable when they're conveyed in several different ways and, at least for a moment during all the general suggestions, made absolutely specific. This is especially important as a way of ensuring that the whole 'cheating' process doesn't backfire; after all, it's fine to change your information into bizarre images and amazing stories, but it's not much use if you can't change it back into the original words, numbers or names on the page.

There are two easy ways to stop this being a problem. The first is to *highlight* – to take a moment during the creation of each image or scene to concentrate on the key element, the bit that needs to be remembered most of all.

Imagine you're trying to remember CHIMNEY, as a word on a list or as part of a memory story. True to the system, you turn the word into a three-dimensional object and make your image unusual and distinctive – the chimney on top of Buckingham Palace, made from gold bricks and covered with royal crests. You involve plenty of senses, using imagination to feel the rough brick and smell the smoke. But when it comes to recalling the image, exactly which *part* of it are you supposed to remember? ROYAL? SMOKE? BRICKS?

To avoid confusion, take a few seconds to highlight the key word. Imagine the lights have gone out on everything except the chimney. Just for a moment you can see nothing except the chimney-stack itself – not the palace, not the smoke, not even the crests on the stone. As always you are in full control, so imagine flicking a light switch on and off.

In the *on* position the whole scene is visible, lots of different reminders pointing to the centre-piece of the scene. But in the *off* position, the only light you see is a spotlight illuminating the chimney.

To make doubly sure, this technique can be combined with another. Many of the tricks you use to help remember a piece of information are likely to be making it more and more general, so amongst them all it's important to have at least one reminder that remains explicit and precise.

Imagine you need to remember the word PARIS. Your imagination will probably bring in many things typically French; you smell the croissants, taste the garlic and hear the accordion music as you look up at the Eiffel Tower. But you need something extra to remind you that you're not trying to recall FRANCE or FRENCH – or even CROISSANT or EIFFEL TOWER!

The key lies in returning to the original word, PARIS. Why not imagine the whole scene covered in plaster-of-Paris? Or perhaps you can come up with an image for the character Paris from classical mythology. These additions would stand out sharply from the general imagery, and play a vital role in avoiding confusion.

To your CHIMNEY picture you could add a member of the royal family, sitting on the roof and smoking cigarette after cigarette – in other words, smoking *like a chimney*. If every image you create involves at least one specific reminder, you'll get into the habit of looking for it each time, and confirming for yourself the precise piece of information to be remembered.

Avoiding the Pitfalls

If there's a problem with stoytelling, it's that the technique can be just too easy! It's possible to write a story that doesn't make your material easier to remember at all.

As an example of this, the story below is an imaginary attempt to remember the following sequence of words:

DENTIST, GARAGE, MILK, EGGS, NEWSPAPER,
CHOCOLATE, HAIRDRESSER, LIBRARY BOOKS.

'A man walks into the dentist's surgery, and sits down in the chair. Suddenly, as he looks around him, he realises that he's actually in a garage, and he jumps up to run away – but the doorway is blocked by a giant carton of milk, and the window is jammed shut by a huge egg. Luckily he has a newspaper in his pocket, and he rolls it up and smashes the egg, opens the window, and climbs outside.

Unfortunately the dentist's surgery is on the second floor, and he has to jump down to the ground. He lands on a bar of chocolate, making his feet stick to the pavement as he walks down the street. He goes into the hairdresser's shop, and reads some library books as he waits to be served.'

Clearly this story fulfils some of the requirements of the *Mindpower System*. The events are certainly unusual, many different emotional responses are involved, and all the words on the page have been brought to life in some way.

But imagine trying to use this story to remember the list, even a few hours after learning it. The first question is going to be: where does the story start?

What's the use of having a powerful story lodged in your mind if you can't remember where to begin? The story to learn the colours on the London Underground map began with the map itself, and when you learned the order of the planets from the sun, the sun was where you began. The best practice is simply to pick the most obvious place to start.

The list above looks like a collection of things to do on a trip to town, so why not start your story where the trip itself will begin – in a car-park, perhaps, or the place where you get off the bus. When you learn a list that has no connection with a real location, a good idea is to choose your own object or place to act as a 'symbol' and obvious starting-place for the story.

If you were learning a list of books of the Bible, for example, you could start with an image of your local church or a cross. If you were working with countries or continents, your starting point could be an old-fashioned globe, or even Atlas himself, standing with the world on his shoulders.

But the main problem with this story lies in its connections. The idea of the dentist's surgery changing into a garage might be unusual enough to stay in the memory for a while, but there is no *connection* between the two places. You might go on to remember that the doorway is blocked – but by what? What does the man land on in the street? What happens in the hairdresser's?

When the story was created, the connections seemed obvious enough, but unless they are formed with special care, connections like these quickly dissolve, and the memorised list disappears.

My experience tells me that there are three main sorts of connection which work – **transformation, combination and interaction**.

Transformation

Think of some of the most memorable horror stories of all time. Do you remember the Incredible Hulk? In this comic strip and television series, the crucial moment in each episode came when Doctor David Banner shredded his shirt and turned into the muscle-bound Hulk. The central idea of the programme only worked because you could *see* the change as it took place – the muscles sprouting, the eyes changing, the clothes ripping.

Then there's the legend of the werewolf, featured in countless books and films. Once again the interest lies in the transformation itself, as hair grows, teeth lengthen and claws appear.

The important idea in all such stories is that Banner and Hulk, ordinary man and werewolf – even mild-mannered Clark Kent and Superman! – are really one and the same. There is change, astounding change, but there is also continuity and a connection between the 'before' and 'after'.

This connection has to be maintained in imaginative stories. Transformation is a very memorable event – after all, according to natural laws, it's one of the least likely things to happen. A chair doesn't suddenly become a bus, nor does a dentist's surgery change into a garage. There also needs to be some sort of reason for the transformation. David Banner transformed when he was angry, and the werewolf appeared at full moon.

Transformation has great potential for use in a story – but only when used correctly. Going back to the story above, how much more memorable it would have been if the following had happened.

Sitting down in the dentist's chair, the man was told that its lifting mechanism wasn't working properly. What was needed was something else to jack him up – so the dentist led him downstairs to an underground garage, and made him lie down on a rusty old wheel-jack . . .

The surgery has still become a garage, but the link is now stronger and more memorable.

So much for a location, but what about when objects or people transform? The key again is to include a reason, but also to make the process gradual, taking care that the connection between the 'before' and 'after' is always clear.

Imagine that CAR and ELEPHANT were two images you'd created from a list of abstract ideas, and they now needed connecting. This is the perfect situation for transformation, since there are similarities as well as obvious differences between these two modes of transport.

Imagine you are sitting in your car, when suddenly you hear what sounds like a horn. You look in your mirror and there's nothing behind you, but the trumpeting sound continues. You double check by using your wing mirrors – and, to your amazement, the mirrors start changing as you watch . . . into *ears*, one at each side. With a jerk the roof pulls back and you find yourself sitting high up in the open air. Bit by bit your car falls apart around you, until you are left sitting on top of this huge, trumpeting elephant, clutching a steering-wheel that's no longer attached to anything.

This last remnant is important, a constant reminder that the car hasn't simply been swapped for an elephant; it has *become* an elephant!

Practise your transformations

Printed below are five pairs of images. Spend a few minutes working out the best ways to make one transform into the other. In each case, look for similarities that can be used, and concentrate on maintaining the connections throughout.

To test yourself, cover up the right hand column, then take each of the words on the left in turn, recalling the scene that unfolded and retrieving the second word in each pair.

1. HAT   POSTBOX
2. TIGER   TABLE
3. BICYCLE   BIRD
4. TELEPHONE   FACE
5. COAT   BEAR

Combination:

Combination occurs, as the name suggests, when one thing is added to another. Again, there needs to be a reason for the process to take place, and it has to be clear how it has happened. Combination is a particularly powerful technique because it forces the mind to notice details, and to concentrate on the necessary connection between one piece of information and the next.

Imagine you must learn the following list of countries, in the order they appear here:

CHINA, FRANCE, HOLLAND, ENGLAND, WALES, GERMANY, SCOTLAND, EGYPT

Using combination alone, it's possible to link them all together memorably – and, as always, the first step is to make each word into something that can be moulded and controlled. A simple idea is to choose an object to symbolise each country. My immediate suggestions would be:

CHINA: Great Wall   FRANCE: Eiffel Tower
HOLLAND: Edam cheese   ENGLAND: Bowler hat
WALES: Leek   GERMANY: Frankfurter sausage
SCOTLAND: Kilt   EGYPT: Pyramid

Now the process of combination can take place. You begin with the **Great Wall of China** – imagine looking at it and thinking that it needs to be made a little higher. There are turrets at intervals along the whole length of the wall, so why not bolt a higher tower – the **Eiffel Tower** – on to each one? Imagine the work that would have to be done and the machinery that would be needed. For added effect, paint each replica tower a different colour.

If you take a closer look at one of the towers, you'll see that the top is sharp enough to cause disaster if a hot-air balloon flies too close. You need something to cover the points, and it ought to be something red to emphasise the danger. The answer: use a lorry-load of **Edam cheeses!** Imagine the sound as a cheese is squashed on to each of the sharp tops! The problem, of course, is that the cheeses will melt in the sun. By delicately placing a **bowler hat** on top of each one you can prevent that happening.

But suddenly it begins to rain. As you watch, it becomes clear that dangerous amounts of water are collecting in the brims of the hats. What you need now is something long and tubular to act as a drainage system – so instruct your workmen to use hundreds of **leeks!** They quickly hollow out each vegetable and then glue them all together to form a vast system of tubes, stretching from hat to hat and carrying away the water. True to their name, the leeks have hundreds of tiny holes drilled in them, allowing the water to leak away freely!

But what happens when the water on the ground becomes a problem? More and more is flowing down the bankside, and the workmen are becoming agitated. You need to build an inflatable platform, keeping you connected to the rest of the structure but making sure that you stay on top of the water – and **sausages** turn out to be the ideal material. You squeeze all the meat out of the skins, blow up each empty skin like a balloon, and then tape them all together in rows.

Everyone climbs aboard, but soon the inflatable platform is rocking precariously from side to side. Just in time you realise how to stabilise it – you order all the workmen to remove the **kilts** they are wearing, then sew them together to form a long skirt that trails around the platform on all sides. This seems to do the trick – but then, disaster strikes.

With a loud bang, the platform bursts and begins to sink, forcing you to cling on to the nearest tower. As you hang there, you see that your mistake was to build the platform just too near the point of a partially submerged **pyramid**!

To recall the list of countries in order, simply remember the sequence in which this huge and unusual structure was built, highlighting the key objects and then substituting the countries they represent. In this example the connections *are* the story, and the sequence is memorable both forwards and in reverse.

For longer lists you should only use combination for some of the connections, each time concentrating on the reason and the method, and always making sure that you combine things forcefully and memorably. By nailing, squashing, glueing or welding things together you force them to remain connected, and anchor them just as strongly to your mind.

Practise your combinations

As with the list of countries, take the following items and *combine* them, maintaining their order by joining one to the next, to the next, and so on. Use as many different combining techniques as possible – glueing, sewing, nailing, bolting – and find out which ones work best for you.

When you've finished, check through your images and combinations, then test yourself by returning to the original list.

UMBRELLA, FOOTBALL, PENCIL, CHEESE, TEA, COAL, TELEVISION, JELLY, MAGAZINE, FISH

Interaction

Since imagination places you at the centre of every story, moulding and controlling what goes on, it's not surprising that the third sort of connection involves your own relationship with the events. This is the perfect opportunity to imagine powerful emotional responses to the action taking place, and to make *yourself* the connection between images.

The more links you can develop with your own thoughts and reactions the better. In the earlier 'shopping' story, the man pulled a newspaper out of his pocket to smash the egg – but what *reason* is there for this to be a newspaper, and not a torch or a stick? And why should you remember that he walked into a hairdresser's, and not a butcher's or a bank? This story involves many emotional responses, but few of them are used to stress the chain of connections. In the best sort of *Mindpower* story, things change around you, but always in connection *with* you: this is the importance of interaction.

How much more memorable it would have been if the following had happened.

'Realising that he couldn't escape from the room because of the milk in the doorway, the man decided to open the carton and have a drink'. Imagine this idea springing up in *your* mind, and link your own response with what happened next.

'He decided to make a meal of it; pulling up a chair and table, he began to eat breakfast' – the meal, after all, when milk is most likely to be used. Imagine expecting the daily paper to be delivered soon, since the milk has already arrived.

Your own expectations can be a powerful part of the story,

sometimes being fulfilled, but at other times coming up against disappointments and surprises. On this occasion a newspaper does arrive, but it crashes through the roof and lands on your head . . .

Your own responses allow you to be both director and star. As the story continues, you view and react to the events from outside – yet at the same time you're *inside* the action, responding as the hero or heroine to whom all the strange events are happening.

As you read the paper, imagine expecting the newsprint to rub off on your hands. You look to see how dirty they are . . . and realise suddenly that they're covered not in ink, but in thick, sticky chocolate! All your senses can be brought into play at this point – but, as always, a specific reminder must also be included. 'To your surprise, you see that each page of the paper contains an advert for some well-known brand of chocolate. As you touch each one, it melts in your hand.'

The technique of interaction is a powerful means of remembering items in a precise sequence. In daily life our minds work on a series of connections, and often we only think of one thing after it's been suggested by something else.

This is especially noticeable during one of those conversations where both people suddenly lose track of what they were talking about. The traditional thing to do is to go back a few steps in the chain, and then work forward until you return to the forgotten place. 'We were talking about your party, and that got us on to Simon's father – then you said something about his car, and that reminded me about *my* car and going to the garage . . .'

This natural tendency of the mind can be made an effective force in remembering the story. If sequence hadn't been important, you could simply have pictured the items on the breakfast table, and then linked them together by combination. But, clearly, a sequence can just as easily be confirmed.

The milk made you think generally about breakfast, and specifically about the things being delivered. The paper *was* delivered, if in a slightly unorthodox way. Then the paper made you think about dirty newsprint – and your expectations ended in surprise when you felt the chocolate . . .

As an example of the importance of interaction, imagine you needed to learn the following list of presents. To save time on your trip to town, you've worked out the order of the shops you'll have to visit, so the sequence of the items needs to be maintained.

SCARF, SNORKEL, TEAPOT, BRANDY, COAT, WATCH, GOLF BALLS, PICTURE

Since you're about to go on a shopping trip, why not start by imagining yourself getting ready to leave.

A SCARF would come in handy on such a cold day, so imagine wrapping one around your neck. Unfortunately you seem to be wrapping it a little *too* tightly – what you need now is something to stop you suffocating! Luckily you have a SNORKEL in your pocket, the perfect life-saver, and by putting it in your mouth you can breathe freely for long enough to remove the scarf.

Now that you no longer need the snorkel, you can make use of its shape and hang it up on a hook – but there's still some water inside, and it starts pouring on to the floor in a long stream.

The answer is to put a TEAPOT underneath to catch the water through its spout. You hear the sound of the pot being filled, and you start to feel thirsty – a sensation which gets worse and worse until you feel you're about to collapse.

Just when it seems too late, into the room bounds a huge St Bernard with a delivery of BRANDY. You gulp it down, feeling it glow inside you. In fact, when you look down at your chest you see that the top half of your body has begun to glow bright red!

Desperate to cover yourself up, you pull on a long COAT, but unfortunately the coat is so long that it trips you up when you try to walk. You're falling, but the director of this film seems to have become very artistic at this point because your fall happens in slow-motion. This gives you time to prepare to hit the ground, and your thoughts turn to the only breakable thing you have with you – your WATCH. Pulling it off, you throw it into some grass so that it has a soft landing.

Finding the watch again proves harder than you'd imagined. You look everywhere, and you're starting to get cross, when suddenly it occurs to you that it might have fallen down a hole.

At that moment, as if controlled by your thoughts, the grass around you begins to turn into a golf-course, and holes appear wherever you look. None of them, though, seems to contain the watch – in fact, every single one has a GOLF BALL in it instead. The more balls you find, the more frustrated you become. Finally, in your anger, you hurl all the balls into the distance . . . and hear the terrible sound of breaking glass. Running to look, you see that the balls have gone through the window of a house, smashing the glass on every expensive PICTURE inside.

This whole story is based on interaction. You are altering things around you, but *you* are also being altered and affected by the events, and strong connection is maintained. The sequence of images is also clear, and even if the exact order of items on a list isn't important, by thinking in sequence you make sure that none of them is missed off.

Practise your interactions
Try the technique yourself by learning the list of words below.

Look at the 'reason' for knowing the words, decide on an appropriate starting-point, then let the story take shape. At every stage involve your own responses; allow the action to affect you at the same time as you affect *it*, and enjoy being both the director and the star of your own memory-movie.

Items To Bid For In An Auction,
In Order Of Appearance:
LAMP, CLOCK, BIBLE, DOLLS' HOUSE, MUG,
TABLE, POKER, VASE, TOY TRAIN, LANTERN

The personal control at the heart of *Mindpower* means that stories only work to their full potential when you invent and visualise them yourself. You can bring in people and places that you know well, and can include your own specific likes and dislikes, fears and hatreds, loves and pleasures.

But to prove that any sort of factual information can be made memorable, below are two examples of the way real lists can be made into effective stories. Stand by to pass tests, win at quizzes and impress your friends, because here are the ten longest rivers in the U.K., in order, and the sequence of British Prime Ministers since the Second World War. The stories created allow you to learn both lists forwards and backwards, and they prove that even the most abstract and boring information can be controlled and remembered.

If you can learn material like this, there should be no problem recalling the sort of lists you have to remember every day.

For both examples there's a description of the imagined story in full. See how many of the key elements you can spot, and notice all the techniques used to make these stories effective. At the same time, think about other techniques that could be employed – ways to bring in more of the senses, or opportunities for reinforcing the connections with *you*.

The Ten Longest Rivers In The U.K.
 1. Severn 2. Thames 3. Trent 4. Aire 5. Ouse
 6. Wye 7. Tay 8. Nene 9. Clyde 10. Spey

The first step, as always, is to turn this abstract information into material that can be moulded and controlled, and can form the basis for a story. The best way to begin is to find suggestions for images within the words on the page.

SEVERN	The number seven and, from that, the Magnificent Seven.
THAMES	'Teams'; perhaps a range of different sporting teams, complete with uniforms and equipment.
TRENT	'Trench'; either the pit or the coat.
AIRE	'Air', or anything to do with breathing.
OUSE	To 'ooze' or seep out. This could be represented by any sort of runny, sticky liquid.
WYE	The letter 'Y', or even a pair of Y-fronts!
TAY	'Tail' or 'tray'.
NENE	The number nine, or the German word 'Nein!'
CLYDE	The male half of the gangster duo Bonnie and Clyde.
SPEY	'Spray' or 'Spain'.

Next, a memorable starting point has to be chosen. Since this is a list of rivers, the obvious place to begin would be on a river bank.

Set the whole scene in your mind: it's a beautiful summer's day, and you're sitting by the side of a slow-moving river. Birds are singing and you can hear a village cricket-match in the distance. You feel relaxed and have nothing to do, so you decide to exercise your memory . . .

Suddenly the peace is shattered. Birds are scared into flight all around you as a group of figures approaches, on horseback, riding up the centre of the river. For a while you can't quite see who they are, but as you watch a few details begin to stand out.

They're wearing cowboy-suits and carrying guns, and when you recognise a few of the faces you realise that this is the Magnificent Seven! Powerful 'Western' music booms out as they come alongside you, and, as if to confirm the key word here, you notice that they're all drinking Seven-Up! One of them hands you a can, and for a moment the frame is frozen. Everything disappears except the number seven on the drinks can.

The focus of this scene is the number seven, and the river to be remembered is the SEVERN.

The group has reached the end of its river journey, and needs to climb out on to the bank. You suspect that this might be harder than they imagine, though, and you're right – they've taken on so much water that their horses simply aren't strong enough to lift them on to dry land.

You offer to help. Running off through the fields, you come across the local cricket teams and enlist their assistance. As you lead them back towards the river you also meet a hockey and a rugby team, all practising in the sunshine. They come along too, and their combined strength is enough to pull the horsemen from the water. Imagine all the struggling and straining, and decide how you would organise the teams to get the most out of them.

A few onlookers have gathered, so, while the rescue operation continues, you put up a few signs, each printed with the word 'teams' to explain what's going on. To reward them for their efforts, you present each team member with a model of Tower Bridge, and there's one left over which you stand on top of one of the signs. The story pauses here for a moment; everything disappears except for the sign and the model, focusing your memory on the word 'teams' and, from that, on the river THAMES.

Making the prize models has been difficult at such short notice, and you're interested to see what the teams do with them. To your annoyance, they throw them into a nearby trench! Determined to get them out again you pull on your trench-coat for protection and dive headlong towards the broken ground.

For extra effect this happens in slow-motion – and the story freezes completely for a moment at the point when you touch the earth. Your coat is the same colour as the mud, and for a couple of seconds everything disappears except this combined image. The focus is on 'trench', so this is the river TRENT.

Scratching away at the mud with your hands, you manage to dig through to where the prizes have been buried. But suddenly, to your horror, you realise that the earth is falling in on you. Within seconds you're buried, and there's only one thought in your mind: air! In the darkness, the word itself lights up and flashes in your mind, and the next river on the list is confirmed as the AIRE.

Just when you think you can hold out no longer, you feel something warm and sticky dripping on to you through the earth. Some sort of liquid is oozing through the soil, and it feels rather pleasant – so much so, that you let out a series of 'ooh!'s. As you do so, you realise that you can breathe again; by making these noises, you've blown little air-holes in the mud. Each time one is formed, everything else in the picture disappears for a moment. The focus is on the 'ooh!'s, the ooze, and, of course, the OUSE.

Unfortunately, holes are beginning to form underneath you as well. More and more liquid oozes down from above, and you let out a scream when you realise that the weight on top of you is finally too much. You're falling, and you land with a bump in an underground cavern.

The light here hurts your eyes, and to make matters worse all the walls in the cavern are painted bright yellow. You notice some objects littered around the room: to your left a pot of yoghurt, in front of you a yo-yo, and to your right a toy yacht. The room itself seems to be Y-shaped . . . and then the significance of it all dawns on you. Everything here begins with the letter 'Y'; and, sure enough, when the freeze-frame happens, all you can see is the fluorescent 'Y' outline of the room. The river to be remembered here is the WYE.

You need to escape. The only item here that doesn't begin with a 'Y' is an old tin tray, which you discover when you trip over it. You decide to put it to use, and by pulling and stretching the metal you manage to mould it around your body. It feels uncomfortable, but soon you've constructed your own personal armoured vehicle, using yo-yos for wheels!

To remind yourself that this is still really a tray you place some crockery on the roof, and you have the idea of attaching a tail to the back to make it look like a giant metal mouse! The tail is clearly the most unusual element of all, and for a moment you pause to focus on the point where it connects with the tray. The river to be remembered here is the TAY.

With a crash of breaking rock you drive your new vehicle through the wall of the cavern and out into the open air. But your happiness is short-lived, because immediately you're stopped by nine German guards, three rows of three, who tell you that you'll have to do it all again; your first attempt wasn't good enough. You try to argue with them, but it's no use – they all shout 'Nein!'. 'Nein!'.

To remind yourself of their instructions, you write the number nine on your hand. Pause for a few seconds to concentrate on the writing: the river here is the NENE.

With some difficulty you reverse the vehicle, allowing you to drive out of the cavern again. You feel nervous, hoping that the guards will praise your escape this time. As you drive out, you wind down your window – but to your surprise you find a sawn-off shotgun levelled at your face.

The guards have gone, and standing there now is **Clyde** Barrow, the notorious gangster. Perhaps he was disguised as one of the Germans earlier on, because he still seems to be wearing bits of their uniform. He opens the door and pulls you out, and then seems to *glide* into the driver's seat. As he drives off he hangs a tattered sign out of the window to display the name of the vehicle's new owner. The sign, on which you focus for a moment, says CLYDE – the name of the next river.

As he drives away, you're determined to see what he's going to do next. He seems to be stopping every so often to pick people up from the roadside – first a group of Spanish dancers, then a matador . . . even a huge, snorting bull! The animal must be slightly smelly, because one of the dancers is having to spray an air-freshener.

There can be no doubt where they're all going; you make a quick diary note to remind yourself. The single word you write down is 'Spain', and, as the story ends, this word is all that remains in focus. The final river must be the SPEY.

British Prime Ministers Since The War

Clement ATLEE, Sir Winston CHURCHILL, Sir Anthony EDEN, Harold MACMILLAN, Sir Alec DOUGLAS-HOME, Harold WILSON, Edward HEATH, Harold WILSON, James CALLAGHAN, Margaret THATCHER, John MAJOR

Once again, the first step is to turn these abstract words into material for a story. Several of the words here are more complicated than those in the previous list, and the best idea is often to break them up into separate parts.

ATLEE	Perhaps 'hat' and 'Lee' – the 'Lee' could be Bruce Lee.
CHURCHILL	He suggests his own images: thick cigar and victory-sign.
EDEN	The Garden of Eden, or maybe Edam cheese.
MACMILLAN	The 'Mac' could be a raincoat; the rest of the name suggests 'millinery' – hats.
DOUGLAS-HOME	For the first part, why not use Kirk or Michael Douglas. The second part is pronounced 'hume', so 'humour' could be suggested.
WILSON	He appears twice on the list, so you'll need to use two different images. One possibility would be a picture based on the words 'will' and 'son'; another could be a horse-racing fan who 'wills on' his chosen winner.
HEATH	A patch of heath-land would be the

	obvious image – perhaps also involving the word 'heat'.
CALLAGHAN	'Calla' suggests Calor gas, and 'han' could become 'hand' or 'ham'.
THATCHER	Imagine the thatcher himself, hard at work on a roof of straw.
MAJOR	Perhaps you think of a sergeant-major, or picture a band of majorettes.

A memorable place to begin the story would be the debating chamber of the House of Commons.

Set the scene in your imagination: people are sitting on the benches to left and right, and a noisy and passionate debate is in progress. Determined to work out what's happening, you ask one of the MPs who points towards the very centre of the hall.

From where you're standing you can see a huge cowboy hat, and a man who's trying to get into it! Looking closer, you recognise him as the martial-arts expert Bruce Lee. With the crowd cheering him on he performs jumps and kicks, and tries his hardest to leap into the hat. He's having difficulties, though, and this could take all day! Your eyes are getting tired, and all you can focus on are the central elements of the scene – the hat and Lee. The first Prime Minister on the list must be ATLEE.

Soon you're so tired that you have to sit down. The MP sitting next to you sees that you need to relax, and hands you the largest cigar you've ever seen! You only just manage to squeeze it between two of your fingers, which are forced out into a V-shape. When you bring the cigar close to your face, the only things you can see are the cigar itself and your fingers – and since the focus is clearly on his two trademarks, the next Prime Minister can only be CHURCHILL.

Smoke from the cigar is becoming thicker and thicker. Eventually it clears, but you're astonished to see that the scene has changed. All the MPs are still there, but now their benches are standing among trees and flowers. Instead of being in a 'house', you're in a *garden*, and you hunt around for clues about exactly where you are.

You wander amongst the trees, clumsily crashing into one as

you turn a corner, and bringing a single apple falling down on to your head. The fruit is bright red and perfectly round; when you take a bite, though, you discover that it's not an apple at all, but a whole Edam cheese! You munch your way through it, and for a while it's all you can think about. Edam is the focus of the scene, so the name of this garden – and the next Prime Minister – must be EDEN.

The cheese was delicious. Still, you expected an apple, and you feel you deserve some sort of refund. Experience tells you that refunds are made in shops, so you wander through the garden in search of one.

It's beginning to rain, and you're doubly glad that the first shop you see has raincoats in the window. This shop has the interesting name 'Macs and Millinery', and, sure enough, the room inside is divided into two halves: on the left are the macs, and on the right are the hats – thousands of them, in all shapes and sizes. You take your time, choosing a coat and hat that suit you, and you look at yourself again and again in the mirror. Each time, your eyes focus on the mac and the millinery, and clearly the Prime Minister in question is MACMILLAN.

You're the only customer in this large shop, and, naturally, you'd like to know why. The assistant explains that everyone is at home watching the Oscar ceremony on television, and to prove it she switches on the TV in the shop.

On the stage you see Kirk and Michael Douglas laughing and joking with each other. It seems to you that the audience laughter is a little artificial, though – and sure enough you notice a sign above the stage that says 'humour!', flashing on and off to tell the audience when to respond. The importance of the whole scene dawns on you: the next Prime Minister is DOUGLAS-HOME.

You reach out to switch off the television – but somehow your hand goes right through the glass, and you find yourself crashing noisily into the ceremony itself!

Everyone is looking at you, including the two famous actors, and you hurry to find a seat. After a moment the proceedings continue; true to form, they're still going on five hours later . . .

You find your eyes wandering to the people sitting near you, and you notice a man handing something to his son. Looking closer, you see that it's a *will*; he's so convinced he won't make it through the whole show alive that he's giving his will to his son for safe-keeping. For a moment this little scene is the focus of your attention. The next Prime Minister is WILSON.

After a few more hours you can take no more. The episode with the will has made you realise that you need to escape, and you ask the lady sitting next to you to show you the way out. She points at a door on the left, and as you walk towards it you notice that the floor is changing from wood to sandy grass.

Your clothes are changing, too, and soon the formal suit you wore for the awards ceremony has turned into an outfit more suited to hiking! You pass through the door, and find yourself standing in the middle of a vast heath. In contrast to the crowded hall, the only thing you can see here is a signpost confirming your new location, and it focuses your mind on the next Prime Minister: HEATH.

You take a closer look at the sign. There's a length of white ribbon attached to the post, stretching for about ten metres and then hanging, magically, in mid-air. Desperate to have all of this explained to you, you're delighted to see a man running in your direction.

You can also hear the sound of hooves. A horse-race is approaching, and the man – in between shouts of support for the horses – tells you that this is the finishing-line. About twenty horses are galloping nearer and nearer, but all of your attention is on the man as he becomes more and more excited. He 'wills on' his favourite horse – and so, for the second time, the Prime Minister to be remembered is WILSON.

As the race comes to an end, the man collapses, exhausted. He needs some food to revive him, so you're relieved to see the perfect equipment lying on the ground nearby; a box of food and a gas stove. Unfortunately, the gas-bottle seems to have run out because you can't get the stove to light – but the man tells you not to worry. He lifts up his hand, and out shoots a powerful blast of Calor gas which hits the stove and makes it burst into flames! You decide there and then to buy one of these amazing hands yourself, and write down a reminder in your diary: 'Calor hand'. The next Prime Minister on the list is CALLAGHAN.

The bad news is that the heath has also caught fire, and flames are spreading away into the distance. You run with them, determined to warn people of the approaching hazard, but unfortunately you're too slow to stop the fire reaching a cottage, and suddenly the whole place is ablaze. Worst affected is the straw on the roof, and the thatcher who is working there is forced to leap into your arms. Imagine your surprise when you realise that you're actually holding *Margaret* THATCHER!

She is not at all pleased, and you decide to make a hasty exit. What you need more than anything is a diversion – so you're delighted to hear the sound of drums, and to see that a military band is approaching along the lane.

As it comes closer, you notice that it's led from the front by a fierce-looking sergeant-major, who shouts loudly to a group of majorettes as they twirl their batons. You slip in among their ranks, and attempt to disguise yourself by pinning a badge to your chest that identifies you as a MAJOR – the final Prime Minister on the list.

Once you've visualised both of these stories, go back through them a few times in your mind to emphasise all the important elements. Story-telling like this may take a little more time than you're used to spending on memory, but it's time well spent, and you'll soon find your speed improving as the techniques come to seem more natural.

I can make fifty-two playing cards into items in a story and connect them all together in less than forty-five seconds. With a little practice, you'll discover that you can retain any sort of information in your memory for ever.

MEMORY ROUTES

When I memorise vast amounts of information, to save time I often use sequences that I've designed already. These take away the need to create connections between bits of material; the connections are already there, and the pieces of information only have to be made real and controllable and then 'fitted into the slots'.

The sequences I've worked out are all based on routes that I know well from real experience – routes around rooms, towns, even whole countries – and they make use of the memory's love of patterns and places.

Imagine you had a portable, wipe-clean white-board and a set of pens. Printed indelibly on the board, from top to bottom, were ten lines, each given a number on the left-hand side. Whenever you were presented with information that needed to be retained you could write it on the board, putting one or more items on each of the lines. This information would then be stored until it could be wiped off and more items written in its place.

This is the effect I create with my routes. Each is simply a list of ten places, ten 'spaces' ready to be filled with information, and the ten are connected together in a definite sequence. When information is placed in the spaces, it too becomes patterned and ordered. Unlike the storytelling techniques described already, these routes have restrictions on size: when all ten spaces are filled up, I need to move to another route if I want to continue memorising, and when I re-use a route I have to wipe out anything written there already. But for reasonably small amounts of information, and for ease and speed, the use of routes is an invaluable element in the *Mindpower System*. The first step is to create a route – if you like, to draw up the lines on your 'board'. Choose a place that you know well. It could be the house where you live, the place where you work, or maybe the home you grew up in. It could be a whole town, a walk you know well, even a single room – just as long as the place can be divided into ten clear sections.

The nature of these 'sections' depends upon the sort of place you've chosen. In the most obvious example, they could be the separate rooms in a house. On a walk they might be the most memorable landmarks, or in a town they could be a combination of shops, parks and streets. The important thing is to use as much of the space as possible.

If your house has more than ten rooms, group some of them together in a single 'area'. Rather than just using ten rooms and leaving wasted space, you might group together several children's bedrooms as one area, or combine the garage and the utility room. All the available space in a country could be utilised by using whole counties, states, or even 'regions' as your ten sections. The more space dedicated to each area, the more possibilities you will have when it comes to filling them with items.

Large sections have a tendency to feel a little vague, though, and I find that a single building is usually the best setting to choose. There's enough room to manoeuvre, but there's also sufficient connection between the sections.

Larger or smaller places can still be made to work well. If you've chosen a whole town, mark out the sections as logically as possible, making sure you remember where one ends and another begins. At the other extreme, if you use a single room, bring in as much variation as possible. A drawer within a piece of furniture might be one of the 'areas', but using more than one drawer would be confusing.

Make all the sections different, separated by location and by the sort of place they are, and use your imagination. Although items will have to be fitted into these places, there are no laws of physics that have to be followed – in fact, the very act of squeezing an elephant into your desk drawer would be pretty memorable in itself!

When you've decided on your sections, the next thing to do is to work out their order. Once this has been arranged it will be dangerous to make any changes, so a little time needs to be spent getting it right.

To make use of the memory's love of patterns and connections, it's best to start by looking for any sequences that already exist. One of the benefits of choosing a walk is that the order of the various areas is already worked out, but in most buildings there is at least a general sense of the way round.

Imagine your chosen place is a house. The path outside could be the first section, and the front porch the second. From there you move into the hallway and through into the kitchen, and this leads straight into the utility area. There isn't actually a door here into the dining-room, but that's still the next section because it's just through the wall. This room leads to the lounge, and from there you start climbing the staircase, the next section on your route. The stairs take you to the bathroom, and your final section might be the bedrooms, or perhaps even the loft.

If your chosen place is a single room, a good idea is to move around it in a generally clockwise direction. The first section could be the doorway, the second a table by the door, the third a wardrobe, and so on. If you're using a town or city, there are almost certainly regular routes you take through or around it that can form a basis for the order of your sections.

*   *   *

Use your imagination to mark out your territory. Walk from section to section in your mind, reminding yourself of the boundaries, and moving from the first to the tenth.

As you go, notice the things that make each section unique: the cooker in the kitchen, the shower-stall in the bathroom, the washing-machine in the garage. Perhaps on your walk one area has an especially tall tree, or you go past a garden where a particularly vicious dog is chained to a post. These details are important because the next step is to fill the ten sections with the information you need to remember, and to use these fixed details as anchoring points.

As always, abstract material must be made real, and prepared to be fixed into the route.

Next, the information needs to be divided up so that you can make efficient use of the space available. Ten items would be perfect, one for each section, although it is possible to place more than one in each. The important thing is that there are the *same* number of items in each area; otherwise it's all too easy to miss some of them out.

I suggest you work out two routes that you can trust completely. By placing two items in each space, you can learn the list of forty words printed at the very start of the book.

To do that, the items must be securely fixed. All of the techniques of *Mindpower* can be used to great effect – bring in all the senses, for example, and remember to highlight and reinforce the focus of each scene.

You can also be as untidy as you like as you deal with your material in unusual and memorable ways. Rather than simply placing a football in the bath, imagine squeezing it in between the taps, only to see it shoot out and roll around the slippery sides, splashing water on to the carpet. Nail a loaf of bread to the wall of your office; splash tomato sauce on to your bedside cabinet, or pour custard across the front of the town hall. You no longer have to think about connections, so throw all of your imaginative energy into fixing the items in place.

The more experienced you become, the more items you'll be able to place within a single section. Two in each area isn't difficult, as long as you always put the first on the left and the second on the right. If possible, make some connection between the two items, the one on the left affecting the other in some way, and always appearing before it.

If you need to learn large amounts of information, your route-system can be combined with all the techniques of story-telling. Make each section the starting-place for a story, and an ordinary semi-detached house in the suburbs can become home to ten long, fantastic stories, each containing perhaps twenty pieces of information! The possibilities are endless.

When your route has been filled, take another quick walk through the sections, checking as you go that you can see all of the items, and making sure that they're all still there in the correct locations.

As you become familiar with your routes you'll find it easy to walk quickly through them, forwards and backwards – even to find a numbered item on the list simply by counting through to its allotted place. Remember, *any* material can be fixed inside the route – names, words, numbers – just as soon as it's been made real and controllable. It will stay there for a while, and although you can make it stay fixed for longer by reminding yourself of the route's contents, this 'limited life' tends to be useful. The material is there for long enough to be used, but the memory's white-board has been wiped clean when you come to it again with more information to be learned.

PUT IT TO THE TEST

When you're comfortable with your two routes, and have decided which of them will always come first, why not turn back to the start of the book and try learning the list of forty items. It's likely that you won't manage it perfectly straight away, but you'll certainly remember many more items than you did the first time around.

If you do make a few mistakes, find out which bits are missing and think up some new ways to anchor them into your route. Once you can remember the entire list in order, you can feel justly proud – it's no mean feat.

You'll have changed even the most abstract pieces of information – SMELL, HOT, EIGHT – into real objects that can come under your control. You'll have let your imagination run riot, forcing these objects into sections along the route, two in each. You'll have stressed to yourself the focus of each image, allowing you to convert the pictures back into words when the time arrives.

Most important of all, you'll have taken control.

The first step is to realise that, like the car that won't drive itself, the mind will never do what you want until you learn how to use it. Good driving comes with practice, as the basic techniques are applied to more and more real-life situations – and the same holds true for the memory. Techniques may seem awkward in the beginning, but before long they'll have become second nature.

Practice makes perfect, and the following sections show how the techniques of memory can be *put* into practice in countless everyday situations. The principles learnt in Part One are the foundations on which more specific techniques can be built.

If you have an imagination, then you possess everything you need to set off on the road to *Mindpower*.

Part Two

MINDPOWER for WORDS

Central to Mindpower is the need to turn dry words on the page into living, moving, colourful pictures. At the same time, many of the examples in Part One showed the importance of using the original words themselves – of manipulating their spellings and sounds to allow images to be formed and to create hooks for the memory. Rather than moving away from language altogether, the *Mindpower System* focuses on language as its very basis. What it aims to replace is a reliance on words alone.

A powerful mind *uses* words by taking control of them, moulding them into individual memory tools and making full use of their potential to fuel the imagination.

It's ironic that many people find words so difficult to learn, struggling to hold on to them by vague means rather than seeing their value as a basis of memory. So much of the information we all have to learn comes in the form of words, and one of the keys to *Mindpower* is to become aware of the power of words themselves.

We have to learn the names of people, places, companies, books. Every day we spend time searching through address lists and dictionaries, often for information we've looked up many times before and will undoubtedly need to find again in the future.

Added to the words we need to know are the words we could benefit from knowing – foreign words; useful new words in our own language; the words that make up essays, quotations, articles and notes. Words can be plain, complicated, illogical, confusing – yet the *Mindpower System* makes it possible to find *within* words the most effective means to remember them.

Since language is often shifting and inconsistent, why not make use of its scope?

Advertisers do this all the time, writing slogans that carry more than one meaning – and, because of that, more than one way to be remembered: 'Everything We Do is Driven by You', 'Roses Grow on You'. They understand how puns, plays-on-words – even anagrams – catch our attention and make us concentrate on the names of particular brands: 'Guinness – Pure Genius', 'SEGA: It Takes AGES to be This Good', 'Ninteresting Ninnovative Nintendo'. They even create new words designed to be easily remembered.

George Eastman, for example, needed to invent a memorable word to name and advertise his new process of photography. He used unusual letters, a simple but distinctive construction – even the 'clicking' sound of a camera – to come up with his solution: Kodak!

Remembering words becomes easier when you're used to concentrating on them, looking carefully at their shapes and listening closely to their sounds. The English language we use today combines elements from a great many sources, including Greek, Latin, French and German – and when you're used to looking for it, words can be seen to come alive with the energy of their origins and parts.

There are words within words, links between words, unusual constructions, memorable patterns of letters. As seen already in many of the examples in Part One, the more images a word suggests, the more successfully it can be remembered as part of a list or incorporated into a story. By combining imagination with an eye for detail you can take any word under your control.

See The Possibilities

In some cases the process relies most on sight. As an example, consider three words: THEATRE, INSTRUMENT and CHAMBER. All three have a number of words similar to them in spelling, sound or meaning, threatening confusion when you try to incorporate them into some memory task.

But things start to become clearer once you notice the heat

in T*HEAT*RE. Your image can now involve a fire blazing on the stage, or a play set in the Sahara Desert, and your memory is given another 'hook' – as well as confirmation of the precise word being learned.

In your imagination you can see someone strum an IN*STRUM*ENT – and why not visualise a large ham roasting in the middle of the C*HAM*BER? Suddenly the words have become more alive, and the vital extra senses of touch, hearing and smell have been brought into play.

Hear The Clues

In other cases, new dimensions can be added to words by *hearing* the possibilities.

Sometimes you can discover alternative meanings for all or part of a word. The two syllables of CROSSBRED, for example, are the same in sound as several other words, and a memorable image could easily be formed of an angry loaf – cross bread – or of the dough you would have to mix to bake a wholemeal crucifix!

Perhaps you're learning a list of American states, and need to remember the word ARIZONA. You might imagine a horse or greyhound called Harry (maybe he looks like Harry Belafonte) being patted by his owner. After all, it only takes a slight change of sound to turn ARIZONA into *'Harry's owner'*!

TENNESSEE suggests an ocean full of ten pound notes: *'tenner sea'*; MINNESOTA could be a *'mini soda'*, . . . and so on, until the whole list has been manipulated and taken under your control.

Try It Yourself

Practise manipulating the following list of words, looking – and listening – for images and reminders. Use all the techniques at your disposal to turn abstract words into memorable pictures.

ALASKA, FULHAM, CARPENTER, GENESIS, INTER-
CEDE, DELAWARE, TONAL, FILTRATE

Understanding Words

As well as allowing you to create new 'meanings' for words, this sort of attention to detail can sometimes bring to light *real* meanings. If you understand something about a word's origin or construction it can make it much easier to remember – especially its spelling – and such discoveries usually come when you split a word apart.

Students learning to speak English, for example, would find CUPBOARD much easier to remember and spell if they separated the 'cup' from the 'board' and deduced the origin of the word. Similarly HANDKERCHIEF splits up into 'hand' and 'kerchief'; even for native English-speakers this simple step can help with difficult spellings, and make complicated new words far easier to learn.

LEARNING FOREIGN LANGUAGES

With a little imagination you can also learn to see some of the real links between words in different languages. Again, this is sometimes possible by looking at the written word, and at other times only by concentrating on its sound. You might *see* that the French word LETTRE means 'letter', for instance, but you would probably have to *hear* the German word BOOT to help you remember that it means 'boat'.

Imagination is even more important when an extra 'step' exists between words in different languages. We tend to remember information much more easily when we feel we understand it, so a moment or two thinking about a word can prove to be time well spent. I will never forget that the German word for harbour is 'Hafen' – but only because a teacher once pointed out its link with the English word 'haven'.

Similarly, 'tapis', from French, translates as 'carpet' – understandable, when you think that the first rug-carpets had originally been hung on the wall like *tapes*tries! When links like this exist it makes sense to use them. And when you can't see a connection? Take the information under your control and *invent* one. You can create your own reason for one word in English meaning another in some foreign language, and you can also invent logic for tricky spellings where none seems to exist.

Memory techniques are especially important when you learn a new language, since even very tenuous reminders can be enough to help you towards more instinctive recall. By using

Mindpower techniques you can learn a word, put it into practice a few times – from memory, rather than looking it up – and find eventually that you remember the word with ease, even if you can't remember *why*.

There are three main steps involved in using the *Mindpower System* to learn a foreign language.

Step One

The first step is to build up your reason for an unfamiliar word having a particular translation in English. As explained above, this should be done by concentrating on the word, discovering all the possibilities of appearance, sound and meaning.

Sometimes, especially with the words you use regularly, a single connecting picture is all you need to trigger the memory. This picture must combine two elements: the image you create by manipulating the foreign word, and the real definition in English. The picture becomes your reason for remembering that one word means the other – a form of logic to act as memory's foundation.

Below are two sets of examples – the first from French, the second from German. In each case begin by looking through the ten foreign words, then read through the memory suggestions, trying to form the images in your mind. Finally, return to the original ten words to test yourself on their meanings. This is especially effective if you're learning the words for the first time – but even if you do know them already, it's useful to remember the pictures and to experience the power of imagination.

French

PORTE, MAISON, LIVRE, LIT, SOEUR, MAIN, SUD, PAIN, MATIN, VENT

PORTE means DOOR

Take a look at the door closest to you as you read this. Imagine pushing it open . . . and being hit by a huge tidal wave which smashes against you, knocking you to the ground. Water is pouring through the doorway, and several boats are being carried along in the waves. The reason? This is the door to a *port* – and, as if to confirm it, an expensive bottle of port wine bobs through the water around your feet.

This picture will act as a powerful prompt whenever you need to remember the French word for 'door'. It's always useful if the scene involves some sort of discovery or sudden experience, since the overall aim is to create a flash of understanding. Here, you open the door to learn what lies behind it – just as you use these memory techniques to find out what foreign translation lies behind a particular word. My experience tells me that a mental trigger is much more likely to be successful if the images it involves are themselves linked with discovery.

Clearly this 'doorway' must also open both ways. The scene described above will remind you of the word in French, but an extra moment's thought is needed to help you translate from French into English.

After concentrating on the door and what comes from behind it, look specifically at the port itself. Perhaps this door is just one of many dotted around the harbour. If you listen carefully, can you hear Jim Morrison and the Doors playing a concert in one of the warehouses?

By creating strong, connected images for both key elements – DOOR and PORTE – this one scene will work as a powerful reminder, whichever word you need to translate. When you think of the door, you remember discovering the *port* behind it; and if you're faced with the word 'porte', simply recall what made this particular port so distinctive: the doors, and the *Doors*.

MAISON means HOUSE

Think of a house you know well. Imagine walking towards it, and seeing a large crowd of people standing outside. They're all looking excitedly at the building – and, as you come close enough, you're able to see why.

A stone-mason is dangling on a rope from the roof, chipping away at the surface of the house and carving a huge face in the stone. Gradually the features become clear, and you realise that the portrait is of James Mason.

Once again, spend a moment concentrating on the other 'side' of the image. The dangling mason keeps swinging against the house, harder and harder, until finally he hits a window and crashes into the building – landing in the middle of a bingo-game as someone is shouting 'house!' . . .

LIVRE means BOOK

Your favourite book is smelling a little odd today. Imagine opening it up, and finding inside it a piece of freshly cooked liver! Some of the pages have been stuck together by the gravy, and you decide to lift out the meat and start cleaning the book.

When you look closely at the liver itself you notice that the pressure of the pages has caused whole lines of writing to be printed across it, turning it into a strange, edible book . . .

LIT means BED

You wake up in the middle of the night feeling hot – and find to your horror that someone has *lit* the bed! Flames are licking around you, and smoke billows on all sides. The bed is quickly eaten away, and you leap to safety before nothing remains but a *lit*tle pile of ash.

Searching around for some evidence, you come across a huge box of matches – and, amazingly, some of them are still lit! An idea hits you. You light each of the matches in turn to make them safe, and then begin the painstaking task of sticking them all together . . . to build a replacement bed!

SOEUR means SISTER

Picture yourself lying in hospital, when the ward sister (who could also be *your* sister, if you have one) comes into your room. She tells you that your bed is needed by someone else, but promises to take you to another area of the hospital.

Climbing out of bed, you follow behind her, trying to guess where you're being put. You walk down several flights of stairs, then through what seems to be a manhole-cover . . . and suddenly it dawns on you that your new bed is in the *sewer*! The smell is terrible down here, so you turn your attention to the woman herself, threatening to *sue her* unless she finds you somewhere else to sleep.

MAIN means HAND

Look closely at one of your hands – the one you use most; your 'main' hand. Imagine how you would feel if water started to gush from the end of your index finger, and you realised that your hand had become a water-main!

A sudden tingling feeling in your other hand reminds you not to touch it, because *that* one carries mains electricity! Concentrate for a moment on these two mains outlets, and imagine watching someone else use their hands to switch off the currents. Whenever you see another mains switch or tap you'll remember seeing those hands save your life.

SUD means SOUTH
You're looking at a map of Britain when you notice something strange about the southern half of the map. The whole of the south is covered in soap suds, bubbling and expanding as you watch. There's a bar of soap lying by the side, still covered by most of its wrapper, and you read the label to find out more about the suds. You discover that the company which makes the soap is based in South Africa, South America . . . and Southend!

PAIN means BREAD
Every time you reach for a slice of bread you feel a sharp pain in your hand. Looking closer, you discover the reason: embedded in the loaf is a jagged pane of glass. As you carefully remove it and throw it away, an idea begins to form in your mind. To make windows more safe, why not replace the glass with thin slices of bread? Within minutes you have transformed your house, and from then on every time you see a *pane* of glass you replace it with *bread*.

MATIN means MORNING
Every morning, as soon as it gets light, you walk out into your garden and cross to the washing-line. There you carefully unpeg one of the mats you washed the previous evening. Sometimes it's a door-mat or a bath-mat; on other occasions, you unpeg a beer-mat or a place-mat.

Walking back to the house you take the *mat in*, just as you do every day, and iron it while you watch early morning television. Unfortunately, you seem to be handling it a little roughly; you hear a wailing sound, and, looking closely at the mat, you see that it's started to cry – in *mourning*. Even the television presenter has put on black clothes and is sobbing into the morning papers . . .

VENT means WIND

The obvious choice here is to imagine the wind as it whistles through a vent in a wall or door. You might try blocking it up to shut out the draught, but nothing seems to work. Every time you step back from it you find that the material you've used falls away, and the wind rushes through even more powerfully than before.

To help you remember the translation when you begin with the English word, imagine carrying a metal vent around in your pocket. Every time you feel a breeze, take out the vent and hold it up to gauge the strength of the wind. Whenever you feel the wind you automatically think of your vent – your portable wind-gauge and, now, portable memory aid!

German
LOCH, BEIN, HUT, BROT, LEITER, VIERTEL, RICHTER, FEIERTAG, BECHER, BILD.

LOCH means HOLE

Picture the scene: a hole in the road, surrounded by sand-bags, warning signs, and workmen leaning on their spades. Suddenly, from the depths of the hole, the Loch Ness Monster rises up, towering over the men and sending them running for cover. As you look closer you can see that the hole is full of water: this is a *loch*, and there's even a stray caber floating at one side!

As it is, this great water-filled hole is a danger to traffic. Luckily the workmen realise this too, and return with a huge lock and key. Covering the hole with some old tarpaulins, they lock it down tightly – and afterwards, whenever you see a lock, you're reminded of that monstrous *hole*.

BEIN means LEG

Your leg is covered in baked beans; you knocked over a can of them as you were about to put them in a pan, and now they've dribbled down one of your bare legs. You consider the situation for a moment, then decide to go all the way and attach the can to your leg as well!

Using some string, you *bind* the can tightly against your skin, then look in the cupboard for more beans to fasten on to your leg.

When you've finished, you feel so proud of your creation that you want to tell people about it. Picking up the telephone, you dial the number of your best friend, hoping desperately to get an answer; 'Be in, please *be in* . . .', you mutter as the phone starts to ring.

HUT means HAT

Imagine looking through the window of a hat shop to find out about the latest fashions. Hats shaped like little wooden *huts* seem to be popular this season, and you go in to try one on. Not surprisingly it feels rather heavy, but you find one made of canvas and designed like a workman's hut. To see how authentic it is, you carry it out into the street and compare it with one of the real huts. You examine the full-size hut carefully – and, when you look inside, find that it's full of every possible design of *hat*.

BROT means BREAD

There's a terrible smell coming from your bread-bin. When you open it you see that the answer is simple: the bread has started to rot, and it's covered with green mould. To remind yourself to throw it away, you take a pen and write the key word, 'rot', on to the bread-packet, starting under the first letter of 'bread' and going downwards to create a new word: BROT. If you see this word again, you'll have no problem remembering how you invented it!

LEITER means LADDER

The higher up your ladder you climb, the *lighter* you feel. At the very top, you're so light that you can step out into the air and float with ease. The ladder has also become lighter and it floats around by your side, getting in your way and spoiling the view.

Taking out your cigarette-lighter, you set fire to the ladder and watch it burn to nothing.

To remind yourself of this bright idea you draw a picture of the ladder on the side of the lighter, and from that moment on, whenever you take it out, you're reminded of your ladder – and feel the urge to find another one to set on fire . . .

VIERTEL means QUARTER

Imagine yourself sitting peacefully, quartering some fruit and eating a quarter of boiled sweets. Suddenly, a piece of apple skids off your knife, flies into the air . . . and you watch with horror as it *veers* towards the *tele*vision, crashing against the screen. You examine the set to see if any damage has been done – but, as you look on, more objects rise up and veer towards it: an American 'quarter' coin, a quarter-light from a car, part of a ship's quarter-deck . . .

RICHTER means JUDGE

You're sitting in a courtroom, watching a famous judge sentence a long line of prisoners. His voice is getting louder and louder, he begins to jump up and down with rage, and the result of his fury is that an earthquake is caused, forcing huge cracks to appear in the walls and floor and sending the prisoners running back to their cells for safety.

Equipment is set up to measure the strength of the quake on the *Richter*-scale. Someone even puts the judge's wig on top of the box of electronics. Everyone gathers round to look at the Richter-scale reading; and the only person that disagrees with it is the judge himself, certain that his earthquake was much more intense . . .

FEIERTAG means HOLIDAY

Picture yourself walking through an airport, suitcases in tow, heading off on a well-earned holiday. At the customs desk, a fire-safety officer, dressed in full protective gear, is checking everyone's luggage, making sure that each case has a *'fire tag'*. Your holiday depends on this tag, so you're relieved when he tells you that your cases are safe.

Out of interest you have a look yourself, and see that the fire-tag is covered with pictures of famous holiday destinations. When you finally board the plane, the person sitting next to you turns out to be the fire-officer himself, armed with some of the fire-tags he's collected, and jetting off for a holiday of his own.

BECHER means CUP

From your front-row seat at Wembley you can see all the action in the Cup Final. At the end of an exciting match the cup is presented to the winning captain. But there seems to have been some mistake, because Boris *Becker*, in his tennis gear, steps up to accept it instead!

He runs around the stadium on a lap of honour, but the disgruntled fans throw their tea-cups at him, forcing him to stop. Fearing that he might drop his trophy, he fastens the huge silver cup on to his head – and whenever you see him again you always remember how ridiculous he looked . . .

BILD means PICTURE

Imagine you're walking round an art gallery, trying to find a suitable picture to buy. Unfortunately, they all seem to be on the subject of *building*; one shows a builder sitting in a lorry, another is a sketch of a pile of building bricks, and everywhere you look the paintings are of buildings and building tools.

You're also shocked to find yourself being charged just to *look* at the artworks; each time you move on from a painting you are *billed*, the curator running up to you and demanding a fee. On closer inspection you discover that the bill itself has quite a pretty picture on it – and you decide to save money by hanging that up instead!

SIMILARITIES AND CONFUSIONS

All of these examples involve using strong images to trigger the memory, creating new connections between words in different languages. But sometimes it can be even harder to remember words which already have connections – words, for example, which are almost identical in spelling from one language to another.

Now the difficulty isn't in remembering an entirely new word, but rather in recalling the precise differences in spelling. The memory technique needs to concentrate less on general reminders, and more on the details of the word.

The best way to begin is to decide exactly what you need to remember. Often a foreign word will have only a couple of letters different from the English spelling. By creating triggers to help you remember these, the rest of the word falls quickly into place.

In French, for example, the word for 'chocolate' is CHOCOLAT. All you have to remember is that the 'e' has been lost.

Imagine reading the list of ingredients on a chocolate-bar wrapper, and noticing that there are hundreds of 'E-numbers'. To make the bar healthier, take a pen and cross each one off, forcefully removing the 'E's. This act of deleting the letter is more memorable than just imagining it being absent in the first place; once again you take control of the word, and an uncertain spelling becomes definite.

In German, the word for 'jacket' is JACKETT. This time the key point to remember is the extra 'T'.

An effective trigger for the memory would be to imagine a jacket designed specifically for the TT motorcycle race. The jacket itself is roughly a 'T'-shape, so visualise it painted with a different colour 'T' on each side, front and back. *You* do the painting; when you think of the word, you'll remember what you did to emphasise the vital element of spelling.

Below are two more lists of examples, each featuring words with similar spellings in two different languages. Again, read through the memory suggestions, then return to the original lists to check your success.

French
PAPIER, TOMATE, LIMONADE, COTON, BANQUE, FORET, HISTOIRE.

Papier/paper
KEY POINT: The presence of the letter I

Imagine opening up a packet of white paper, ready for use in a printer or typewriter, when you realise to your annoyance that the sheets have already been used. Amazingly, *your* picture is printed on every one! 'I am on the paper!', you say aloud.

On some of the sheets you're walking along a *pier*, and on others you're eating a *pie* – points which help you recall the exact position of the 'I'. Imagine colouring in the pictures – even hanging some on the wall – to reinforce the images and confirm the spelling in your mind.

Tomate/tomato
KEY POINT: The O has changed into an E

In this case, why not make use of the fact that the French word can be split into two English words: *To Mate*.

Imagine arranging your tomato plants close together, in the hope that they'll start *to mate*. In a couple of weeks your plan seems to have worked; there are baby tomato-plants everywhere . . .! Perhaps you even write a book on the subject: 'How *To Mate Tomato* Plants'.

Limonade/lemonade
KEY POINT: The first E has changed into an I

Again, in this example the change of letters has created a new word: LIMO.

Imagine drinking so much fizzy lemonade that you swell up like a balloon, and need to replace your car with a vast limousine. Even this is only just large enough for you to squeeze into; concentrate on yourself – I – sitting inside your limo, opening yet another bottle of lemonade . . .

Coton/cotton
KEY POINT: There is only one T

An easy reminder would be to imagine buying a cotton T-shirt, and finding that half of it was missing. There's only one of the T-shaped pieces of material, and you have to tape it on to your chest rather than pulling it over your head!

Banque/bank
KEY POINT: The K has been replaced by QUE

Again, an obvious image springs to mind. Your local bank seems very noisy as you walk past, so you open the door to find out what's going on. Inside, the usually peaceful room has been filled with noise and commotion by a huge QUEUE, snaking around all four walls of the bank. Most surprising of all is that even the Kitchen has been taken over and filled by a section of the queue . . .

Foret/forest
KEY POINT: The absence of the S

The letter S not only starts the word 'snake' but even *looks* like a snake, so that's often the most powerful image to use.

Imagine organising a hunting party to rid the forest of snakes, searching through the undergrowth and working through the whole forest until all the snakes have been killed. Only when the last S has been removed can you RETurn home.

Histoire/history
KEY POINT: RY has changed to IRE

Again, the change in letters has highlighted a new word: IRE, or anger.

Picture yourself sitting in the most angry history lesson imaginable. As you browse through your textbook you see that each page contains pictures of war and violence. The students sitting around you are becoming more and more unruly, and the teacher is positively irate!

As always, it's important to include your own response, so imagine becoming so angry, so filled with ire, that you storm out of the room, putting an end to this imaginary *story* . . .

German
GRAS, DOKTOR, FELD, DEZIMAL, JOCKEI, ALLEE, FISCH

Gras/Grass
KEY POINT: One letter S has been lost

In this case, rather than a new word being formed by the change of spelling, the opposite has happened. The 'ass' or donkey visible in the English word has been lost – yet this too can be the basis for a memory trigger.

Imagine looking into a field of long grass and hearing an animal approaching . . . but when it arrives, it turns out to be only *half* an animal; the front half of an ass! It has only one pair or legs and half a body, and shuffles through the grass with great difficulty – especially since an *A*rabian *S*tallion is riding on its back . . .!

Doktor/Doctor
KEY POINT: The C has changed into a K

Picture yourself entering the doctor's surgery, only to find him preoccupied with mending a *K*ite! He's using some strange things to try to fix it: a *K*ey, a *K*ettle, a *K*ennel – even his *K*nee! All you want is for him to see – *C* – you, but there seems to be no chance of that, especially when he starts putting all his energy into *K*icking his *K*ite!

Feld/Field
KEY POINT: The absence of the I

Imagine looking out across a beautiful field on a hot summer's day. You'd love to walk through the gate and sit there for a while – but when you try, a farmer rushes out and orders you off his land. You try to sneak under the hedge, then between some trees – but the farmer sees you every time and turns you away. '*I* am never going to be in that field', you mutter to yourself as you walk away, taking out an axe and *FEL*ling one of the trees out of spite . . .

Dezimal/Decimal
KEY POINT: The C has changed into a Z

Imagine you're at school, sitting in a boring maths lesson that seems to be going on for weeks. The subject is decimals – the blackboard is covered with decimal points – but nobody seems to be paying any attention. One by one the pupils are falling asleep and, just as in a cartoon, lines of *ZZZZZZ*s are appearing above their heads.

More and more people slump in a heap on the floor, and soon there's no-one left sitting in a *C*hair. The snoring gets louder and louder, and in the end all the *C*hildren are hidden behind a cloud of *ZZZZZZ*s . . .

Jockei/Jockey
KEY POINT: The Y has changed into an I

In this example, the KEY in jockey has been lost. Picture the jockey, still on his horse, trying to open his stable door but finding that the key has broken . . . into *EI*ght pieces! He realises that the key can never be mended, and nails all eight pieces on to his door-frame – next to the horse-shoes – to remind him to be more careful in future!

Allee/Alley
KEY POINT: The Y has changed into an E

In the English word there was already one man's name – AL – but the change in spelling has added another: LEE. Imagine hearing a commotion in a dark alley, and peering in to find out why there's so much noise. It's not long before your 'why?' – *Y* – has been answered and silenced: the actors AL Pacino and LEE Majors are fighting amongst the dustbins! During a pause in the action, you ask each of them for their autograph, as a memento to take home . . .

Fisch/Fish
KEY POINT: The presence of the C

Since '*C*' sounds exactly like 'sea', an obvious image presents itself.

You've been at sea for hours, so imagine your delight when you reel in the biggest fish you've ever seen. The effort has made you hungry and you decide to cook the fish there and then. But when you start eating it you find that most of the fish's weight is *sea*-water, pouring off your plate and soaking the deck. In the end there's nothing for it: you supplement your meal with CHeddar CHeese and CHocolate!

Step two
Once you've created the main base of imagery, either as a reminder of the foreign word or as a prompt for its spelling, the second step involves confirming the GENDER.

Unlike in English, words in French, German and many other languages have genders; in French, either masculine or feminine, and, in German, masculine, feminine or neuter. A word's gender is important, since it controls much of the grammar in a sentence, and students of language often find gender one of the hardest elements to remember.

But if you're used to making imagery part of the learning process, then there's an easy way to be sure of the gender of any word.

In Part One, the first rule of *Mindpower* was: You Remember Things That Happen to *You*. Since all of us are either male or female, our own part in a set of images can be used to stress the gender of a word.

If you're male, make sure that every scene you create to remember a masculine word involves *you* at the very centre, affecting the action and controlling what goes on. When you're faced with a feminine word, construct the scene so that the events involve someone else, while you just stand back and watch.

If you're female, simply do the opposite: make yourself the controller of scenes built around feminine words, and remain a spectator when masculine words are being remembered. Even when you're only watching a scene you can still involve yourself through emotions and reactions – just avoid imagining yourself becoming physically involved.

If the language you're learning presents you with neuter words to remember, simply create your scene so that an animal or an object is the source of the action.

As examples of this technique, consider three words from the lists above:

LA PORTE

The French word for 'door' is feminine. If you yourself are female, then the earlier suggestions for imagery still work. *You* open the door, *you* are hit by the huge tidal wave, *you* hear the music . . . The whole scene emphasises your role at the centre of the action, and confirms that the gender of the word is the same as your own: FEMININE.

If, on the other hand, you're a *male*, then a few changes need to be made. Choose someone else to control what happens, while you watch from the sidelines.

Perhaps you make this a famous door – the entrance to Number Ten Downing Street, for example, or the door to Buckingham Palace – allowing you to use the Prime Minister or the Queen to open it up. When the waters rush in, imagine that person's reactions, and think about how you would feel as a spectator. Concentrate on your own vantage point, stressing all the time that you can see everything, but have no physical role in what goes on.

DER FISCH

In German, the word for 'fish' is masculine. The story suggested earlier involved you as the controller of the scene, sailing your boat, catching the fish and then discovering it to be full of sea-water. This is fine, as long as you yourself are male; the story confirms your place at the centre of events, and stresses that the word is masculine, too.

But if you're female, then you have to become a spectator. Think back to a boat trip you've made, or a film you've seen set on the high seas, and decide on a character to take centre stage. Watch as that person has all the experiences and controls the action, and imagine your feelings when you're unable to get to the food! You're forced to stay on the outside, so the word for 'fish' must be masculine.

DAS GRAS

The German word for 'grass' is neuter. No matter what your own gender, the images used to remember this word need to feature some animal or object as the central force in the story. The earlier suggestion is perfect; the two-legged, half-bodied ass is the focus of interest, emerging from the long grass and catching your attention. You only watch, astonished – and your amazement is aroused even more when you see the Arabian stallion, yet another reminder that the word in question is neuter.

Step Three

The final step is to confirm which word is part of which language.

Many of us learn new languages at school and college, and these days more and more people are learning several at once. Your imagery may be strong for individual words, but, if you're learning French and German at the same time, how do you separate one image for 'house' or 'dog' or 'car' from another?

You might see the word 'door' and think instantly of a port – but perhaps that's your trigger for the word in German . . .

The answer is to involve *place* – seen already to be so effective in the route-making in Part One.

Choose a single location for each language you learn. If you've visited the country in question, your location could be a town or city you know reasonably well. If you're still at school, why not turn a classroom into the location for the language you learn there? Select a place you can visualise clearly – because this final step involves fixing each word into your chosen location.

Whenever you create an image to help you remember a word, spend a moment anchoring it to the appropriate place. If you are learning French and German, for example, you might decide upon Paris as the location for all your French words, and your German classroom as a venue for the words in German. When you've finished inventing the watery images to help remember 'porte', work out a way to have the whole scene happening in Paris. Perhaps the door you open is the lift-door in the Eiffel Tower, and the water and boats pour down from a great height!

When you've visualised the scene to remind you of the German word 'leiter', picture the ladder leaning precariously in the corner of your classroom, and imagine hiding the cigarette-lighter before it's confiscated! Use the same techniques as when you use a memory route to anchor your scene in the appropriate place. This way, you create a huge storehouse of language information. Each location can contain thousands of images and scenes, every one reminding you of a foreign word's meaning, spelling and gender.

To recap: every time you're faced with a foreign word to learn, work through the three key rules.

One Work out exactly what you need to remember about a word, either its meaning or spelling, or both, and create an imagined scene to act as a 'trigger'. Involve all the techniques of *Mindpower* to make the pictures as striking and as memorable as you can.

Two Find out the gender of the word, and construct your scene accordingly – either with you in control, if you share the same gender as the word, or with you as a spectator if you don't. Make use of animals or objects at the centre of the scene if you're remembering a neuter word.

Three Anchor the whole scene in one of your chosen locations, fixing it in place so that you never confuse words from one language with those from another.

Language Lists:

Once foreign words have been taken under the control of *Mindpower*, given life and shape and moulded into memorable scenes, it's possible to use story-telling and route-making techniques to remember them in lists. Being able to reel off sequences like the days of the week or months of the year can be a useful skill – yet many people waste time trying to remember them parrot-fashion, and by lengthy repetition.

A much more efficient way is to turn them into brief stories, linking the individual images with a chain of memorable events, and then practising the list a few times from memory until it's fixed for good – just like the list of planets in Part One.

To round off this section on foreign languages, here are the lists of days of the week in French and German, and suggestions for stories to commit them to memory.

French
DIMANCHE, LUNDI, MARDI, MERCREDI, JEUDI, VEN-DREDI, SAMEDI

As always, the first step is to change the words on the page into lively, three-dimensional images. Since the aim is to be able to read the list aloud from memory, concentrate on images that will help you recall the sounds of the words. Often, remembering the first couple of syllables will be enough to trigger the whole word.

DIMANCHE   The first two syllables suggest a strong image: a 'demon'.

LUNDI   An action-word would be useful next in the story, so use the first syllable here to create 'lunge'.

MARDI	The obvious image here would be a huge 'mardi-gras' carnival.
MERCREDI	This word looks like an anagram of 'Mercedes'!
JEUDI	The story could use another character, so transform this word into Punch's wife 'Judy'.
VENDREDI	The first two syllables here are words already: 'Vend' and 'Red'. You need to combine them into a single image, though, so why not imagine a bright red vending-machine, selling tomatoes, cherries, red-noses . . .
SAMEDI	A slight change of pronunciation gives you 'Sammy D' – Sammy Davis Junior!

As a memorable starting-point for the story, imagine looking at a notice-board fastened to the Eiffel Tower, trying to find out which days of the week it is open. You quickly learn that it's open *every* day, and take the lift to the top floor to enjoy the wonderful views of Paris.

Your attention is caught by a plume of black smoke. There's a fire burning in the middle of the city, and as you look closer you see a DEMON rising up from the flames, then racing around the busy streets – he's a speed-demon! Suddenly he stops and LUNGES into a crowd of people, who shout at him and call him a LUNatic . . .

As the crowds part, you see that they're all watching a MARDI-GRAS procession; imagine all the colours and sounds and smells. As you focus on one of the floats, you notice that it's been built on the back of an expensive MERCEDES car, driven by a MERCenary dressed in full battle-gear!

The float itself has been made into a huge puppet theatre. A Punch and Judy show is being performed – but, for once, Judy seems to be coming out best. Punch has been thrown off the stage and is lying battered in the road: the show has become a one-woman performance of the JUDY show!

With only one puppet there can hardly be much violence, so the puppeteer decides to sell off all his stage blood. Judy is seen to wheel a bright RED VENDING-MACHINE on to the stage, and to start selling bottles of fake blood to the audience. When those run out, other pieces of red merchandise appear: cherries, tomatoes, strawberry-jam . . .

The sale is going well – until suddenly the audience jumps to its feet. A rumour had gone round earlier that a star guest would be performing in the procession, so they're delighted to see SAMMY DAVIS JUNIOR dancing down the street towards them. Everyone crowds round as he does his cabaret routine – and you decide to run down the steps of the Eiffel Tower and across the city to catch the last part of his act.

Once you've visualised the story, run back through it in your mind to confirm the key points. As you reach each of the main images, say aloud the French word that's been triggered.

You see the demon – DIMANCHE – who lunges – LUNDI – into a crowd watching the Mardi-Gras – MARDI. The main float is built on a Mercedes – MERCREDI – and features a puppet show with Judy – JEUDI – as the star. She brings out her red vending-machine – VENDREDI – but her sale is interrupted by the appearance of Sammy Davis Junior – SAMEDI.

As you repeat this to yourself a few times your speed will increase, and soon you'll know the French weekdays as surely and instinctively as their equivalents in English!

German
SONNTAG, MONTAG, DIENSTAG, MITTWOCH, DON-NERSTAG, FREITAG, SAMSTAG.

SONNTAG	The key first syllable is already a word: 'Son'.
MONTAG	Perhaps the first part of the word here suggests 'money' or 'monkey'.
DIENSTAG	To bring in an action-word, 'diens' could be changed into the similar-looking and sounding word 'denies'.
MITTWOCH	Since this is the only part of the list without the 'tag' ending, it's important to learn both halves of the word. Imagine a Chinese wok used for cooking woollen gloves: a 'mitt-wok'!
DONNERSTAG	This word suggests 'donations' or 'doner-kebabs'!

| FREITAG | Another action-word could be created by turning the first syllable here into FRY. |
| SAMSTAG | The SAM in question could be Sam Spade, Sam Cooke – even Uncle Sam! |

As an appropriate starting-point for the story, imagine standing on the site of the old Berlin Wall, asking a passer-by how many *days* it took to build, and on what *day* of the week it was knocked down. She doesn't seem to know, but you ask her young SON instead and he tells you the details, putting all the facts into SONg!

His singing is wonderful, and you decide to reward him with some MONEY. He thanks you when you hand him some coins, and puts them straight into his MONKEY-shaped money-box!

You're interested to see what he does with the money. You follow behind him as he walks into a restaurant to spend it on a meal – but the waiter approaches angrily and DENIES him entry! The boy is accused of being the thief who stole food earlier that morning, even though he *denies* it vigorously; in the end, the waiter says that he can only eat at a table in the cloakroom.

The boy is so hungry that he agrees, and eats people's woollen mittens, cooked in a specially-made MITT-WOK . . .

You feel guilty about the state of affairs, and sorry for the boy, and decide to make a charitable DONATION. You buy a DONER-KEBAB, and throw it into the wok.

The food sizzles noisily, and the sound of FRYing gets louder and louder. People start leaping up from their seats in FRIght! Soon there are only a few people left in the whole restaurant – and you notice with interest that they all have something in common: they're all called SAM!

Sam Cooke is singing at one side, Sam Spade is looking for clues at the other, and in the middle Uncle Sam, dressed in stars and stripes, is singing the American National Anthem.

Repeat the main elements of the story to yourself, and start to practise recalling the German words.

You were standing by the Berlin Wall when the woman's son answered your questions – SONNTAG. You gave him some money – MONTAG – which he tried to spend in a restaurant, but was denied entry – DIENSTAG – and had to eat from a mitt-wok – MITTWOCH – in the cloakroom. You were the donor of a doner-kebab – DONNERSTAG – which started to fry so loudly – FREITAG – that only the Sams were left in the building – SAMSTAG.

The beauty of these stories is that, as soon as you've visualised them, you can do away with the words on paper, and practise the list to yourself wherever you happen to be. I used to learn the majority of my foreign vocabulary on my morning walk to school!

REMEMBERING ENGLISH WORDS

As well as helping you to learn foreign words, *Mindpower* techniques can also be used to remember difficult spellings in English. Once again the trick is to be aware of *details*; to work out exactly which elements of a word you need to remember, and then to use the imagination to create triggers and prompts.

Every time you look up a word in the dictionary, make a point of learning it so that you never waste time looking for it again. Words that are commonly misspelt fall into a number of main categories.

The Surprises
These are words which seem to catch most people out. English is often described as a language with very little logic to it – and these examples demonstrate that well.

Agoraphobia
This word, meaning 'the abnormal fear of crossing open spaces', is often misspelt by people leaving out the first 'O' – especially since this letter is glossed over in pronunciation. An obvious reminder is contained within the word, though, since the correct spelling forms the word 'GO'.

Imagine an agoraphobia sufferer being encouraged to leave the house. A crowd has gathered outside, each member holding up a green placard bearing the word GO! They start chanting this, too, and in the end they're successful; the householder throws open the door and runs out into the street, to do a wild *go-go* dance in the open space . . .

This example demonstrates a very effective approach. Where possible, concentrate on an element within the main word – in this case 'GO' – which *only* remains when the spelling is correct. This gives the memory a positive target to aim for, rather than a pitfall to avoid, and helps confirm when the spelling is right. But whatever technique you use, always make sure your images tie in with the word in question, so that the mere sight of it in future will remind you of the specific prompts you've designed.

Aqueduct
Here, a connection with the word 'aqua' leads many people to replace the 'E' with an 'A'. Although the correct spelling contains only half of the word 'queue', an image based on queuing would be enough to remind you of the 'E' – especially since it allows you to form a powerful picture.

Imagine looking up at an aqueduct and seeing a long line of people *queuing* to carry water across. Some people are trying to skip the queue by pushing to the front, forcing other people to spill their water-jars as they're knocked aside . . .

Boycott
The second letter 'T' is easy to miss off in this word. It's always good to involve real people in your imaginary scenes, so why not have *Geoff* Boycott wearing motorcycle leathers and helmet, and taking part in the TT race! Perhaps he enjoys the gear so much that he uses it even when he plays cricket, riding his motorbike between the wickets!

Refrigerator
Although 'fridge' has a 'D' in it, 'refrigerator' doesn't, and catches many people unawares. It's useful to create a scene featuring *both* words, and highlighting their differences.

Imagine walking into your kitchen at home or work, and finding that someone has delivered two new fridges: a small one on the left side of the room, with the word FRIDGE written on it, and a large one on the right with space for the whole word: REFRIGERATOR. The small model seems to be misshapen; there's a curved RIDGE in the top of the case. The large model, on the other hand, is perfectly made – but so huge that a scaffolding RIG has had to be put up around it to keep it from toppling over!

The 'Alternatives'

These are words which take on a different meaning when spelled in a different way, and include some of the most regularly confused words. As in the previous example, a useful technique is to combine the pair of words within one imagined scene – especially since this highlights the differences, and reminds you that there *is* a choice to be made between the two.

Effect/Affect

'Effect' is a noun, and means something that happens as the result of something else. 'Affect', on the other hand, is a verb, an action word describing the act of *causing* an effect.

Once you understand the difference between the two words, it's easy to create a prompt to remind yourself of their spellings.

Picture yourself sitting in a cinema, watching a film that's full of exciting special effects. Unfortunately, something seems to have gone wrong; the effects are taking a long time to work, and there's an almost *E*ndless wait before each one *E*ventually works.

In the end, you're so tired of waiting that you decide to take *A*ction. You jump up next to the screen and start *A*ctivating the effects yourself.

'E' is for *E*ventual *E*njoyment, but 'A' is for *A*ctual *A*ctivity!

Dessert/Desert

'Dessert', meaning a sweet course, is often confused with the 'desert' of sand and camels. This time the difference is between single and double 'S'.

Picture yourself eating your pudding in the middle of the Sahara. To while away the time, notice the main difference between the dessert and the desert. Your *dessert* is made up of many ingredients: sugar, shortbread, sherry, spices;

multiple 'S's. But the *desert* has only one ingredient, only one 'S': sand.

Calendar/Calender

The difference here is again between an 'A' and an 'E'. 'Calendar' means a chart of days and dates, but a 'calender' is a machine for rolling cloth or paper.

Visualise a scene that involves both words. You're sitting in your workshop, busy with your *calender*, but also gazing at a *calendar* as you long for your next holiday. When you think about it, the difference between the two words is clear.

The 'E' in calender stands for *E*quipment, *E*nergy, *E*ffort and *E*lbow-grease, so you paint a large letter E on to the side. But the 'A' in calendar is for *A*way-day, *A*dventure, *A*irport and *A*merica – so you circle the 'A' in August to remind you that your holiday to the USA isn't too far away.

Practice/practise

Like 'effect' and 'affect', the first word here, 'practice', is a noun, and the second, 'practise', a verb.

A good way to combine both words is to imagine yourself hard at work in a cold rehearsal-room – singing, dancing, and then playing an instrument. Everything static – like a noun – begins with 'C': your *C*hair, your *C*opy of the music, your *C*larinet . . . But all the movement and action you do begins with an 'S': your *S*ong, your *S*amba, your *S*olo *S*onata. You stay warm by moving and performing energetically, but the room is so cold that ICE starts forming on every static object . . .

Double Letters

This category includes some of the hardest spellings of all – words with a mixture of single and multiple letters. A useful technique is to look for famous initials amongst all the pairs of letters.

Embarrass

As in all of these examples, the first step is to decide on the specific elements of the word that need to be remembered. In this case it's the final two syllables, taking in the two 'R's and the two 'S's.

To be embarrassed you need to have people watching – so choose a setting with a large audience. The Oscar ceremony is one of the world's most watched programmes, so imagine something embarrassing happening to one of the stars.

Robert Redford – R.R. – was meant to arrive in a long limousine, but it crashed on the way to the theatre. In the end he had to settle for making his entrance on a decrepit old ASS! Imagine his face turning a bright shade of red as everyone looks at him, confirming the focus of the whole scene: RR – ASS!

Commitment

A scene is required to remind you of two key elements in this word: the double 'M's and the single 'T'.

Any performer needs commitment, – but especially so if he has no props – other than his own body – and he's not allowed to say a word! *M*arcel *M*arceau, the mime artist, is just such a man; picture him practising his act, showing so much commitment that he goes back to the same mimes again and again.

In fact, he makes each one so perfect that it becomes the 'definitive' version – and receives a TradeMark! The letters *T.M.* are stamped on to his body every time he creates a new mime . . .

Accommodation

This time there are two pairs of letters, 'C's and 'M's, so your image can involve two very famous characters.

Picture your own accommodation, the place where you live. When you arrive home, two passers-by are waiting outside, wanting to know if they can have accommodation for the night. You recognise them instantly: Charlie Chaplin and Mickey Mouse! Imagine what it would be like to talk to them, and think where you might put them to sleep.

Address

The last example in this section also has two pairs of letters. Visualise yourself addressing an envelope. To make doubly sure it reaches its destination, you write the address on both sides: everything is doubled.

When you've finished, the envelope looks a little plain, so you decide to include some artwork. On the front you draw a large ADDition sign, and on the back you sketch a beautiful DRESS – two words that can only appear if your spelling is correct.

Confusing Vowels
With some words, the more you think about them, the less sure you feel about which vowel goes where . . .

Relevant
In this word, the second 'E' and the 'A' are often confused. To find out relevant information you would probably go to a library, so picture your local branch.

Imagine walking into the building and noticing that the doors have been widened and a ramp has been built, making the whole place very *E*asily *A*ccessible. The librarian is called EVA – she's wearing a huge name-badge – but when you ask her questions she seems to be very EVAsive . . .

Dependent
This time only one vowel is really in question – the final 'E'. If one thing is dependent on another they could be said to lean together – but what happens if they lean against each other a little too forcefully?

Imagine a small, flimsy shack leaning against a huge sky-scraper, entirely dependent on it for support. The shack's owner is worried that the connection isn't strong enough, and puts all his weight into pressing his building against the wall of the other – so much so that a large DENT forms in the towering structure. He tries to mend it before anyone notices, borrowing a drill from the DENTist next door . . .

Apparent
To make sure you never mistake the 'E' for another 'A', notice that the word 'parent' appears here if the spelling is correct. To tie this in with the original word, consider that the very first information you receive about the world is usually made apparent by your *parents*. Picture a baby being told about birds

and trees; the information is clearly apparent to you, but to the child it's all new and exciting.

Appearance
This time, the opposite is true: the vowel with a tendency to cause confusion, the final 'A', can easily be mistaken for an 'E'. To remember the true spelling, imagine that your favourite movie star has put in a surprise *appearance* at one of your parties.

To your horror you realise that you're wearing your oldest, dirtiest jumper. Later you'll tell people how you RAN upstairs to change, and made a much more appropriate appearance when you returned wearing a brand new ARAN sweater!

Strange Spellings
Some words are just plain hard to spell. You think of them, and know instantly that you'll have to find a dictionary. You've probably been having difficulty with them since you first learned to read and write – so why not take a moment now to work out their spelling once and for all.

I'll never forget how to spell the word 'beautiful', because someone once taught me the following sentence: *B*ig *E*lephants *A*re *U*seful *T*o *I*ndians *F*or *U*nloading *L*ogs. Memory phrases like this can be fun to invent, and they tend to be especially effective when you work them out yourself. It can take a few minutes to come up with a good one – a sentence which, if possible, ties in with the word in question, and uses unusual words rather than 'the' 'it' and 'a'. But if you do it well, you'll never wonder about the spelling again.

Below are four famously tricky words, and four sentences I've come up with. I'm sure you can do better . . .

Rhythm
I began here by looking for a letter which could transform into a word linked with the theme of 'rhythm'. I chose 'M' for 'music'. Next, I spotted a famous pair of initials – RH for Rolf Harris, himself a musician – and formed my sentence around these key points.

*R*OLF *H*ARRIS *Y*EARNS *T*O *H*EAR *M*USIC!

Jodhpurs
This time I picked 'H' for 'horse', as well as 'J' for 'jockey' and 'R' for 'riding'. The result is a warning about what to wear on your next ride.

JOCKEYS OVER-DRESS –
HORSES PREFER UNDERSTATED RIDING-SLACKS!

Yacht
Here, I concentrated on 'A' for 'anchor'. If you're having trouble controlling your yacht as well as spelling it, then

YOUR ANCHOR COULD HAVE TANGLED!

Syllable
My key-letters this time were 'L' for 'language' and 'lines', and 'S' for 'speak'. To count syllables, as well as to spell them:

SPEAK YOUR LINES LOUDLY –
ALWAYS BREAK LANGUAGE EVENLY!

Meaningful Memory

As well as learning difficult spellings, *Mindpower* techniques can help you recall the meanings of unusual or obscure words. These tend to be words bearing little resemblance to usual English constructions, and are often even harder to learn than foreign words since their origins are vague and their meanings difficult to guess. Again, the best approach is to invent reasons for one word meaning another. Try to bring the sounds and spellings alive, and exercise your imagination.

Learning the meanings of rare words can prove very useful in crosswords and other language games, as well as bringing variety and interest to writing and conversation.

Below is a game to try straight away. Test yourself on the ten questions below, trying in each case to work out which of the possible meanings – a, b or c – is the correct one. When you've finished, see how well you scored by checking the answers at the end – then set about learning the meanings so that you'll never be confused again.

Read through the suggestions, improve on them and invent some of your own, then go back and try the ten questions for a second time. Your accuracy target is a hundred per cent.

Questions
What do the following words mean:
1) SAKER
   a) A highly alcoholic Eastern drink
   b) A large migratory falcon
   c) A formal gown worn by women in the Middle Ages

2) CLEAM
   a) Plaster
   b) Porridge
   c) Pig-manure

3) FESCUE
   a) To be mouldy or rotten
   b) Something small or trivial
   c) The underside of a bird's nest

4) INKLE
   a) A small Victorian pen
   b) A type of igloo
   c) A kind of linen tape

5) RUNANGA
   a) An African dance
   b) A Maori council
   c) An Aboriginal spear

6) GLOUT
   a) To frown or scowl
   b) To affix tiles
   c) To dig out weeds or unwanted plants

7) MUGA
   a) A form of Middle Eastern pottery, baked in an oven
   b) The young of the house-fly
   c) A wild silk, obtained from the cocoon of a moth

8) HAMBLE
a) To maim or mutilate
b) To cook gently on a low heat
c) To separate animals into different pens

9) CHOWK
a) A Native American battle-axe
b) A market-place or main street in India
c) A small sea-bird native to Scandinavia

10) DEASIL
a) In curtain-making, the width of material required
b) The most fertile layer of soil
c) Clockwise, in the direction of the sun

Answers
1) b   2) a   3) b   4) c   5) b   6) a   7) c   8) a   9) b   10) c

Mindpower Suggestions

1) SAKER: *A large migratory falcon.*
Change the word slightly into 'sacker'. Imagine that this word describes someone whose job it is to put things in sacks.

Imagine looking at a 'sacker', a woman whose clothes are also made out of old sacks, struggling to hold on to something alive in one of her sacks. Suddenly she loses control; the sack opens and a huge *falcon* flies out and off into the distance. *'Sack her!'*, cries the disgruntled crowd . . .

2) CLEAM: *Plaster.*
A useful technique for remembering rare words like this is to 'squash' two words together. Imagine which pair of words might have been combined to create this strange word.

'Cleam' suggests a mixture of 'clean' and 'gleam', so the next step is to imagine a picture which connects both of them – and the original word in question.

Visualise yourself carrying out the most extensive spring-clean imaginable. You scrub and polish, rub and scrape until everything is so *clean* that it *gleams* – and you have to put on your sunglasses against this new bright glare! Unfortunately, you've gone a little too far: all the wallpaper has been pulled off, and you're left with bare plaster.

3) FESCUE: *Something small or trivial.*
Again, decide on two words which could have been joined together to create 'fescue'. One is obvious – 'rescue' – and the other could be anything appropriate beginning with the letter 'F'.

Think of your favourite disaster movie, or recall the last rescue you saw on the news. Imagine all the emergency services being called out to this accident or hazard – only to find that their task is something completely trivial: rescuing somebody's flower from behind the fridge, or reaching up to mend a fan! This is a Futile *rescue*, a Failed *rescue*, a Farcical *rescue* – so 'fescue' is something trivial or small.

4) INKLE: *A kind of linen tape.*
This time, the two words could be 'ink' and 'wrinkle'. Imagine trying to clean and iron a dress that seems to be a little worse for wear. It's covered in huge patches of INK and criss-crossed with WRINKLES, and although your efforts are effective, the dress is still not perfect. So, to cover up the last few blemishes, bind the offending parts in a few layers of special *linen tape* . . .

5) RUNANGA: *A Maori council.*
With a slight alteration of spelling, two regular words can be found here: 'run' and 'anger'.

Imagine sitting around a fire in New Zealand, taking part in the meeting of a Maori council. Suddenly, someone notices that you're the only one without a painted face, and all the other members of the council start to laugh at you. You feel your *anger* rising, and in the end you can take no more, RUNning out of the circle and off into the night . . .

6) GLOUT: *To frown or scowl.*
Two powerful words suggested here are 'glow' and 'gout'! Imagine watching an amazing transformation of the sun taking place.

This is the sun seen in children's picture-books, with a smiling

face surrounded by glowing rays of light. But today the sun is
unwell, suffering from a terrible case of *gout*. The glowing rays
start to disappear, consumed by the gout, and the happy smile
turns quickly to a frowning scowl . . .

7) MUGA: A wild silk, obtained from the cocoon of a moth.

The emotive word 'mugger' is the obvious suggestion here.
Imagine walking home through a dark city, and being witness
to a mugging. The mugger snatches his victim's bag and throws
it open – only to find it full of sheets and sheets of *silk* . . .

8) HAMBLE: To maim or mutilate.

'Hamble' could be made from a mixture of 'ham' and 'ramble'.
Imagine walking out in the countryside on a beautiful summer's
day, and stopping around lunchtime to eat your sandwiches. As
you sit there, you spot another rambler perched on the top of a
mountain to eat his food – but when he drops a piece of ham from
his sandwich it falls on to a sheep and injures it badly. Another
piece maims a goat, and a third piece of ham lands on *you*. The
combination of *rambler* and *ham* is dangerous indeed!

9) CHOWK: A market-place or main street in India

The obvious technique here would be to transform 'chowk' into
'choke'. Imagine wandering around a busy city in India, enjoying
the sights and sounds but being less impressed by the smells.
There's traffic everywhere, cars and lorries and motorbikes
blocking the streets and creating clouds of fumes. You can
feel your throat tightening, and in the end you have to leave
for home before you *choke* . . .

10) DEASIL: Clockwise, in the direction of the sun.

Since this example suggests the word 'diesel', it maintains the
toxic theme of the last!

Imagine sitting in the carriage of a diesel train, staring out of
the window to while away the time. You keep glancing at the
clock on the wall, wishing your journey could be over, and you
find yourself looking out at the clouds of diesel smoke rising up
into the sky. It's a windy day and the smoke is blown in circles
around the sun . . .

REMEMBERING TEXTS

So far, Part Two has concentrated on using the techniques of *Mindpower* to remember individual words. An awareness of detail is important, along with the ability to break words down into parts, and to find 'hooks' within the individual sections of a word. The trick is always to work *with* the memory – to find the easiest and shortest means to take hold of a word – and the same basic techniques can be applied to learning larger portions of text.

Again, the key is simplification. Even long passages of print can be broken down into a few vital points, then rearranged into a form which is much easier to remember. The first stage is always a practical one. Decide what you need to remember from a text, so that you can use the most efficient memory techniques and find the easiest methods of recall.

For many people, the same approach is used every time – no matter what they're trying to remember. More often than not this is the hit-and-miss technique of endless repetition, wasting time and effort and bringing only partial success. The more you have to learn, the more it all blurs together. You fool yourself into thinking that the material has been learned, until the dreaded moment comes to recall it. And even the information you *do* remember will not be there for long.

A great deal of time and energy can be saved, and a much greater level of success achieved, if you take a moment to find the most suitable approach. Always look ahead to the time when you'll have to start recalling the information. Will you have to know it word for word? If it's an essay, will it be useful to know the order of the points in an argument? If you're learning a play, will it be enough just to learn your own lines and cues? Decide on the *form* your recall will take, then adapt your techniques to suit it.

When I revised for my final university exams, I spent about half my time preparing to learn before I actually started memorising. I was studying English Literature, and I needed to know about fifty long essays that I'd written during the previous two years. Some of these were carefully constructed arguments, and I would have to know the sequence of all the major points.

Others were more general collections of information, including quotations and references. I needed to know the names of novels and plays, writers and poets. I had a desk full of piles of paper, and many different sorts of information to be learnt.

When I eventually went into the exam hall, I felt very confident. I had taken control of all the information, moulding it into a form in which it was at my disposal. In a minute or so I could write down all the main points in any of the essays, in sequence if need be, and remember any useful references or quotes.

Every time I thought of a particular section of information, my memory was prompted to cross to other relevant areas of knowledge. Every time I answered a question, I felt sure that I was including every appropriate piece of information I'd learnt.

I was making use of all the techniques *of Mindpower*. Each of my essays had been broken down into a list of key words, and the words moulded into a memorable story. Each story had its own location, which I stocked full of useful images to remind me of relevant quotations and facts, and each location was close to others holding similar information. I had created a vast, interlinked 'database' – and I actually enjoyed putting it to use in the exams!

Imagine, for example, that I had to answer a question on Shakespeare. All of my Shakespearean essays had been turned into stories, and all their locations were in the same area of my home town. I could pin-point any essay, since each one's story began in a particular shop, and I could easily include information brought in from other stories nearby.

As well as the essay points, each shop also contained reminders for quotations, and I could walk through the buildings in my mind to find the appropriate material. When I needed to remember an essay, I simply recalled the starting place for its story, wrote out the list of words as I went from image to image, then made this list the 'template' for my answer – adding some of the 'extra' information along the way.

I use similar techniques when I have to give talks, go through job interviews – even present radio programmes. Any information can be broken down, rearranged, then compiled into a form ideally suited to the way you have to remember it. You can hold business meetings without fumbling with tattered notes, or carry out presentations without breaking eye-contact with your audience. As long as you finish up with the information you need, who cares if you've been remembering fantastic stories, and taking mental journeys through imaginary lands?

LEARNING ESSAYS

My degree was in English Literature, but the beauty of the *Mindpower System* is that its techniques can be applied to any sort of essay on any subject, at any level. I was only able to revise efficiently for my university exams because I'd practised the same techniques when I studied for 'A' levels and GCSEs.

The system may take a little work to begin with, but soon you'll realise how much time you can save. Once you've taken an essay under your control and moulded it to fit the memory, you can link it with others, or add new elements at any time. By grouping together sets of information you'll also start to see more links within your work, and become more observant and creative. Most important, you'll finish your revision feeling confident that all your learning is at your fingertips.

When you're faced with an essay or passage of text to learn, the first step is to decide what sort of material it is. There are three main categories, each requiring a slightly different approach.

Category One: A Collection of Information.

This is an essay where a number of points of information are gathered together, and where their *order* isn't as important as the details themselves. This isn't an argument or an ordered explanation, but rather a collection of key points on a particular subject. At the same time, it is important to remember *all* the points, and you can combine them together into the material for a story without having to worry about the precise details of a sequence.

As an example, printed below is part of an essay about nuclear physics. The subject may seem complicated, but *Mindpower* techniques make it as easy to learn as any collection of words and ideas. Although there is a sequence to the events described here, it's more likely that a science student would have to remember just the key factual points about early atomic experiments. The power of the *Mindpower System* is that the perfect approach can be found, stressing these points, but adding to your understanding by reminding you of the general order in which they happened.

ERNEST RUTHERFORD AND THE ATOM

(The paragraphs have been numbered for reference later on).

1. Sometimes even scientists have to use imagination and instinct as they struggle to probe further than the human eye can see. That was certainly the case in the early years of the twentieth century when Ernest Rutherford investigated the structure of the atom. In just a few years he formed an understanding of atomic physics that laid the foundations for much of modern science, and the work he and his students carried out forms one of the most important periods in experimentation and discovery.

2. Rutherford's earliest experiments involved alpha particles – the positively charged emissions from radioactive materials such as radium. He noticed that these could pass through a thin sheet of mica, even though this seemed to be impossible; there were no holes in the material and it seemed solid enough to prevent any such movement of particles. Yet the particles did pass through – some travelling on a straight course, but a few others being deflected or scattered along the way. And it was these scatterings that interested the scientist most of all. Why did the particles veer off course only *some* of the time?

3. Although Rutherford had very little precise data to support his thinking, a new idea was taking shape in his mind. Perhaps atoms had a tiny core or nucleus with an electric charge strong enough to deflect the alpha particles – but only when they came very near to it. Around this nucleus, it followed, the electricity would have an opposite charge, through which the alpha particles could pass as if it were empty space.

4. To help take his ideas further, Rutherford enlisted the help of two of his assistants – H. Geiger and E. Marsden. Their job would be to investigate further the scattering of alpha particles as they passed through metals, looking especially at the number of particles changing direction and the angles at which they were scattered. Once again, the source of the alpha particles was radium; its radioactive products were held in a small glass tube. The experiment itself took place within the vacuum of a metal box, as a thin beam of particles was directed against a metal sheet – sometimes platinum, on other occasions silver or gold. A microscope fitted with a zinc sulphide screen detected the particles, which made a tiny flash of light each time one connected with the screen.

5. As soon as the experiment was underway, the scientists began the task of counting the flashes, and measuring the angles of deflection from the original straight line.

Reading through an essay like this provides you with a rough understanding of the material. The next step is to break it down into its key points, working out which are the important pieces of information and summarising them in a couple of words. Time spent *preparing* the essay to be memorised is vital; by deciding on the best way to simplify the text, you make the rest of the process quicker and easier.

Always remember to put yourself in control. Don't be confused by paragraph breaks in the text. Sometimes a printed section can be summed up in a single word, but on other occasions it might contain ten key points. As you go back through the essay, you're looking to strike a balance; you can't miss out the vital points, but there's no sense in repetition, or in including facts that you'll never need to know. Decide what you need, and simplify *that*.

Paragraph One. This is quite a general start to the essay, and the information here can be summed up quickly. The name of ERNEST RUTHERFORD will be anchored to the story when you link the essay's title to its imaginary location, so it can be left aside for now. Other than that, the only important point remaining in this first paragraph can be summarised in one word: IMAGINATION. This combines all the ideas here about the great scientist's 'instinct' and vision, and this single word will remind you about the themes at the beginning of the essay.

If it's possible, every time you decide on a key word, write it on to the essay. You can use pencil if you'll have to remove it later, but the very act of writing the word is important, forming an early step in the memory process.

Sometimes, as with 'imagination', the word will be present in the text itself, and you can underline it or enclose it in a circle. But, on other occasions, the best summarising word is one that you make up yourself, and it has to be added at the side of the page.

A third possibility is that the key word will already be in the text, but seems to be too scientific or unusual to go into your story unchanged. In that case, put to use all the language skills you developed in the earlier sections of Part Two, playing around with the word and re-shaping it until it can be included. Several examples of this appear in paragraph two.

Paragraph Two. I can pick out four key points here. The first is perhaps the most important item in the whole essay, one which reappears on several occasions: ALPHA PARTICLES. This is one of the times when a little imagination needs to be used.

As well as underlining these words in the text, why not create a 'reminder' image to add as well – perhaps the grumpy TV character Alf Garnett, or lovable alien A.L.F. Either of these characters could be made to sprinkle PARTICLES of sand, or find themselves covered in flour or salt, giving you a range of possibilities when you come to create your story. For now, just write the word 'Alf' alongside the text.

RADIUM is the second word I would underline here. Since it's another scientific term, perhaps you might jot down 'Radio' or 'Radiator' as an extra image for your story.

The next point is slightly more complicated, involving the idea of particles passing through a sheet of mica, but even this can be summarised neatly by underlining just two words: THROUGH and MICA. Perhaps MICA is changed to 'Mike A.' – the cricketer Mike Atherton, or motor-racing star Mario Andretti. Once again, as well as underlining the two key words, make a margin-note of the extra image your imagination suggests.

The final point in this paragraph involves the strange scattering of the particles. An easy way to summarise this is simply to underline the word SCATTERINGS, and then to add a large question-mark. In your story, there can be some great mystery about whatever it is that's being scattered.

Paragraph Three contains another four main points. NUCLEUS is described here as a 'tiny core', so your extra image could be of a little *apple* core. The second point, ELECTRIC CHARGE, might suggest an electricity bill! After that, the third key concept relates to the particles being deflected – perhaps like a goalkeeper deflecting a shot in football or hockey – when they come near to the core. By writing down the words NEAR and DEFLECTION you can neatly summarise the whole idea.

Finally, the word OPPOSITE sums up the rest of the paragraph: the opposite electric charge, and the opposite effect on the particles.

Paragraph Four contains a number of important points, yet most of them are simple additions to your growing list of words.

The first two are names: GEIGER and MARSDEN. GEIGER suggests the Geiger-Counter, clicking away in so many science-fiction films, and MARSDEN could become a *Den* for hiding *Mars*-bars! Make a note of each suggestion alongside the underlined words.

In the experiment, the two things being measured are NUMBER and ANGLES – two simple words to be used in your story. The equipment being used provides you with six more: TUBE, VACUUM, PLATINUM (perhaps suggesting a *platypus*), SILVER, GOLD and MICROSCOPE.

Finally in this paragraph, the ZINC SULPHIDE is an important part of the scientific process. To make the words suitable for your story, why not change Zinc to *Sink*, and Sulphide to a phrase like '*Sell Fido* . . .!

Paragraph Five simply recaps the details of the experiment. Since the appropriate memory techniques are being brought into play, it's the sort of reminder that you no longer need.

A couple of minutes spent simplifying the essay turns out to be time well spent. This complicated scientific text has been reduced to the following list of words and image-suggestions:

IMAGINATION, ALPHA-PARTICLES (Alf), RADIUM (Radio), THROUGH MICA (Mike A.), SCATTERINGS?,

NUCLEUS (Core), ELECTRIC CHARGE (Bill), NEAR DEFLECTION, OPPOSITE, GEIGER (-Counter), MARSDEN (Mars-Den), NUMBER, ANGLES, TUBE, VACUUM, PLATINUM (Platypus), SILVER, GOLD, MICROSCOPE, ZINC SULPHIDE (Sink/Sell Fido!).

This list looks more complicated than it is. Remember, the suggestions in brackets will become *replacements* for the more technical words when you create your story, so this is really a collection of just twenty images – half as long as the list learned at the end of Part One.

The first step in creating the story is to find an appropriate starting point, connected in some way with the essay's title. 'Atom' makes me think immediately of an atom-*bomb*, so why not start the story at a bomb testing-site on some isolated island? Visualise the scene in detail, and zoom in to see a scientist stuck up to his neck in a huge rut in the road. This is RUT herford, and the process of turning the list into a story can now begin.

The scientist is stuck fast in his rut. It's clear that he's thinking hard, trying to use his IMAGINATION to come up with a means of escape; his eyes are rolling, and every so often a shower of sparks and a cloud of smoke bursts out through his ears! The smoke is starting to dirty the ground around him, and you decide to do a bit of cleaning up – but you're beaten to it by ALF Garnett, himself covered in PARTICLES of dirt, and swearing and grumbling as he mops down the sand.

You watch him as he works. Suddenly he finds something unusual: a glowing piece of material marked RADIUM. As if to confirm its identity, this substance is shaped like a RADIO – and it even seems to be playing music . . .

You decide to test its strength. The next two people to come along are both MIKE A.'s – Mike Atherton, dressed in his cricket pads, and Mario Andretti, wearing a fire-proof racing suit and helmet. Amazingly, even with all that protection, the radium goes right THROUGH them, leaving them with gaping holes in their middles! This seems certain to affect Mario Andretti's racing career – and, sure enough, he climbs into his car and crashes instantly, smashing the vehicle into thousands of pieces which SCATTER in all directions across the sand.

These scatterings intrigue you. How come there are so many, and why have they scattered so far? The mystery is cleared up when you look closer: the car actually hit something in the road – the TINY CORE of an apple. The core is wrapped in an old ELECTRICITY BILL, complete with all its itemised CHARGES. Just in case *you're* asked to pay this bill you quickly throw it away – but it bounces back, again and again, DEFLECTING off NEARBY objects.

You finally solve the problem when you find an open space with nothing near. In fact, the OPPOSITE now happens; when you let go of the bill, it flies away into the distance and disappears.

Rather than leave litter on this deserted island, you decide to search for the bill. The only piece of detection-equipment you have is an old GEIGER-COUNTER, and unfortunately it seems to be a little faulty. Instead of leading you to the bill, it locates a secret stash of chocolate-bars: a 'MARS-DEN'.

Your interest has been excited. You count the NUMBER of bars, and measure the ANGLES of each one with a protractor.

All the bars are exactly the same – except one. This bar is shaped more like a hollow TUBE, and you decide it will come in very handy as a replacement part for your VACUUM-cleaner! To protect it, you cover its surfaces with the three most precious metals you can think of: GOLD on the inside, SILVER on the outside, and PLATINUM on the edges at either end. You could even use the left-over platinum to draw a PLATYPUS on the outside, before fixing it to the vacuum cleaner and checking that it works . . .

When you're tired of cleaning, borrow a MICROSCOPE to check that you've sucked up every last speck of dirt. This microscope is the most expensive model on the market, and you'd love to buy it – so much so that you decide to sell up everything you own. Soon you find yourself bargaining away your last two possessions; the kitchen SINK, and your dog. Yes, you've even had to SELL FIDO!

When you've visualised the story and repeated it to yourself a few times, practise using it to remember the list of twenty points. Once again, this is something you can do wherever you are; you can make full use of spare moments spent waiting in queues or on journeys, and you'll soon be able to reel off the list in a few seconds.

It's important to have at least one 'dry-run' at reconstructing the essay. Begin by writing down the list from memory, then take each point in turn, explaining to yourself what it means and what part it plays in the essay. If you have time, you can write it all down, but otherwise simply think through the points, returning every so often to the original essay to check your progress.

'IMAGINATION: Rutherford needed to use imagination and instinct in his atomic experiments. ALF – ALPHA PARTICLES: He used these in his first tests. RADIUM: This was the source of the particles. THROUGH MICA: Rutherford's interest was sparked when he saw that the particles could pass through a sheet of mica. SCATTERINGS?: He was especially interested to find out why some of the particles veered off a straight course . . .'

You'll find that the key-points prompt you to remember more and more of the detail of the essay, stressing the most important areas, but reminding you, too, of the more general areas of interest. You may have spent a while on the initial preparation and on creating and visualising the story, but now you *know* it, and the essay has been taken under your control once and for all.

Before a test or exam you can glance back through the list of words to confirm them one last time, rather than skimming through pages and pages of unsimplified text, and you can be confident that this and other sections of information are at your fingertips.

In the examination itself you may need to combine several essays. Since each one will have been given its own memorable story, you can easily write down the appropriate lists of points, then pick and choose which ones to include in your answer. Suddenly all the information is there before you, and you can start to be creative, finding links between essays and making comparisions and cross-references.

Having the key words in front of you creates a great sense of confidence, and provides you with a plan to work from. I always found it far easier to control my time during an exam if I could see how many points I still had available to make.

Category Two:
Different Angles on One Topic

This sort of essay includes a number of different 'mini-essays' on one specific subject. It's also the style used by many people when they take notes or summarise information from a book, so it's especially useful to be able to learn this sort of text. By understanding the construction of an essay, and using the appropriate memory techniques, you make it much easier for yourself to reconstruct the material from a list of key points, and to retrieve the information in a very convenient form.

In the following essay, each paragraph looks at a different composer, and describes the links he had with the piano.

'COMPOSERS FOR THE PIANO'.

1. 'Johann Nepomuk Hummel influenced an entire generation of pianists. He received widespread praise for his compositions, and his influence on the development of playing techniques was especially great. His books of studies proved extremely popular with students, as did his systems for fingering and the playing of ornaments, and he published structured routines for daily practice.

2. John Baptist Cramer was brought up in a musical home. His father, a renowned violinist, influenced his musical development, and Cramer achieved great skill as a performer at the keyboard. But it was as a publisher and composer that he was best known. He produced books of studies for students, along with a large number of 'display pieces' designed to improve piano technique. His contemporaries praised him for his interpretation of works by other well-known composers.

3. Adolf Henselt was mostly self-taught as a pianist, and achieved a remarkable level of musicianship. But he disliked playing in public; he worked hard instead on keyboard studies, and invented exercises to increase the stretch of the hand and flexibility of the fingers. Smoothness of playing was always his goal.

4. Stephen Heller was another prolific composer for the piano. What his work lacked in quality was more than

made up for by its sincerity and style, and contemporary writers pointed to a very individual sound. One described it as 'the music of good breeding . . . replete with imagination, charm.'

In an essay like this, the separate paragraphs or sections are of more value. Each one relates to a particular composer, and it's important to keep them as individual units of information, even though they're all connected by a central theme. When you come to reconstruct the material, having the sections as distinct 'chunks' will be of great use.

As before, the first stage is to highlight the key points.

Paragraph One. The first point is clearly the composer's name: HUMMEL. The word INFLUENCE sums up his importance at the time, and then five words can be picked out to describe the key elements of his work: TECHNIQUES (he helped develop playing techniques); STUDIES (he published books of studies); FINGERING, ORNAMENTS and ROUTINES (he wrote systems for each).

Paragraph Two. This also begins with a name, CRAMER, and the information about his background can be simplified into two words: VIOLINIST FATHER. His own skills are divided into three main areas – PERFORMER, PUBLISHER, COMPOSER – and another three words sum up the rest of this section: STUDIES, TECHNIQUE and INTERPRETATION.

Paragraph Three. The composer featured is HENSELT. His education at the piano can be spelled out in just one word, SELF, and then four key words stress his interests and aims: STUDIES, STRETCH, FLEXIBILITY and SMOOTHNESS.

Paragraph Four. The final paragraph centres on HELLER. His role was simply as a COMPOSER, and his qualities are summed up by SINCERITY, STYLE and INDIVIDUAL. The final quotation might be useful to know; its key points are BREEDING, IMAGINATION and CHARM.

An essay like this, written in note-taking style, is packed with important points. Several of them reappear, and there are often only subtle differences between the composers described. Each group of facts must remain separate, yet all four need to be brought together, connected to the central theme and providing contrasts and comparisons.

An effective technique is to make use of the characters already present. By creating a strong location, each of the composers can have his own sequence of events, and your imagination can make four different stories come to life in the same place.

The location must be linked with the subject. In this case, think of a room you know that contains a piano. It might be the room where you practise, a concert-hall where you've watched a pianist perform – even a room in your local pub! The piano has to be the focal point; each composer's 'story' will revolve around it.

Once you've visualised the location, the next step is to concentrate on the characters.

Begin with their names. As demonstrated in the earlier sections of Part Two, just a single syllable is often enough to remind you of a whole word – and this is especially true when real names are involved. Here, each name can be simplified into its initial syllable, and four words are formed, each capable of becoming the starting point for a story: HUM *(Hum*mel), CRAM *(Cram*er), HENS *(Hens*elt), HELL *(Hell*er).

Before you create each story, make a note of its starting point and the words it needs to include.

HUMMEL:
> *HUM*, INFLUENCE, TECHNIQUES, STUDIES, FINGER-ING, ORNAMENTS, ROUTINES

Imagine the room you have chosen is a huge concert hall, filled to bursting-point with eager music-lovers. How disappointed they are when, rather than play the piano, all the star performer will do is HUM! Someone sitting next to you suggests that the man is 'under the INFLUENCE' – and, sure enough, he's seen by the crowd to take a long swig from a bottle of wine! This *influences* the audience's decision to stand up from their seats and leave.

They do this in different ways. Some of them jump up, then skip to the door; others climb up slowly before hopping out of the hall. You watch all these different TECHNIQUES in amazement, and decide to record them. You make detailed notes as you watch, determined to publish your STUDIES as soon as you can.

Unfortunately you fumble with your papers and spill them all over the floor. You curse your careless FINGERING – especially when you hear a crash, and realise that some of the sheets have hit a row of priceless ORNAMENTS and brought them tumbling to the ground. To make matters worse, a dance-troupe has come into the hall. The dancers start practising their ROUTINES amongst the broken bits of china and glass, and you think back in annoyance to the humming performer who started this disastrous tale . . .

CRAMER:
CRAM, VIOLINIST FATHER, PERFORMER, PUBLISHER, COMPOSER, STUDIES, TECHNIQUE, INTERPRETATION

On another day, as the audience sits waiting, champion runner Steve CRAM sprints into the hall and starts to *cram* even more people in between the rows of seats. He has personal reasons for wanting a large crowd: his VIOLINIST FATHER is about to perform. The audience waits, hushed – and when the star of the show eventually arrives, they're not disappointed.

The show is made up of three sections; two halves, with an interval between. In the first half, the man – helped all the way by Steve Cram – shows off his talents as a PERFORMER.

In the interval he sits by a photo-copier, hurriedly running off booklets to sell and proving his skill as a PUBLISHER.

Finally, in the second half, he demonstrates his composition techniques, allowing the audience to watch a COMPOSER at work.

As a grand finale, he holds up pictures of his house. Among the many rooms there are several STUDIES where he can work in peace, and he explains that he has a different TECHNIQUE for working, depending on which room he's in.

In one he might lie on the floor; in another he prefers to walk around, lean against the desk or stand on his head! The only thing common to every room is a trained interpreter, who sits at his own little desk and translates the musician's work into different languages. Wherever he goes, this famous player and composer always has someone to do his INTERPRETATION . . .

HENSELT:
  HENS, SELF, STUDIES, STRETCH, FLEXIBILITY, SMOOTHNESS

On one famous occasion, the concert hall nearly had to be evacuated when it was invaded by a flock of HENS. Luckily, the pianist there that day was able to catch them all himSELF, explaining that he was entirely *self-taught* as he pushed them all into *Self*ridges carrier-bags. When all the hens were caught, he concentrated on each one in turn, carrying out a detailed series of STUDIES.

One hen was so large that he had to STRETCH out both his hands to hold it. The audience were fascinated by his hands, and he demonstrated that each one had a quality of its own. His right hand had great FLEXIBILITY; he could bend each finger without moving any of the others. And his left hand had the sort of SMOOTHNESS that only a certain brand of washing-up liquid creates . . .!

HELLER:
  HELL, COMPOSER, SINCERITY, STYLE, INDIVIDUAL, BREEDING, IMAGINATION, CHARM

One Halloween, the concert hall was decorated to look like HELL. The role of the Devil was played by a famous COMPOSER, who wrote some special hellish music and then spiked the sheets on to the prongs of his pitchfork! He invited the audience-members individually, sending each of them a letter marked '*Yours sincerely*', and concealed his identity when they arrived with a show of fake SINCERITY.

Each of the guests was dressed in a different STYLE. Some wore modern clothes; others had found old-fashioned costumes, swimwear or overalls. The devilish composer inspected each of them in turn noting their individual characteristic, and only one was turned away – for ignoring the 'no pets' rule, and bringing along a BREEDING pair of rabbits!

Finally, when the audience was fully assembled, he told them all to start exercising their IMAGINATION. He began to perform a mime, pretending to be a snake-*charmer*, and told them all to imagine that he was able to CHARM a gigantic snake . . .

As ever, the more weird and wonderful the stories are the better! Make sure that you highlight each key point in your mind, and think up extra ways to confirm each word on the list.

When it comes to remembering the essay, a number of possibilities are open to you. You can pick any single composer, reel off the words in his 'story', then write your answer based on those central points. You can combine several of the lists to write a more comprehensive answer if need be. And perhaps most usefully of all, you can pick out any word, and find out how many of the sections contain it.

For example, an examination question might ask you to write about composers who wrote books of studies for the piano. In just a few seconds you could remind yourself of each of the stories, and learn that your essay could include Hummel (remember your *studies* of the people leaving the hall . . .), Cramer (the many *studies* in the performer's house), and Henselt (visualise the pianist *study*ing the hens!).

Or the question might be more precise: 'Which of the composers you have studied was known for his sincerity and individual style?'. Faced with that question, simply go through the stories until the 'target' information appears. You remember someone writing 'Yours *sincerely*' on a letter, you recall his fake *sincerity* – it was the composer in *Hell*, Heller!

The beauty of this sort of story-group is that you can add on more sections whenever you want. Each time you read about a composer who wrote for the piano, simply connect a new story with the main location. You create the equivalent of a 'piano file'; you can open it up with ease, and any linked topics can be located nearby.

You might learn about some *organ* players, and choose to house their stories in a room upstairs. The street outside the concert hall might be your location for great piano *makers*, each unloading his van and revealing another sequence of key points. Gradually your mental data-base grows, and the resources available to you become more and more powerful.

Category Three:
Essays With a Sequence of Points.
Some essays have a definite shape to them that needs to be maintained. This might be a carefully worked out argument,

or perhaps a historical sequence of events. The strength of the story-telling technique is that any sort of sequence, once it's been found, can be kept intact, and the order of key points stressed.

Graham Greene's novel *The Power and the Glory* is read by students at many different levels, and forms the subject of the following essay. The argument here has been carefully worked out, and valuable exam time could be saved by knowing the exact order of points.

'IS GRAHAM GREENE "UNFAIR" IN HIS PORTRAYAL OF THE LIEUTENANT IN THE POWER AND THE GLORY?'

1. The lieutenant's goal is clear: to wipe out every last trace of Catholic faith in Mexico. This means that it would be possible to portray his actions in strikingly different ways. On one hand the author could write from the Catholic viewpoint, condemning the lieutentant and all he stands for, and presenting his character as thoroughly bad. But from another position, in which no judgement was passed on a character's actions, the lieutenant could be seen as a strong man, triumphant in the pursuit of his goal. These are the simple extremes; Graham Greene chooses neither of them.

2. Instead, the lieutenant's character is presented in a more complicated way, and the reader learns of his good qualities as well as his flaws. Most importantly of all, although the novel suggests from early on that this man's actions are wrong, it remains to be seen whether he himself will realise that, and perhaps even try to change. That possibility is where much of the interest lies.

3. The portrayal of this character, then, is itself changeable. Sometimes the lieutenant is shown to be an admirable man. The reader is led to sympathise with him because of his difficult upbringing and the struggle he has made through hardship and poverty. He is dedicated and strong-willed, avoiding luxury and never thinking of personal gain, and his generosity is seen when he gives money to the priest. He even breaks the law to bring a gift of brandy to the man's lonely cell.

4. Above all, the lieutenant follows a noble aim: to create a better life for the children of Mexico. Greene gives him

some powerful arguments about the need to ease suffering, and clearly the lieutenant is never wholly condemned.

5. But at the same time he is shown to be a very bitter man. He follows an idea, but seems incapable of feeling love for real people. He may respect the priest, but he is determined to kill him for his beliefs. Most of all, he loses his confidence. Rather than being 'unfair', Greene simply refuses to allow the lieutenant any easy way out, and shows the man's own worries eating away at his character. His 'love' is described as the force which moved only his 'trigger-finger'; he questions his own motives, struggling with the complications of life.

6. Rather than being 'unfair', by judging him too harshly or giving only a partial picture, Greene shows the lieutenant's character in all its complexity. Most of all, his novel achieves a great deal of its power when the lieutenant starts to pass judgement on *himself*.'

As with all of these examples, an essay like this will always be much easier to learn if you've written it yourself or studied the subject. Yet the techniques of *Mindpower* can make *anything* much more memorable; atomic physics, music history, literature . . . The same basic rules apply whatever you need to learn.

With an essay like this, based firmly on a sequence of points, the first step is to work out exactly what that sequence is.

Paragraph One can be summed up in just three carefully-chosen words: GOAL, POSSIBILITIES and NEITHER. All three are very abstract ideas, yet they work as powerful prompts to help reconstruct the argument.

GOAL is the most straightforward of the three, and will be especially important as a reminder of where the sequence starts. The lieutenant has a clear goal, which means there are several POSSIBILITIES when it comes to portraying his character. The third word, NEITHER, is especially powerful, since it stresses that there are *two* main possibilities – a negative portrayal, and a positive view.

The three words chosen here remind you of everything you need to know about this opening paragraph, as well as the best way of ordering the points into an effective argument. Since the lieutenant's goal was so clear, the novelist *could* have taken one of two extreme views – but didn't.

This is stressed by the first of two words summing up

Paragraph Two: COMPLEX. The whole essay is going to concentrate on the complexities of the man's character, and, most importantly of all, on his SELF-AWARENESS.

Paragraph Three centres on his ADMIRABLE qualities. There are four more specific key words here: UPBRINGING, DEDICATION, FRUGAL and GENEROSITY, all of which simplify powerful points in just a single word.

Paragraph Four is an important one, even though it contains just one main point: the lieutenant's care for the CHILDREN of Mexico.

There is a shift in **Paragraph Five** towards the negative side of the lieutenant's character. Two words, BITTER and UNLOVING, remind you of very important themes, and WOR-RIES makes the argument even more specific. The interesting point being made is that the man's loss of *confidence* is the most negative thing of all, and TRIGGER-FINGER reminds you of a quotation which sums up the whole idea.

The phrase which encapsulates **Paragraph Six**, SELF-JUDGEMENT, sums up both the ending of the essay, and the thrust of the whole argument. There is a clear sequence of points, worked through from paragraph to paragraph, and the story you create needs to make this clear. For once, the paragraphs in the text are important; your story must make it clear where one section ends and the next begins.

As well as the markings you've made on the essay or article itself, always make a point of writing down the list of key words on a separate piece of paper. This allows you a clear view of the points to be included – and means that you can compile your own 'revision booklet', a handy collection of the simplified versions of all your essays. At the top of each page make a clear note of the main elements of the essay's title.

GRAHAM GREENE/POWER AND GLORY/UNFAIR PORTRAYAL OF LIEUTENANT?

(GOAL, POSSIBILITIES, NEITHER,) (COMPLEX, SELF-AWARENESS,) (ADMIRABLE, UPBRINGING, DEDICA-TION, FRUGAL, GENEROSITY,) (CHILDREN,) (BIT-TER, UNLOVING, WORRIES, TRIGGER-FINGER,) (SELF-JUDGEMENT)

In this list, the words bracketed together represent the key words in a particular paragraph. By learning these sixteen words, in six distinct sections, you can become confident that the whole complex essay is completely under your control.

Since the question is all about a 'fair' or 'unfair' portrayal, why not set it in a law court? This is especially appropriate, since the final point, the conclusion, is all about judgement. To remind yourself of the author in question, everything and everybody in the court could be *green* – and perhaps there's a picture of a *power*-station on the wall to confirm the title of the book.

Visualise the scene in your mind, bringing in as many senses and emotions as possible. Picture the lieutenant standing chained in the dock. This essay is about whether he's being treated fairly or not, so imagine feeling great interest in his plight.

The judge climbs down from his seat, and sets up a huge football GOAL in the middle of the room. He explains to the audience that there are two clear POSSIBILITIES; either the lieutenant will be able to score a goal, or he'll miss – the result will be clearly positive or negative.

Unfortunately, though, things don't quite go according to plan. The lieutenant kicks the ball, and, miraculously, it lands on *top* of the goal. NEITHER possibility has come true; he hasn't scored, but then again he hasn't entirely missed.

The judge decides that more football testing is required. He leads the audience to a nearby sports COMPLEX, through a complicated maze of passageways and doors, and into a sports hall. But the hall is already in use; a SELF-AWARENESS group is being held, according to the huge banner across the ceiling.

A new location is required, but, apart from the sports-hall, the only other large room in the complex is the swimming-pool. When they arrive there, the audience watches with interest as a huge ship, being steered by a fierce-looking *Admiral*, sails down the pool. The judge declares this room to be perfect: 'ADMIRABLE!', he shouts, and instructs everyone to watch the action on board ship.

The Admiral is teaching his young children how to sail, completing a vital stage in their UPBRINGING. They're so small that he has to lift them in his arms to *bring* them *up* to the level of the wheel. .

Once this training is over, the ship's DEDICATION-ceremony can be carried out and it can sail off on its maiden voyage. You watch as a bottle is swung against the ship's bow – but, as it smashes, only water pours out. The organisers have been very FRUGAL, much to the judge's delight, and he explains that by saving money like this, the rest of the celebrations can be all the more *generous*. Sure enough, a huge feast is laid on – and you decide to send the Admiral a card to thank him for his GENEROSITY.

It's time to leave the sports-centre. As the audience files back outside, they pass a huge group of noisy CHILDREN coming in for a birthday-party and filling the corridor . . .

It takes hours to weave through the crowds of children and arrive back in the street. The judge is furious; he tells everyone how BITTER he feels at the delay, and opens a bottle of *bitter*-lemon to help drown his sorrows. He criticises the sports-complex for being uncaring about their customers, UNLOVING, and even scrawls the word in red paint on the front door!

Not surprisingly, you start to have WORRIES about his sanity. A number of worried murmurs pass through the crowd. Suddenly, someone lets out a scream. The judge has brought out a gun, and is aiming it at your head! His TRIGGER-FINGER quivers . . .

Meanwhile, everyone has forgotten about the lieutenant. Amid all the confusion and excitement, he has been left in the court-house, forced to pass JUDGEMENT on HIMSELF.

This story is based on a definite sequence, with one thing leading clearly to another. One of the most important elements is that each of the six initial paragraphs has its own location: the courthouse, the sports-hall, the swimming-pool, the corridor, the street-and, finally, the courthouse again. Even if you forget one of the details within a section, you can still remember the overall flow of points by moving to the location that follows.

When it comes to reconstructing the essay, simply go back through the story in your mind, write out the key points, and bracket them together, section by section. Within seconds you have in front of you all the main parts of the essay, the sequence in which they appear – even a reminder of the original paragraphs!

Once again, other essays can be made to link up with this one. If you learn more information about the same novel, the new stories you create can be set in and around the same area. Other material about Graham Greene can also be put nearby, and the opening scenes painted green. If you want to add new points to an essay, simply find the appropriate part of the story and use your imagination, making an opening in the action or fitting in an extra stage.

REMEMBERING QUOTATIONS

Often it can be useful – and impressive – to include relevant quotations in your essays and examination answers. Once again, the trick is to make the text come alive, looking for the 'hooks' that already exist within individual words and phrases. Quotations need to be remembered exactly, and a few moments spent concentrating on detail is invaluable.

There are three main steps when you need to learn a quotation. The first is to create a general image for the sentence or phrase. Let your imagination run riot, creating puns and plays-on-words, and turning abstract text into pictures.

Printed below are ten real quotations, followed by imagery suggestions. Practise bringing them to life in your imagination, and think up some variations of your own.

1. 'The curate; he was fatter than his cure'. (Tennyson, *Edwin Morris*)
2. 'Round numbers are always false'. (Johnson)
3. 'Truth never hurts the teller'. (Browning, *Fifine at the Fair*)
4. 'Patch grief with proverbs'. (Shakespeare, *Othello*)
5. 'You're not a man, you're a machine'. (Shaw)
6. 'A brain of feathers, and a heart of lead'. (Pope, *The Dunciad*)
7. 'Where more is meant than meets the ear'. (Milton, *L'Allegro*)
8. 'We be of one blood, thou and I'. (Kipling)

9. 'Your sister is given to government'. (Dickens, *Great Expectations*)
10. 'Oh Rome! my country! city of the soul!' (Byron, *Childe Harold's Pilgrimage*)

Suggestions

1. As a first, general image, picture a *curate* in a dog-collar sitting next to a *cure* he's invented. Notice the difference in size; the tiny bottle of medicine is overshadowed by the huge bulk of the curate!

2. Imagine marking the sums in a young child's maths book. You put ticks by the side of most of the questions – except the ones where the numbers have been given *rounded* sides and put in circles. These sums are always wrong, the answers clearly *false*.

3. If you remove the 'T', 'Truth' becomes 'Ruth'. Imagine a girl called Ruth – perhaps someone you know – staging a violent bank robbery, but changing her mind at the last minute. She could never hurt the bank-*teller*!

4. 'Grief' sounds a little like 'Greece', so picture an old map of the world with ugly holes where Greece should be. Tear up an old book of proverbs, and use the pages to patch up Greece.

5. As a man turns round, you see that his back is a mass of wires, levers and cogs. Confront him with his true identity!

6. This quotation is already very visual. Add to the words by bringing in as many senses as possible. What would it *feel* like to have a brain of feathers? How would you walk if you had a heart of lead?

7. In this quotation, 'more' could become 'Moore'. Imagine a huge ear, and a long line of people filing into it. Only one person hangs back; *Patrick* Moore, the astronomer . . .

8. 'We be' could become '*Wee bee*' – a tiny buzzing insect.

Imagine trying to persuade someone that you both share a likeness with this little creature . . .

9. Imagine a nursing-sister – or a nun – being physically handed over to Parliament.

10. Change 'soul' to '*sole*', and you can visualise the whole of ancient Rome covered in fish . . .!

Once you've developed the quotation into a memorable, visible image, the new scene can be incorporated into the story you write for any sort of essay.

To make it part of the history of music for the piano, for example, simply connect your pictures with the concert-hall location. Imagine the nun being passed over the heads of the crowd, towards a government committee sitting inside the piano! Perhaps the tatty map is blowing across the stage, or the pianist himself turns out to be a clanking machine . . .

If your quotation needs to appear at a particular point in the essay, anchor the images to the appropriate event or location. In the Graham Greene essay, for instance, quotation number two could be fixed to the third paragraph by giving the maths book to one of the children on-board ship. The curate and his medicine bottle could be sitting at either side of the courthouse, to include that quotation in the first paragraph, or Ruth's bank-robbery could be staged on the street of paragraph five.

The final step is designed to make you word perfect. The general images will help you rememember the gist of the quotation, but a few moments more need to be spent confirming the precise words.

Try to guess which words you're likely to get wrong; the plain words, the unusual words, the strange spellings. Highlight the difficult elements, then add detailed reminders to the larger pictures.

In quotation one, you might mistake 'fatter' for 'bigger' or 'larger'. To make sure you don't, picture streams of melted bacon-*fat* pouring down the curate's head!

The first two words of the fifth quotation might be confused with 'You aren't' or 'weren't'. By visualising a k*not*ted handkerchief on the man's head you can confirm the words in your mind.

In quotation seven, see the people munching hunks of meat – '*meets*' – as they walk into the ear; in quotation eight, change 'thou' into '*thought*', 'I' into 'eye', and imagine sensing the person's *thoughts* from the look in their *eyes*.

Quotations quickly become easier with practice, and these techniques give your memory the solid foundations it needs.

In examinations, memory is at its most powerful when it's used as a springboard for success. Clearly you have to find, read or write the information in the first place, understand it and have your own views and ideas. But the *Mindpower System* makes sure that you *use* all your hard work; that you remember all the right things in the exam, and have all the resources you need to be *creative* with the material you know.

So many people waste time struggling with the vaguest sorts of learning. They come out of exams realising they've missed important points and, ultimately, let themselves down. All too often, memory is a neglected, wasted resource.

By deciding to *use* your mind, to take control of information and to mould it to your advantage, you might just be taking the vital, rising step towards success.

PART THREE

MINDPOWER FOR NUMBERS

If words worry people, numbers *terrify* them. Their responses revolve around three main points.

The first is to insist that numbers are mostly impossible to learn. Perhaps a few telephone numbers are within reason, but beyond that there's little point in even trying. Numbers are dry, colourless, abstract shapes on a page, and the human memory simply can't cope.

The second involves the excuse that there's no *need* to remember numbers. All you have to do is find the right bit of paper, open a telephone directory or press a few buttons on a computer.

The third response is that, unless you're a mathematician or a nuclear-physicist, there are very few important numbers anyway. A handful of telephone numbers, the P.I.N. on your bank-card, a date or two in your history exam – other than that, numbers play very little part in everyday life.

All three points are wrong.

One: numbers may seem difficult and confusing, but it's possible to take control of them more efficiently and effectively than any other sort of information.

Two: you may think you can write down every number you need and always have it to hand – but how many times have you found yourself searching for the phone-pad, cursing yourself for not bringing your address book on holiday, or wasting hours finding out the numbers on the credit-cards, passport, aeroplane tickets or driving-licence that were on the seat of your car . . .?

Three: you may not think that numbers feature heavily in your life, but what about the numbers that make up dates and times, price-tags, flight numbers, dialling-codes . . .? You may not have to remember straightforward lists of numbers, but you *do* have to know people's birthdays – 12.2.72 – appointments – 10.30, 25.10.95 – security codes, bus time tables, house numbers, registration plates, measurements . . . The truth is that numbers are everywhere. Being able to learn them easily saves time, creates confidence, and helps you escape from otherwise tricky situations. Rather than being impossible to remember, numbers are the perfect form of information to be ordered, brought to life, and fitted into systems.

There are millions of words, but there are only ten digits. Simply learn ten new 'identities', and you have the hooks on which to hang any number at all.

By putting the *Mindpower System* to work on numbers, you provide yourself with an invaluable resource. As well as allowing you to remember all the numbers you need, these memory techniques make it possible to use numbers to remember other things.

You can number the items on a list, and learn them by using the numbers as prompts for the mind. You can break an essay into separately numbered sections, then learn the *numbers* as a detailed and pliable frame. Most importantly of all, you can combine numbers within all the other material you learn – useful dates and references within essays, phone-numbers alongside addresses, amounts in recipes, employee numbers with names.

Whenever numbers appear, you're confident of remembering them. Whenever they don't, you have the skills to bring them into play, to make use of their potential, and to exercise your control.

Numbers often bring back bad memories of school: maths lessons misunderstood, physics formulas forgotten, dates jumbled. The important thing to realise is that numbers themselves are not difficult. There are just ten differently shaped digits, and you don't have to be a mathematics wizard to deal with them. Most of us already know all the maths we need – and have calculators for the rest! So, numbers are simply another form of information to be *made* memorable.

Numbers are flat and dead – and that's what makes them so easy to control. You start with a clean slate, ten shapes on a page that can be given new identities, manipulated, brought to life in the imagination. There can never be any surprises; once you're familiar with the ten building-blocks, *any* number is just a variation on a theme.

CREATE YOUR OWN NUMBER SYSTEM

When dealing with words, *Mindpower* techniques allow you to work on individual sets of letters, and to choose the best memory methods for any situation you face. But with numbers, the system can be much more rigid. Imagination is still the key force at every level, but now most of the work only needs to be done once. Time spent learning a simple number system is one of the most worthwhile investments you can make.

There are five easy steps to creating a system for remembering numbers. As always, the best system is one you design yourself. Take a piece of paper and a pencil, and use the steps and suggestions that follow to build up your own personal resource.

Step One
Use a ruler to divide your paper into three columns lengthways, then draw horizontal lines to create thirty sections – ten groups of three. At the left-hand side of each group write a digit: 0 at the top of the page, going down towards 9 at the bottom.

Label each of the three columns; the first OBJECTS, the second ACTIONS and the third DESCRIPTIONS.

You now have a template to create an entire number system. Each digit is going to be given its own objects, actions and descriptions. When you've finished, any set of digits will transform in seconds into a memorable story.

Step Two
This whole system is based on the *objects* you choose for each digit. The second step is to make your decisions – to give each of the ten digits an object of its own.

A simple way to do this is to apply your imagination to shapes. Look at each digit in turn, and come up with an object based on its shape – its distinctive lines and curves. The new identity of a digit will be much easier to remember if it *looks* something like the number it represents.

As you choose each object, write its name in the appropriate box – in capital-letters, but leaving plenty of space for other words to be added later on. Use pencil, as you may have to make changes, and work from digit to digit until the whole of the first column has been filled in, the ten objects chosen.

Suggestions

0   is the perfect example of a digit with a powerful shape. My first reaction would be to make its object a BALL. Write a simple word like this under the Objects column alongside **0** then move down to the next.

1   has similarities with several other digits in that it can be written in several ways. In each case, choose the number's simplest form. **1** is really just a single, straight, vertical line – like a PEN.

2   always reminds me of a SWAN, a long, curved neck above a solid body.

3   is a good example of the way shapes can be manipulated. This digit is an unusual shape when it's upright – so why not lie it down? On its side-m – **3** looks like two curved HILLS.

4   can also be put on its side-x – to create a TABLE.

5   has a strong shape as it is. I like to see it as a huge, sharp-pointed HOOK.

6   a musical NOTE – an 'object' on a sheet of music, but also a *sound*, suggesting powerful possibilities later on . . .

7   is a digit made from two sides of a triangle. Perhaps it reminds you of the triangular sail on a YACHT.

8   makes me think of an old-fashioned loaf of BREAD, made from two balls of dough.

9   is made up of a circle and a line – perhaps the head and body of a PERSON.

Clearly, the title 'objects' is only a guideline. This column can include living creatures as well as inanimate 'things'. The trick is to choose words that are simple and distinctive, and which, like PERSON, NOTE or PEN, provide possibilities for a wide range of images, sounds and colours.

As you look back through your list, check that each 'object' is very different from all the others. My suggestions include a variety of shapes: the rounded BALL, the rigid PEN, the spiked HOOK. There are also very different materials: rubber, plastic, feathers, grass, skin. Words like NOTE and BREAD present possibilities for bringing in extra senses, and PERSON will pave the way for a variety of emotional responses.

Feel free to make changes to your list. These first ten words are the most important of all, and it's crucial to choose them well. As the titles of the other columns suggest, these words are going to be connected with *actions* and *descriptions*, so make sure that each of them has sufficient scope.

Step Three

Now begin to expand upon the ideas. Take each word in turn, and fill up the rest of the box with new associations, each based on the initial word but taking the theme in a slightly different direction.

Before you include a new word, glance down the list to make sure it can't be confused with another heading. BALL might well lead you to think of a rounded BOWL, for example, and this is fine to include in the same box. But if you were to make it into a *goldfish* bowl, you couldn't then add FISH to your collection of words to represent **7**, since it would be just too confusing. If your memory story involved a fish, which number would it be prompting you to recall?

Make each initial word the starting-point for some imaginative off-shoots. The more possibilities each number has, the more varied and interesting your stories can be. Each digit should have a certain 'theme', based on its keyword, but spreading out to include many different ideas.

Suggestions

0 : BALL: The central theme here is 'circles' – so other objects could include HOOP, RING, ROLLER – even CLOCK, since it can't be confused with any of the other number-headings.

1 : PEN: As well as other writing- and drawing-implements, like PENCIL, PAINTBRUSH and RULER, this section could be expanded with words like INK, PAINT, PICTURE and BOOK. Once again they all have links to the initial word PEN, and none of them causes confusions with other parts of the system. The addition of BOOK here demonstrates the sort of 'off-shoot' that can take place; the link is maintained, but a whole new area of images is opened up.

2 : SWAN: The theme of this section is 'wings' and 'flying', so *any* bird can be included here – along with anything else that flies: PLANE, KITE, BALLOON. The last word here demonstrates the care that you have to take; if **0** had been linked with 'BUBBLE', or 'BALLOON' itself, then there would have been a confusion between digits. But by using the balloon image only as a *hot-air* balloon, and never simply as an example of something rounded and circular, you ensure that it always prompts you to recall the right number.

3 : HILLS: This could become your 'plant-life' section! Any word linked with the countryside can be included here: FIELDS, FLOWERS, TREES . . . To add an extra dimension, why not expand it to involve the idea of *walking*, in the countryside and elsewhere: SHOES, FEET, LEGS . . .

4 : TABLE: It's often useful to make a specific decision about a category, to help set it apart from all the others. Here, rather than imagining a *wooden* table, which might cause confusion with all the trees and fences of the previous section, why not make this a specifically *metal* table? By doing this you give yourself a whole new set of images; as well as CHAIR and STOOL and other 'furniture' words, you can now include images of the metal itself: IRON, STEEL, GIRDER . . .

5 : HOOK: This is a good example of the need to expand a section with new themes. The key-word here may suggest a few other images, like CLAW, TALON – even FINGER and NAIL – but these would still leave you with quite a limited supply of pictures and ideas when you came to create a story.

The trick, as always, is to activate the imagination. Concentrate on the general themes here, of 'picking up' and 'fastening', and think up some associated ideas.

A VACUUM-CLEANER picks things up, as does a BRUSH; GLUE and TAPE are also used for fastening things, along with DRAWING-PIN and MAGNET. As long as these words don't overlap with the images in other sections, the more ideas you can include the better.

6 : NOTE: The possibilities here are endless. This key-word has a scope wide enough to include GUITAR, TRUMPET, PIANO, RECORD, TAPE, C.D., BAND, MUSICIAN – even SINGER and DANCER. The whole world of music can be included in this one section.

7 : YACHT: This is another key-word full of possibilities. Any sort of BOAT or SHIP can be included here, along with images linked to WATER, LAKE, RIVER and SEA. Even FISH and FISHERMAN are part of the same overall theme, adding to the bank of suggestions, and promising to make the eventual stories easier to write, visualise and remember.

8 : BREAD: Since this is the only section featuring food, almost anything edible can be included – CHEESE, EGGS, MEAT – along with words linked with cookery and food-preparation: STOVE, PAN, KNIFE, SPOON. As an example of the need to fine-tune your system as you build it up, you might have included FURNACE as part of your metal images for **4**, but decide now to rub it out, to avoid confusion with the fire and heat of your STOVE.

As with all of these expanded sections, check each word you add to make sure it doesn't fit under any other heading. FISH, for example, is certainly edible, but it would cause great confusion with the images representing **7**.

9 : PERSON: Rather than involving body parts, which might overlap with the FINGERS of section **5** or the FEET of section **3**, why not expand the theme here to include SHIRT, HAT, COAT – any article of clothing *except* things worn on the hands, feet or legs.

The other off-shoot could be to include the names of specific people. Again, any person can be included – FATHER, SISTER, POLICEMAN, TEACHER – just so long as they don't fit more properly under another heading. GARDENER, for example, would be a powerful image to include in section **3**, and SAILOR in section **7**. There are still many characters to be used; you could even include YOURSELF . . .

When you've finished filling up the boxes in the first column with new ideas and themes, spend a moment looking through all the information you've included so far. All ten digits should now have their own 'bank' of images and pictures, each revolving around a central theme but expanding to include a range of useful ideas. When you've made sure that there are no overlaps between digits, no possibilities for confusion, it's time to start filling up the remaining two columns.

Step Four

The ACTIONS column is based firmly on the OBJECTS. The stories you'll create will be made up of movement and energy as well as memorable images, and this column controls the details of any action that takes place.

Work from section to section, reminding yourself of the information on the left, and adding appropriate action words to the central column. Once again, it's important to avoid overlaps and confusion. Use your imagination to include powerful, memorable actions, always making sure that they have strong links with the objects concerned.

Suggestions

0   The obvious suggestions to suit BALL are words like JUGGLE, KICK and ROLL. Make sure all the actions you choose are linked specifically with balls and hoops; THROW, for example, would be a bad choice, since people throw so many other things, but ROLL is perfect.

Since one of the words in the box on the left is ROLLER, a useful action to include would be FLATTEN; RING, on the other hand, might lead you to add the action of TAGGING – the sort of thing scientists do when they fix rings onto the legs of animals. Links with the original words remain, but new possibilities are being opened up.

1   PEN leads on logically to action-words like WRITE, DRAW and PAINT, and BOOK suggests READ and STUDY. The two columns combined now include any idea linked with the written word.

2   The obvious actions here are FLY and GLIDE, but more variety will be needed when it comes to creating a story. THROW was too vague for section **0**, but it would be perfect here; the idea of *making* something 'fly'! Another powerful, associated word is FALL – especially since it would allow great emotional involvement to be brought into a story.

3 As mentioned above, 'gardening' actions would work well here: DIG, HOE, PLANT, TEND. The other main themes in the OBJECTS column can be represented by WALK and RUN, two very clear and powerful verbs.

4 In this section, obvious actions need to be expanded with imaginative ideas. SIT and LIE are good, solid actions – but SLEEP can be added to give an extra dimension. Linking in with the 'metals' theme, why not make actions like FORGE and MOULD part of the stock of possibilities?

5 Here, most of the imaginative work was done when you filled in the first column. The action words can now follow the two main themes; LIFT, SPEAR and VACUUM on one hand, and, on the other, FASTEN, GLUE, and FIX.

6 As well as all the musical words like PLAY, BLOW, PLUCK and BEAT, you can include more specialised actions: RECORD, TUNE-UP, CONDUCT. In addition, the general theme of musical performance creates possibilities like DANCE and SING.

7 The imagery in this section provides you with another rich seam of actions. SAIL, ROW, SINK and SWIM are obvious ones, but you can expand the themes again to include fishing verbs like CATCH and REEL-IN – and, since WATER is a central idea here, DRINK.

8 To contrast with the drinking of the previous section, the action-words here revolve around eating: EAT, CHEW, SWALLOW, MUNCH. There's also no shortage of powerful words linked with food-preparation – COOK, BOIL, FRY . . . – and a combination of general ideas and specific terms gives you a wide range of actions to choose from.

9 The specific themes in the OBJECTS column suggest some useful words: WEAR, SEW, KNIT. The rest of the section is very general, so why not make use of that, and include here some important actions not used elsewhere? Section **2** involves the written-word, and **6** the sounds of music and singing, but not yet included is the theme of *speaking*. This is the perfect action to include in a section based around people, and it allows you to use a variety of words – SPEAK, WHISPER, RIDICULE – as well as expanding to encompass emotional words, such as LAUGH, CRY, SCREAM.

Once again, check through the whole of this column when you reach the end, looking out for possible confusions, and confirming to yourself the ·details of each section. Concentrate on each word, making sure that its link with the *original* word – BALL, PEN, SWAN and so on – is clear.

When this is done, only one easy step remains.

Step Five

Now finish creating your number-system by filling in the final column: DESCRIPTIONS. As you write your stories, you'll find it useful to be able to use descriptive words from time to time, varying the pictures and including extra detail.

It's best to have at least two adjectives to 'describe' each number – one visual, and the second based on another of the senses – although sometimes *both* forces can be combined within one powerful descriptive word.

Suggestions

0 The visual description here can be chosen from several possibilities, such as CIRCULAR, CURVED, HOLLOW. For the other, why not bring in the sense of *touch*, and imagine the feel of a ball: BOUNCY, SQUASHY – especially since one of the action words in this section is FLATTEN.

1 COLOURFUL would be a powerful description here, associated with the ink and paint, and allowing you to create some very memorable images. Paint also has a very strong, unpleasant smell, so you might choose to make this section include the adjective SMELLY!

2 WINGED is perhaps the most obvious adjective here, and it could be used effectively in a story – especially if you chose to give wings to an otherwise stationary object like a piano or a pen. The linked word FEATHERY could also be included to bring the sense of touch into play.

3 FLOWERY might be the best adjective for this section, allowing you to imagine colours and patterns, and WOODEN could also be used as a strong descriptive word. Both these terms suggest the sense of smell – and, unlike the negative SMELLY of section **1**, the description here is SWEET-SMELLING, PERFUMED.

4 Contrasting with the previous section, the adjective for 4 is

METALLIC, suggesting both the look of an object, and its feel against the skin. If the ball in section **1** is SQUASHY, metal is always going to feel HARD.

5 The hook both *looks* and *feels* SHARP, and the glue and tape feel STICKY on your fingers. Since one of the action-words here is VACUUM, why not also include the description CLEAN?

6 For once, the visual description is the hardest to create! The others are easy: MUSICAL, NOISY, MELODIC, but the visual word takes a little more imagination. Perhaps you could choose a description such as MOVING-RHYTHMICALLY, or SPINNING, like a ballet-dancer.

7 Words like DRENCHED, SOGGY and WET combine a visual description with the sensation of touch.

8 Once again, words like APPETISING and SUCCULENT combine descriptions based on several senses: sight, smell, taste, touch. You could even bring in *hearing* by making SIZZLING part of this section – and, since it's not used elsewhere, another appropriate and powerful word to use here is HOT.

9 CLOTHED, like WINGED in section **2**, could be especially powerful if it was applied to inanimate objects – loaves of bread dressed in jackets, or trees with hats! And finally, since the actions section includes so many 'emotional' words, why not simply turn them into descriptions? LAUGHING, CRYING and WORRIED will allow you to include a range of emotions in your stories – and to create some strange and memorable pictures: a laughing swan, a crying fork, a worried pair or shoes . . .

With this column complete, your number system is ready to use. The sheet of paper in front of you contains everything you need to remember *any* number – whether it's made up of one digit or ten thousand. You may have spent half an hour compiling the three columns, but the time you'll *save* using this system will quickly make up for that – not to mention the efficiency and success you'll be able to enjoy.

Spend a final few moments reading through the groups of words in your system. Each digit has been given its own range of identities, a mixture of objects, actions and descriptions. All the possible words for a single digit are connected through a central theme – the words for **2**, for example, are based on flying, and those for **8** on eating and food – but the range of ideas is enough to give you room for manoeuvre. There may only be ten digits, but this system will allow you to create a vastly different memory-story for any number you need to know.

It's important to keep this sheet of paper – for reference, and so that you can update and alter it if you think up new ideas or useful improvements. You'll need it in front of you the first few times you use the system, but soon you'll know the possibilities for each number off by heart.

It may seem a daunting task in itself to remember these three columns of words, but in reality you're only learning the ten basic themes: BALLS, WORDS, FLYING, NATURE, etc. And since these are based on the shapes of the numbers themselves, the entire system is memorable and familiar from the moment you set it up.

To sum up the five steps needed to create the number system page 131 shows a complete version made from some of the suggestions above.

It's important to remember that not *all* the possible images and ideas are included in this written list. The boxes here contain just the main words and themes, and other pictures can be used when you create your stories – just as long as they fit in with the theme of a particular number, and don't overlap with images used elsewhere.

As you experiment, you'll find that some ideas are more memorable than others, and particular words in a section list will be 'favourites', used more than the rest. With practice, the system will become moulded to your own control.

USING THE NUMBER SYSTEM

If you're used to putting into effect the techniques of *Mindpower* – ordering information, making it memorable, turning it into pictures, sequences and stories – then you'll find your number system easy to use. The three columns provide you with all the ideas and images you need to turn numbers into strange, funny, memorable stories.

The way it works is simple. Whenever you're faced with a number to learn, you deal with it digit by digit.

THE FIVE–STEP NUMBER SYSTEM

	OBJECTS	ACTIONS	DESCRIPTIONS
0	BALL, HOOP, RING, ROLLER, CLOCK	JUGGLE, KICK, ROLL, FLATTEN, TAG	ROUND, HOLLOW, FLAT, SQUASHY
1	PEN, PENCIL, PAINT, INK, PICTURE, BOOK	WRITE, PAINT, DRAW, READ, STUDY	COLOURFUL, BAD-SMELLING
2	SWAN, BIRD, PLANE, KITE, BALLOON	FLY, GLIDE, THROW, FALL	WINGED, FEATHERY
3	HILLS, FIELDS, TREES, FLOWERS, SHOES, FEET, LEGS	DIG, HOE, PLANT, TEND, WALK, RUN	FLOWERY, WOODEN, PERFUMED
4	TABLE, CHAIR, STOOL, IRON, STEEL, GIRDER	SIT, LIE, SLEEP, FORGE, MOULD	METALLIC, HARD
5	HOOK, CLAW, FINGER, VACUUM-CLEANER, BRUSH, GLUE, TAPE	LIFT, SPEAR, VACUUM, GLUE FASTEN	SHARP, CLEAN, STICKY
6	NOTE, GUITAR, TRUMPET, C.D., BAND, SINGER, DANCER	PLAY, BLOW, SING RECORD, DANCE	MUSICAL, NOISY, SPINNING
7	YACHT, SHIP, WATER, LAKE, FISH, ANGLER	SAIL, SWIM, SINK, CATCH, DRINK	WET, SOGGY
8	BREAD, CHEESE, EGGS, MEAT, STOVE, PAN, FORK, CHEF	EAT, SWALLOW, COOK, BOIL, FRY	APPETISING, SUCCULENT, SIZZLING, HOT
9	PERSON, COAT, SHIRT, FATHER, SISTER, TEACHER, YOU!	WEAR, SEW, SPEAK, WHISPER, LAUGH, CRY, SCREAM	CLOTHED, LAUGHING, WORRIED

For each individual digit, choose any word contained within its section in your number system – either an object, an action or a description. The idea is to use the words you choose to build up a story, so pick a word that best suits your needs at any particular point.

If one digit is made to represent a person, the story will be helped along if you make the next one into an action. Before a person, a descriptive word will add detail to the picture. At every point, choose a word that makes the story-writing *easier*.

This sounds far more complicated than it is. The best way to understand the process is to see it in action. Below are several examples – all based on material from the system printed on the previous page.

Imagine you had to learn the number **72506** – the serial-number on a computer, say, or the reference on a form. Each digit is going to become one element in a short story.

For each digit, you have a choice. The **7** can be represented by any word within section **7** in your system. Since it's the first element in the story, it would be useful to make it into a character – a SAILOR, perhaps, or an ANGLER.

On the other hand, you could decide to make it into a descriptive word, allowing the *second* digit in this number to be the 'character' of the story. In this case, the **7** could be represented by the adjective WET, helping to build up detail from the very start. This would be especially useful in a five-digit sequence like this; the construction DESCRIPTION, OBJECT, ACTION, DESCRIPTION, OBJECT would create a clear, straightforward story.

So **7** becomes WET.

As you practise using your number system, it's useful to write down each word you choose, helping you to see the story as it grows and takes shape.

The next digit in the sequence is **2**. Since you've started with a description, you really need to make this digit into an object or a character – the 'thing' controlling the story's action. SWAN is a strong image from the OBJECTS box in section **2**, and it fits well with WET.

So **7** and **2** have become 'a WET SWAN'!

An action word will be useful to include next. The digit in

question is **5** – so why not choose the word LIFTS as the next element in your story?

7.2.5: 'a WET SWAN LIFTS . . .'

There are just two more digits to deal with. An easy way to finish the story, as suggested above, would be to make the first into a description and the second into an object. For **0** you might choose ROUND, and, if you turned **6** into SINGER, your scene would be memorable indeed:

> 'a WET SWAN LIFTS
> a ROUND SINGER!'

You could picture a bedraggled bird reaching its beak into the water and pulling out a hugely fat opera star . . .

As always, connect this scene with your *reason* for remembering the number. If it was a number on your bank-card, you might set the whole scene inside the bank. If it was a security code for a door at work, a beautiful poster of this scene could be mentally pinned to the door itself. In just a few moments the dry, abstract numbers have been brought to life and turned into a memorable story, connected back to the numbers themselves, and fixed firmly into the memory.

To recall the numbers, simply carry through the process in reverse. Bring the picture to mind, and highlight the key elements: WET, SWAN, LIFTS, ROUND, SINGER. Each of these words can refer to one number only: WET has to be **7** the digit with the 'water' theme; SWAN is the key-word itself in section **2**; LIFTS must refer to the hook, **5**; ROUND is clearly the rounded, ball-like **0**; and SINGER, finally, comes from the section based on music: **6**. The picture contains everything you need to remember the number in seconds: **72506**.

The beauty of this system is its scope for endless variety. Since each digit can be turned into any one of a whole range of words, any *group* of digits can be made into a variety of stories. Using exactly the same system, ten people could take the same five digits and create ten wildly different scenes.

The **7** could become a SAILOR. An action word would be useful next, so you might choose to turn **2** into the word THROWS. **5** could become GLUE . . . and a new story is taking shape: 'a SAILOR THROWS GLUE . . .'

What is he throwing the glue *at*? The remaining numbers are
0 and 6, so it could be a HOLLOW GUITAR, a FLATTENED
C.D., or a ROTUND DANCER.

The possibilities are vast; by using your imagination, the most
memorable scenes can be formed.

Any number of digits can be learned using the system.
Sometimes it's necessary to remember just one or two numbers
– in an address, for example, or a lot-number at an auction.

Imagine your friend's new house-number was 98. Rather than
writing it on your hand, or repeating it to yourself as you set out
on the journey, simply turn the digits into a memorable scene.

9 could become your friend, since the system makes it into
a 'person', and 8 would allow you to picture him or her cooking
a meal to celebrate your arrival!

If the number was 41 you might choose the action SIT and
the object BOOK, and picture the two of you sitting on tall piles
of books, waiting for the furniture to arrive . . .

If it was 87, you might visualise your friend opening the door
and handing you a HOT DRINK. The system allows you to turn
even a couple of numbers into a memorable scene – to change
abstract numbers into words and then pictures.

Longer numbers simply need longer stories. All of the
storytelling techniques described in Part One can be brought
into play, and it's important to start thinking about the links
and progressions at the same time as you're deciding on the
words and images to use. Connections are vital, but as long as
each element in the story leads on to the next, even the longest
numbers can be remembered with ease.

Always be on the look-out for ways of connecting a story with
the *reason* for creating it. If that reason involves a person – like
the friend with the new house – make at least one of the 9s *into*
that person. If the number in question is the telephone number
for a jewellery shop, it makes sense to turn any available 0 into
a RING rather than a BALL or HOOP. The idea is always to
make things as easy as possible, to make use of handy prompts
and to spot the memory opportunities already there.

Printed below are excerpts from an imaginary phone-book.
Most of us could benefit from learning just ten of our own
most-called numbers, and a few minutes of imagination can
save a great deal of time spent searching through notebooks

and directories. There's no point in learning information you only use rarely, but the ability to remember a handful of key numbers really can make life a lot easier.

A list of six examples is printed first, followed by suggestions for images and stories. When you've read through them all, practise visualising them and making improvements of your own, turn back to the list and test yourself. Cover up the numbers in the right-hand column, and see how many of them you can read back from memory. The words on the left should be all the prompts you need.

THEATRE	**643872**
LIBRARY	**221854**
SCHOOL	**897545**
DOCTOR	**103479**
HAIRDRESSER	**680033**
CINEMA	**983681**

Suggestions

Theatre: **643872**

The initial step is to notice any useful numbers. The first digit here, **6**, could be a very handy way to connect the story with the theatre, basing the whole thing on music and performance. Combining it with the number **4** creates an appropriate starting-point indeed: 'PIANO STOOL'.

Imagine your reaction if the piano-stool suddenly sprouted feet on the ends of its legs, and began running around the stage! It's possible to put two action-words side by side here: 'RUNS', for **3**, could be followed by 'to EAT' for **8**. Already the first four numbers have been dealt with: 'a PIANO-STOOL RUNS to EAT . . .'

It runs into the theatre's restaurant . . . but what does it find? It's useful to ask questions like this as a way of reminding yourself of the sequence of events. The final two numbers are **7** and **2**, so perhaps it starts munching on a WET PIGEON, splashing water around the room as it gobbles down the bird.

The theatre's phone-number has become a bizarre piece of action: 'A PIANO-STOOL RUNS to EAT a WET PIGEON!'

Visualise the scene, adding extra details or new reminders as you confirm it in your mind.

The piano-stool is sitting on the theatre stage, ready for a concert, when the strange events begin to unfold. By dialling this number a few times from memory rather than from a book, you'd strengthen its link with the theatre as well as its hold in your mind, and find that you never had to look it up again.

If you can remember the scene, you can break it back down into the original six digits.

The PIANO-STOOL is a combination of musical **6** and furniture-based **4**; RUNS is one of the main actions in section **3**; 'to EAT' must represent tasty **8**; WET reminds you of watery **7**; and PIGEON, finally, lives with all the other flying things in section **2**. The theatre's phone number is **643872**.

Library: **221854**

The obvious number to concentrate on here is **1**, since its theme of reading and writing is connected strongly with the library itself. Before that, the double **2**s show the importance of being able to choose a different sort of word for each: why not make the first an object – a BIRD – and the second an action – GLIDES? The books can then become the centre of attention: 'a BIRD GLIDES into a pile of BOOKS'.

This time you might choose to turn the **8** into a person – a CHEF who sees the bird and decides to turn it into dinner! He PICKS it up – **5** – and, struggling with the weight, places it on a TABLE – **4** – for later . . .

Remind yourself that the story takes place at the library. There's a huge pile of new books sitting on the pavement, waiting to be taken inside. The scene is set, and the story can begin.

As you watch, a BIRD GLIDES down through the clouds and crashes into the BOOKS. Apart from you, the only other person nearby is a CHEF, who knows free food when he sees it! He PICKS UP the bird, and sets it down on his TABLE . . .

The next time you needed to order a book from the library, or find out if it was open, you would simply recall this short story and turn the pictures back into numbers. 'A BIRD – **2** – GLIDES – **2** – into some BOOKS – **1**. A CHEF – **8** – PICKS IT UP – **5** – and puts it on his TABLE – **4**. The number for the library must be **221854**.

School: **897545**

A strange thing is happening in the school canteen. The school cook seems to have given up making dinners, and is sewing up the sails from a yacht instead! When the COOK – **8** – has finished SEWING – **9** – the SAILS – **7** – she starts tidying up. She CLEANS UP – **5** – with a METAL – **4** – BRUSH – **5**.

Once again, it's important to reinforce the precise sequence of events. Visualise her seeing the mess she's made and deciding to clean it up, then wondering what to use. Imagine the sound of a metal brush on the floor, and run through the whole story again in your mind to confirm the details.

There are children everywhere, so this must be a *school* canteen. The COOK is clearly representing food-filled section **8**; SEWING comes from the clothes theme of section **9**; the SAIL is what gave section **7** its yachting theme in the first place; CLEANING must be done next, one of the key actions representing **5**; she uses a METAL BRUSH – the metal belongs with the iron chair and steel table in section **4**, and the brush itself, another 'cleaning' word, prompts you to remember another **5**. The number for the school can only be **897545**.

Doctor: **103479**

Sometimes it's possible to let the 'shape' of a number suggest the best way to construct a story. Here, the final digit, the **9**, could be made to represent the doctor himself, allowing the whole story to be based on your struggle to get to him.

As you approach the doctor's surgery, you notice that a hollow oak-tree has been planted in front of the door. The bark is covered in words, and you READ the HOLLOW TREE. Most of the words are meaningless, but after a while you make out a set of instructions: SIT IN THE WATER.

There's a shallow puddle close by, and, reluctantly, you sit down. But this seems to do the trick, because suddenly the door opens and out steps the DOCTOR. Somehow, this strange ritual has won you an appointment right away!

The story is all about finding the doctor – a useful link for when you need to find his number. The story starts when you find your instructions; you READ – **1** – the HOLLOW – **0** – TREE – **3**. The writing tells you to SIT – **4** – in the WATER

– **7** – and the discomfort is worth it because the DOCTOR – **9** – appears. When you next need to get through to the doctor, his number must be **103479**.

Hairdresser: 680033

There's no obvious link here between the hairdresser's salon and any of the digits. Instead, why not use the salon simply as a location for the bizarre set of events that follows.

Spend a moment visualising the place where you have your hair cut. Imagine sitting down in one of the chairs, and watching in amazement at what happens to the person sitting on your left.

You're sitting next to a famous footballer. His problem seems to be his feet; not their smell, because they're actually very pleasantly perfumed, but rather their size. His feet are *huge* – obviously a big drawback for a sportsman – but luckily the hairdresser seems able to help.

She brings out an implement you've never seen before – a spinning spoon! – and sets it going, smoothing down her customer's feet while she goes back to more usual work . . .

It really is a strange and memorable scene. The SPIN-NING SPOON SMOOTHS the FOOTBALLER's PERFUMED FEET! Imagine making a note of this summary to tell your friends. Never again will you forget the hairdresser's phone-number.

SPINNING – like a dancer – comes from section **6**; the SPOON is part of the collection of cookery tools in section **8**; SMOOTHS is one of the actions in section **0**; the FOOT-BALLER is skilled at kicking **0**-shaped footballs; PERFUMED is a pungent description from flowery section **3**; and FEET are firmly planted in section **3** as well. The number of the salon must be **680033**.

Cinema: 983681

This time the number begins with a **9**, so you can choose a strong character to control the action. Since the place in question is a cinema, why not make the 9 into your favourite movie star?

Picture yourself sitting in the front row of your local cinema, watching the latest comedy film. Your favourite ACTOR – **9**

– is the centre of attention – especially since he's doing something rather strange. He's EATING – **8** – a WOODEN – **3** – MUSIC-STAND – **6**! From the look on his face you can tell he's not enjoying it. There's something wrong with the way it's been cooked, and he returns to the kitchen to find the COOK-BOOK – **8** and **1** . . .

The next time you need to telephone the cinema to book some seats, remember this unusual film. As you recall the ACTOR EATING a WOODEN MUSIC-STAND and returning to the COOK-BOOK, you'll know that the number for the cinema must be **983681**.

If you have difficulty remembering any of the six numbers when you return to the initial list, go back to the story in question and make it more memorable. Highlight the elements you find difficult, then work out new prompts and reminders to confirm the sequence in your mind. This is a useful exercise; once you can recall all six numbers, you've memorised 36 random digits – a feat most people would say was impossible!

Most important of all, you've learnt a skill that can be of use to you almost every day. Whenever you're faced with a new number, make a point of learning it. Write it down, certainly, but memorise it as well – and the next time you use it, resist the temptation to look it up. The more you use your memory, the more you'll find that you can rely on it, and become confident in your ability to put any sort of information under your control.

Put it to the Test

Printed below are six more imaginary phone-numbers. Use them to practise all the key stages in the system, choosing appropriate images, deciding upon a starting point, and telling yourself a memorable story.

1. DENTIST 926342
2. TAKE-AWAY 765488
3. SPORTS COMPLEX: 534710
4. COMMUNITY CENTRE: 853826
5. RAILWAY STATION: 212343
6. TOWN HALL: 107539

NUMBERS AND NAMES

The numbers above can all be connected to definite locations – station, cinema, town-hall – and, often, to clearly-defined characters like doctors and hairdressers. This makes it easy to connect them with the stories you create, but the same principles can be used even when the numbers you're calling are less straightforward.

All you may have to go on is a name – Alan Ramsey – but it only takes a moment to create a strong connection.

Bring into play the sort of techniques learnt in Part Two. Play around with the name on the page, looking for ways to create the images you need to build up a strong foundation for the story.

In this case, 'Alan' might expand slightly to 'A LANE' – especially useful since it gives you the beginnings of a location. In the middle of the lane is a RAM, who SEES – *'sey*'s – you and runs away. The story you create to remember Alan's number can revolve around what happens next.

Perhaps his phone-number is 313922. The ram runs away . . . and you decide to RUN – 3 – after it. Unfortunately you don't get very far; as you turn a corner in the lane, you crash into a COLOURFUL – 1 – TREE – 3. You're dazed and, cartoon-like, find yourself TALKING – 9 – to the BIRDS – 2 – FLYING – 2 – around your head!

The next time you have to ring Alan Ramsey, your mind will recall that lane and that ram . . . and the story will unfold!

DIALLING CODES

Although many of the numbers you call regularly will be local and not require a dialling code, it's useful to be able to remember codes for when they do apply. These usually contain just a few digits – but if you create strong images, even just a couple of numbers can be connected firmly to a town or country, and you'll never have to call Directory Inquiries again.

Most codes will have some relevance for you – a town you know well or the home of a relative – giving you enough material for the starting-point to a story. But it's perfectly possible to learn the code for a place you've never been – perhaps never even heard of.

As with the name-example above, play around with the words until you've carved out a hook to hold the story.

Below are four UK dialling codes. As with the earlier list, read through the suggestions and then test your success.

LIVERPOOL: *0151*
PETERBOROUGH: *01733*
NEWCASTLE: *0191*
OXFORD: *01865*

Suggestions

Liverpool: **0151**

The *Mindpower System* is all about making memory easier; and here, as with all of these numbers, the 01 can be kept aside from the learning process. All codes begin with 01, so there's little point in memorising something that *has* to be there!

LIVERPOOL contains many possibilities. It can be broken up into two definite words – LIVER and POOL – but it also has a number of more general associations: the Beatles . . . the Mersey . . . For this example, though, to emphasise that you don't have to know a place to give it an image, concentrate on the liver and the pool.

Imagine you work for a butcher, and your job involves washing pieces of LIVER in a special POOL. It's a complex task, and you need to follow a long list of instructions. Again and again you LIFT your BOOK – 5 and 1 – and, in the end, you HANG it up on a sharp HOOK . . .

The code for Liverpool must be (01) 51.

Peterborough: **01733**

PETER Rabbit is BURROWing into a hillside. He's rushing to take cover from a rowdy group of SAILORS – **7** – going for a WALK – **3** – in the COUNTRYSIDE – **3**.

He manages to get out of the way just in time; suddenly there are hundreds of sailors marching through the fields – each of them carrying a 'Blue PETER' flag . . . !

The code for Peterborough must be (01) **733**.

Newcastle: **0191**

Imagine sitting high up in the tower of your NEW CASTLE, admiring the clean, unused buildings. Suddenly, to your horror, you notice that some young BOYS – **9** – have broken into the courtyard, and are about to scrawl GRAFFITI – **1** – all over the walls! Will you make it down the stairs before it's too late?

The code for Newcastle must be (01) **91**.

Oxford: **01865**

Visualise an OX-FORD – a place for oxen to cross the river. Hundreds of the animals plod from one bank to the other – but things start to go wrong when one of them stops to EAT – **8**.

Take a closer look at exactly *what* it's munching: it's a NOISY – **6** – VACUUM-CLEANER – **5** – that someone has thrown away in the mud! Imagine the chaos as the other oxen pile forward, and the guilty animal keeps chewing, the noise of the vacuum's motor adding to the din . . .

The code for Oxford must be (01) **865**.

When you're faced with country codes to learn, it's a straightforward process to base a story on well-known 'national' images. A good idea is to choose a famous *location* as the basis for remembering each international code.

Below are ten worldwide dialling codes, followed by brief suggestions for ways to remember them.

AUSTRALIA: **61**	INDIA: **91**
USA: **01**	SWITZERLAND: **41**
CHINA: **86**	JAPAN: **81**
FRANCE: **33**	NETHERLANDS: **31**
GERMANY: **49**	DENMARK: **45**

Suggestions

Australia: **61**

A strong location to represent Australia could be Ayers Rock. Imagine looking out on to this magnificent landmark – and seeing a very famous Australian, Rolf Harris, performing beside it for the crowds! He's doing the two things he's most famous for – playing his didgeridoo and painting. Again and again he plays a long, low note before jumping back to add more paint to his canvas. The MUSICIAN – 6 – PAINTS – 1; the code for Australia is **61**.

USA: **01**
This time the location could be the Statue of Liberty. You've been given the daunting task of painting this huge structure, and the paint has just arrived – in equally huge tins. Each one is as tall as you, and you'll have to roll them to the statue from the van. Persuade some of the locals to help you, shouting out your instructions: 'ROLL – **0** – the PAINT TINS! – **1**'. The code for the USA is **01**.

China: **86**
The most famous structure in China is undoubtedly the Great Wall. Imagine yourself on a memorable visit. You arrive at the Great Wall of China to find that a splendid welcome awaits you. A huge band of top Chinese musicians has been assembled to greet your arrival, and you watch and listen with delight. They play on and on and, as the midday sun beats down, you realise the musicians are in great danger from the heat. Their instruments are melting, and more and more of them collapse with exhaustion. This really is a HOT – **8** – BAND – **6**! The code for China is **86**.

France: **33**
Paris is the venue for a large arts festival. Striking, unusual displays have been put up all around the city. The theme seems to be *size*; everything is either very small or incredibly large.

The centre-piece of the whole event is the artwork erected around the Eiffel Tower. A whole team of craftspeople has worked for weeks to create huge wooden roses and daffodils, which surround the tower and reach to its very top. By taking the lift to the highest level you can enjoy the best view of the WOODEN – **3** – FLOWERS – **3** The code for France is **33**.

Germany: **49**
The location you choose to represent Germany might be the site of the demolished Berlin Wall. Bits of this structure have been sold around the world as souvenirs, symbols of unity and

peace, and you decide to look for something in the remains to keep for yourself.

You realise that you're not alone. To your right, an official-looking man is collecting bits of metal into a bag. You decide it might be best to ask his permission before you take anything, and walk over to talk to the 'metal man'. His title is even written on his cap: METAL – **4** – MAN – **9**. The code for Germany is **49**.

India: 91

A famous Indian place, and a famous Indian leader: Mahatma Gandhi is lying on a bench outside the Taj Mahal.

He looks frail and old; as you come closer, you see that he's having to dictate a letter to one of his assistants. You listen carefully to his words of wisdom, and stand there all day as he DICTATES – **9** – LETTER – **1** – after letter . . . The code for India is **91**.

Switzerland: 41

If it's not possible to think of a definite location or character, why not base your scene on a famous national object – or even a whole group of them? Switzerland is known for precision craftwork – clocks, watches, knives . . . so imagine wandering around a Swiss gift-shop, looking for a souvenir to take home.

Everything is very tempting, but rather expensive, and in the end you choose to buy the smallest thing on offer; a Swiss pen made out of shining gold. You scribble on a piece of paper before you leave the shop, just to check it's working, then make your way home – the proud owner of a precision-made GOLD – **4** – PEN – **1**. The code for Switzerland is **41**.

Japan: 81

Another possibility for the basis of a scene is to pick out a national characteristic. The Japanese, for example, are known for their efficiency and hard work.

Imagine being taken on a tour of the busiest factory you've ever seen. Workers are racing around on all sides, anxiously completing job after job. Only one employee is slacking; a tired-looking man, hiding behind his desk to read a newspaper. He knows he mustn't be found out, though, and you watch with amusement as he *eats* the paper when his supervisor appears! It's a good way to destroy evidence, but imagine what it must *feel* like to EAT – **8** – a whole NEWSPAPER – **1**. The code for Japan in **81**.

Netherlands: 31

Visualise yourself re-decorating a huge windmill. To match the tulips in the garden, you've chosen bright red paint for the sails, and yellow for the brick tower. The job has taken weeks of hard work, but now you're almost finished – so imagine your horror when someone walks too close to the paint and rubs out a whole section! This vandal even puts a foot into one of the paint-pots, and trails red and yellow footprints across the paths and through the building. You never imagined that someone would be stupid enough to WALK – **3** – into the PAINT – **1**! The code for the Netherlands is **31**.

Denmark: 45

Imagine taking a day-trip to see Denmark's famous mermaid statue. Unfortunately, many other people have made the same decision, and huge crowds are milling around the harbour, blocking the view.

You have an idea. One of the harbour-cranes is nearby, and its hook is dangling a metre or so off the ground. You climb up on to the hook and sit down. As the hook is raised, you're presented with the best view imaginable! In future, when anyone mentions Denmark, you'll remember your idea and recommend that they SIT – **4** – on a HOOK – **5**. The code for Denmark is **45**.

A DAY TO REMEMBER

If telephone-numbers and dialling codes are the most obvious examples of numbers to remember, dates must come a close second. From history lessons to politics exams, museum tours to coin-collections, dates need to be memorised often in our lives – yet we're more likely to repeat them to ourselves a hundred times than to find a simple way to learn them *once*.

But if you can learn a six-digit phone number, how much

easier it must be to remember the four digits in a date. In fact, dates can be regarded as just *three* digits; the majority of precise dates to learn begin with 1, and you're not likely to confuse one date with another a thousand years away. You could learn the date of the Great Exhibition, for example, as 8,5,1, rather than 1851, and be confident of remembering that it happened in the 19th century rather than the 9th!

The technique for remembering dates is almost exactly the same as for telephone numbers. Each digit is replaced by a word from your system, and the picture you create is linked firmly with events behind the date itself. By using your imagination and choosing the words carefully, appropriate scenes can be drawn; created in minutes, but remembered for years.

Below are ten real dates to impress any history teacher! Read through the memory suggestions, then check your success from the original list.

PEASANTS' REVOLT:	**1381**
GREAT EXHIBITION:	**1851**
DEATH of QUEEN VICTORIA:	**1901**
BATTLE of HASTINGS:	**1066**
GREAT PLAGUE:	**1665**
WORLD WAR II BEGINS:	**1939**
WORLD WAR II ENDS:	**1945**
GREAT FIRE of LONDON:	**1666**
BATTLE of WATERLOO:	**1815**
GUNPOWDER PLOT:	**1605**

Suggestions

Peasants' Revolt: **1381**
Dropping the first 1 leaves you with just three digits to learn: **3**, **8** and **1**.

As always, look for the most useful words to choose. The number **3** can become the peasants themselves – COUNTRY-folk. Imagine hundreds of them gathering in a large field, to revolt against their rulers in the best way they can. They curse the laws, the rules, and the learned men who have made them, and build up a huge fire on which the PEASANTS – **3** – BURN – **8** – all the BOOKS – **1** – they can gather.

The scene is a simple one, but very appropriate. It gives you three numbers – **3**, **8** and **1** – and, by adding the first **1** – since this clearly didn't happen in 381! – you arrive at the date of the Peasants' Revolt: **1381**.

Great Exhibition: **1851**

Again, begin by dropping the first 1 to leave you with **8**, **5** and **1**.

Imagine a day out at the Great Exhibition. There's so much to see; the newest inventions, the finest creations. Everything is designed to impress – so imagine your amazement when you sit down in the restaurant to catch your breath, and notice that your menu is covered with soup-stains! Every single word is obliterated by a brown blotch. Amongst all this splendour, the dirty menu stands out as a memorable exception.

You call for the CHEF – **8** – and he apologises as he CLEANS – **5** – your MENU – **1**. It takes him hours, and you watch intently – but at last you can read the writing, and you order a huge meal to make up for the disappointment . . . The Great Exhibition was in **1851**.

Death of Queen Victoria: **1901**

Whenever the number **9** appears in a date, turn it into an appropriate person. Here, the obvious candidate would be Queen Victoria herself.

Imagine discovering some amazing information. Leafing through some old papers, you find out the shocking truth about how the queen *really* died.

It turns out that she was stuck in her library one day among the dusty old books, and wanted desperately to ease the boredom. Taking three large books down from the shelves, she began to juggle them – slowly at first, but then faster and faster.

Unfortunately, she threw one book so high that it hit a loose shelf, and brought a pile of books showering down on her head . . .

You even find a picture to go with the story. It shows VICTORIA – **9** – JUGGLING – **0** – the BOOKS – **1**. The date of her death was **1901**.

Battle of Hastings: **1066**

Since history is full of battles and wars, it's important to distinguish one conflict from another. The Battle of Hastings is famous for the arrow that killed the king, so your story might concentrate on bowmen and archery.

Picture the scene at Hastings, as the archers practise before the battle. They seem to know already that the events are going to involve an arrow, and they're determined to be skilled and ready when the enemy arrives. Unfortunately, they also enjoy lots of sports besides archery, and most of their time seems to be spent kicking footballs and playing tennis.

Suddenly, they hear trumpets. The other army is approaching. You decide to move away as far as you can, and the last thing you see is the SPORTSMEN (playing BALL-games) – **0** – HEARING – **6** – the TRUMPETS – **6**. The Battle of Hastings was in **1066**.

Great Plague: **1665**

Once again, your imagination allows you to travel back in time. Imagine wandering around the deserted streets of London, realising the devastation that the Plague has brought. There's no-one around, but from one of the houses you can hear singing.

You stop walking and listen carefully, determined to hear what the song's about. Perhaps not surprisingly, it's subject turns out to be the healing and cleaning that will have to happen before London can return to normal. You make a note in your diary: 'HEARD – **6** – SONG – **6** – about CLEANING – **5**'. The Great Plague was in **1665**.

World War II begins: **1939**

World War II ends: **1945**

When you have a pair of dates like these, linked firmly to the same historical event, it's useful to be able to connect their *stories* as well. Look for digits that appear in both dates as your basis for creating the link.

A simple picture for the start of the war might involve one ARMY, lines and lines of men – **9** – MARCHING – **3** – to meet the other mass of TROOPS – **9**. Mould your picture to match the balanced shape of the numbers: one army walks from the left, led by Churchill, the other from the right with Hitler at the front. In a moment World War II will begin when they meet in the middle; the date must be **1939.**

The war *ends* in a very strange way. The German troops sit down for a rest – and realise too late that the Allies have spread glue on their chairs. The Germans are stuck fast; imagine the look on their leader's face! The fighting stopped when one ARMY – **9** – SAT DOWN – **4** – in the GLUE – **5**, the year was **1945.**

Great Fire of London: **1666**

The British have a reputation for bearing up under adversity. Imagine you were present on the day of the Great Fire, and saw the flames starting to take hold. All around you people were rushing into the streets, searching for water and trying to rescue their family and friends.

The noise is deafening, but one particular sound catches your attention. Somewhere you can hear an orchestra tuning-up! You walk towards the sound, and, sure enough, a huge concert is about to take place. Flames are licking around the instruments and water is being thrown over the audience, but the show will go on, no matter what. You spend a few more minutes LISTENING – **6** – to the ORCHESTRA – **6** – TUNING-UP –**6**. The Great Fire of London started in **1666.**

Battle of Waterloo: **1815**

To set this battle apart from any other, why not picture it taking place on the platforms of Waterloo *Station*?

There are soldiers everywhere, fighting on the track, in the ticket office – even on top of the trains! You have a good view from your seat in the platform-cafe, which itself is full of people, and you listen to the cooks grumbling about all the cleaning-up they'll have to do. One of them spots a British Rail vacuum-cleaner, and they study it intently in case it might be of use . . .

You draw a quick sketch of this strange scene on the back of your train ticket. The COOKS – **8** – STUDIED – **1** – the VACUUM-CLEANER – **5**; the Battle of Waterloo was in **1815.**

Gunpowder plot: **1605**

It's 5th November, and the organisers of your local bonfire-party are having problems. They've had great difficulty finding wood this year, and the bonfire is only a couple of feet high. It seems that the whole event will have to be called off – until, at the very last moment, a local celebrity comes to the rescue.

A famous pianist lives nearby, and he decides to donate his old piano to be burned on the fire. He drags it to the field, but as he hauls it on to the pile he slips, and drops the whole instrument on to his hand. His career is ruined; the PIANIST – **6** – has FLATTENED – **O** – his FINGERS –**5**! The original bonfire, the Gunpowder Plot, was in **1605**.

HIDDEN NUMBERS

So far, Part Three has concentrated on the most obvious examples of numbers to be learned: telephone numbers, codes and historical dates. But sometimes numbers can be found below the surface of information. Once you've developed your own number system, it's sensible to use it whenever you can, and this often means changing information *into* a numeric form.

The simplest example of this comes when you need to remember the day and month as well as the year. Your next important conference might be on 18 November 1995, but you're much more likely to remember the details if you change them all into numbers: 18.11.95. This allows you to take the information under the control of your number system – to turn them into words and pictures, then connect the images with the conference itself.

It's important to carry out exactly the same process with every date you need to learn. Always put the numbers in the same order: for most people this is DAY, MONTH, YEAR. If every date you learn has the same shape and the same number of digits, it's much easier to make sure that you never make a mistake.

If you need to remember a large number of dates, it's useful to make a few additions to your number system. By creating objects, actions and descriptions for the numbers **10**, **11** and **12**, you can make your stories much easier to create.

*   *   *

If there's space on your original piece of paper, add three more sections underneath the boxes for **9**; otherwise, continue on another sheet. The method for filling in the new sections is roughly the same as before, and you begin by concentrating on the numbers themselves.

With double digits, it's sometimes necessary to use the *sounds* of the numbers as much as their shapes. Experiment with associations that come to mind until each of the numbers has been given its own key image, and remember to use the main list to check for overlaps and similarities.

As before, give each number a distinct character, precise enough to be clear and memorable, but with enough scope and variety to create memorable stories.

Suggestions

Objects:
10   The most famous 10 in the world is probably fixed to the British Prime Minister's door. Why not make DOOR the main object here? Alongside it you could include HOUSE, TENT and CASTLE, and perhaps also LOCK and KEY.

11   The two digits here look like the uprights in a LADDER. The theme could include STEPS and STAIRS, and expand to bring in other means of ascending and descending: ROPE, POLE, ESCALATOR . . .

12   With a little imagination, 'twelve' can be made to sound like 'travel'. This allows you to use CAR as your key word, and to include any mode of road transport: VAN, BUS, BICYCLE . . . You can even include ROAD and MOTORWAY!

Actions
10   The OBJECTS column here gives you all the suggestions you need. Actions like OPEN and CLOSE are strong and memorable, and, along with LOCK and SET FREE, will provide you with useful new elements for your stories.

11   The obvious words to include in this box are CLIMB and DESCEND, and the more unusual objects – pole and rope – allow you to include SLIDE and SWING!

12   TRAVEL is itself an action word, and you can add to it

with DRIVE, BRAKE and FREE-WHEEL, as well as SKID
and WHEELIE!

Descriptions:
10   OPEN and LOCKED are useful words to include –
and why not CREAKY, like a castle door . . .?
11   The ladder could be UNSTABLE and WOBBLY—
and the pole SLIPPERY!
12   Since it doesn't appear anywhere else on
the list, the main description here could be FAST
– like a sports-car or powerful motorbike. Other
possibilities are CONVERTIBLE, and either FOUR- or
TWO-WHEELED.

As before, for ease of reference, these three new
sections are printed below in table-form.

Objects	Actions	Descriptions
10 DOOR, HOUSE, TENT, CASTLE, LOCK, KEY	OPEN, CLOSED, LOCK, UNLOCK	OPEN, CLOSED, LOCKED, CREAKY
11 LADDER STAIRS, ROPE, POLE	CLIMB, DESCEND, SWING, SLIDE	UNSTABLE, SLIPPERY
12 CAR, BUS, BIKE, ROAD, LANE	DRIVE, STEER, SWERVE, SKID	FAST, TWO-/FOUR-WHEELED

Now that your number-system stretches to 12, the month of
any date can be represented by a single element in the story. Six
ideas become five, and, as seen earlier, a story with five 'parts'
splits up effectively into DESCRIPTION, OBJECT, ACTION,
DESCRIPTION, OBJECT: the fast chef juggles some wet fish,
or a noisy crow sits on a wobbly bus.

Below are five dates, plus imaginary reasons for remembering
them. Read through the suggested stories, and practise putting
the technique for dates into use.

January 7th 1996:	SALES CONFERENCE
12 April 1995:	TRIP TO FRANCE
October 24th 1987:	DAY YOU BEGAN NEW JOB
November 17th 1995:	SCHOOL EXAM
6 July 1996:	FRIEND'S WEDDING

Suggestions

January 7th 1996: **Sales Conference**

The first step is to turn the date into a list of five numbers. No matter how the date has been written in words, always order the numbers in the same way.

The 'day, month, year' sequence turns this date into 07.1.96. The five story elements, are **0**, **7**, **1**, **9** and **6**.

The day here is **07** in order to ensure that there are always 5 numbers; in the 'month' section, on the other hand, the **0** can be left out, since all twelve possible numbers here have a single picture of their own.

Once the five numbers have been highlighted, it's an easy process to bring them to life and to transform them into a story.

Imagine arriving at the sales conference and being greeted by the organiser. He's ready to give a presentation, and has written a speech backed up with slides and music. His chosen CDs are carefully arranged on a desk – but all his plans are ruined with the arrival of an unexpected visitor.

A ROTUND – **0** – SAILOR – **7** – PAINTS – **1** – the ORGANISER's – **9** – CDs – **6**! Visualise the scene in your mind, highlighting all the important parts. This fat seaman splashes paint eveywhere as he vandalises the discs, and the organiser's face is white with rage . . .

By remembering the scene, you remember the whole date. When you're still new to this technique, it helps to write down the five numbers before you turn them back into a date.

In this case the numbers are **0** . . . **7** . . . **1** . . . **9** . . . **6**. The *first* two digits always refer to the day: the 7th. The *final* two digits always point to the year: 1996. And the remaining number, either one digit or two, reminds you of the month: 1 January. Your sales conference is on 07.1.96.: 7 January 1996.

12 April 1995: **Trip to France**

Again, begin by reducing the date to numbers and to five individual 'bits': 12.4.95. Here, the number representing the day already contains two digits, **1** and **2**, so there's no need to add an extra **0**. The five elements are: **1**, **2**, **4**, **9** and **5**.

As you drive off the ferry, you see a French onion-seller putting aside his wares and busily cleaning the road in front of you! As you watch, a brightly coloured bird sits down on the top of his broom. You jot down the details on a postcard: COLOURFUL – **1** – BIRD – **2** – SAT DOWN – **4** – on FRENCHMAN's – **9** – BROOM – **5**.

When the time comes to break the story back down into its key numbers, you write down: **1** . . . **2** . . . **4** . . . **9** . . . **5**.

The first two digits give you the day – 12 – the last two the year – 1995 – and the remaining digits, just one in this case, the month: 4, April. Your day-trip to France is on 12.4.95: 12 April 1995.

October 24th 1987: **Day you began new job**

This date demonstrates the usefulness of having 10, 11 and 12 within the range of your number system. When you break it down it becomes 24.10.87, made up of the five elements **2**, **4**, **10**, **8**, and **7**. October – **10** – can be treated as a single number rather than two separate digits, since it has its own bank of identities in your system.

It's the night before you begin a different job, and you're in the middle of a very worried dream. Unsure about what the new work is going to be like, you imagine all sorts of weird possibilities.

You dream that a strange rule forces you to *fly* to work every day. Your new place of work turns out to be a huge metal fortress, and the first time you arrive, you fly through the door and land straight in the canteen! All there is to eat is plate after plate of raw fish . . .

Run back through the 'dream', concentrating on the five key points.

You FLEW – **2** – to the METAL – **4** – FORTRESS – **10** – and ATE – **8** – FISH – **7**. This story allows you to remember five numbers – **2**, **4**, **10**, **8**, and **7** – and, once you've written them down, it's a simple task to turn them back into a date.

The first two numbers give you the day – 24 – the last two the year – 1987 – and the remaining digits the month – 10, October.

You began your new job on 24.10.87: October 24th 1987.

November 17th 1995: School exam

Once again, the month – the 11th – can be treated as a single element. The full date can be simplified to 17.11.95, and the five key elements are 1, 7, 11, 9 and 5.

You're in the middle of an important examination, when it all goes horribly wrong. There are only a few minutes left to go, you still have a couple of questions to answer – and your ink suddenly turns to water! There's only a slight change at first; the colour of the ink becomes a little bit weaker and you have to press harder on the paper to make the writing clear. But soon the colour has faded completely, and you're left trying to write with watery drips.

The school's supply of ink is kept on a shelf close to where you're sitting, and you pull up a ladder to help you reach. But the teacher has seen you. He reaches out his long, gnarled finger and catches you by the scruff of the neck . . .

This memorable story has five main parts. Your INK – 1 – turned to WATER – 7 – so you tried to use a LADDER – 11. But the TEACHER – 9 – hooked you with his FINGER – 5. The numbers are 1, 7, 11, 9, and 5.

The date of your exam is 17.11.95: November 17th 1995.

6th July 1996: Friend's wedding

As ever, the simplified date – 06.7.96 – gives you five individual elements: 0, 6, 7, 9 and 6.

You're Best Man at your friend's wedding. It's a lavish affair, with a large group of musicians set up at one side of the aisle. Unfortunately, in your nervousness, you drop the ring into the trumpet-player's drink! Thinking this is a signal, the congregation starts to sing . . .

For weeks afterwards your mind returns to the chaotic events. The RING – 0 – went in the MUSICIAN'S – 6 – DRINK – 7 – and the PEOPLE – 9 – started to SING – 6. The five numbers are unforgettable – 0, 6, 7, 9, 6. The date of your friend's wedding is 06.7.96: 6th July 1996.

MONTHLY MEMORY

Rather than counting through all the months every time you have to remember a date, it's useful to know instantly the 5th month, or the 9th, or the 6th.

The easiest way to learn them is simply to create a link between the words and their numbers. One strong connection for each will mean that you never waste time counting from month to month, and never make a mistake.

Below are suggestions for ten of the twelve links. (I'm assuming you can remember that January is the first month, and December the twelfth!)

Month 2: February
The 'bruary' in February could become 'brewery'. Imagine the drunken brewery-workers THROWING – **2** – vats of beer at each other!

Month 3: March
By coincidence, the word 'march' appears in section **3** of the number system. Emphasise the reminder by visualising an army *marching* through the *countryside*.

Month 4: April
On April Fool's Day you're caught unawares by a collapsing CHAIR – **4**.

Month 5: May
The Maypole collapses. Everyone looks at you, because it was your job to fix it with GLUE – **5**.

Month 6: June
Turn 'June' into 'dune'. As you sit on the sand-dunes on a beautiful June day, you battle to hear yourself think above the din. Everybody on the beach is playing a RADIO – **6** . . .

Month 7: July
The first syllable of 'July' could be changed into 'duel'. Imagine taking part in a duel on the sea. You and your opponent each have a SPEEDBOAT – **7** – and race towards each other through the waves . . .

Month 8: **August**
The second syllable of this month gives you a powerful *gust* . . . of delicious cooking – **8**!

Month 9: **September**
As long as you're not eating, picture a *sept*-ic tank . . . and see your least favourite person – **9** – falling in.

Month 10: **October**
As you stand outside your house, admiring the building, an *oct*-opus suddenly bursts forth – a tentacle crashing through every window in the HOUSE – **10**.

Month 11: **November**
At the bonfire-party, disaster strikes a man who climbs on to a ladder to get a better view. He puts it too close, the flames eat through rung after rung and, within minutes, a small pile of ash is all that's left of the LADDER – **11** . . .

When you've visualised these ten brief scenes, you can recall the number of any month within seconds. October points you to the octopus, the house, and the number **10**; April to the joke chair and the number **4**; and your skill at remembering dates is greatly improved.

THE ZODIAC
When you're confident in your ability to commit any date to memory, it's possible to learn whole lists of dates. As an example of the vast possibilities of *Mindpower*, printed below are the signs of the zodiac, alongside the official start and finish-dates for each one. This is the sort of information that would require hours to learn without an efficient technique to rely on. But with the *Mindpower System*, a few minutes is all it takes.

AQUARIUS:	20 January to 18 February
PISCES:	19 February to 20 March
ARIES:	21 March to 20 April
TAURUS:	21 April to 20 May
GEMINI:	21 May to 20 June
CANCER:	21 June to 21 July

LEO:	22 July to 21 August
VIRGO:	22 August to 21 September
LIBRA:	22 September to 22 October
SCORPIO:	23 October to 21 November
SAGITTARIUS:	22 November to 20 December
CAPRICORN:	21 December to 19 January

The easiest way to approach this material is to take it sign by sign. For each one, change the word into a picture, and turn the two dates into two parts of a story, the picture suggesting the theme.

Aquarius: 20 January to 18 February

Using the same system as before, each of these dates can be changed into three separate elements: **2**, **0**, **1** for the first, and **1**, **8**, **2** for the second. The first two digits in each refer to the day, and the remaining figure or figures, to the month.

A good image to use for the zodiacal sign here would be an AQUARIUM.

When you've simplified the dates, and decided upon a central image, the remaining step is to create a memorable story. The first three numbers provide the material for the first half, and the second three describe the conclusion.

You're sitting in an exclusive restaurant, at a table next to the AQUARIUM. Behind the glass are all the lobsters, crabs and fish that you can choose to have cooked. You're just about to make your decision when something happens to put you off the whole idea.

Someone throws an empty paint-tin into the water! Bits of rust flake off the sides, and the water turns a dirty brown. You take a napkin and make a note on it to have chicken instead . . .

This story can be divided into two clear halves, two actions: one to cause an effect, the other to give a response. Someone THREW – **2** – an EMPTY – **0** – PAINT-TIN – **1**, and, in response, you MADE A NOTE – **1** – to EAT – **8** – CHICKEN – **2**.

As with all these stories, the three central elements in each action are all that concern you. Everything else – the restaurant, the fish, the napkin – is there purely to add detail and colour.

When you think of Aquarius you remember the aquarium, and the story that follows gives you two sets of numbers: **2**, **0**, **1** and **1**, **8**, **2**. In each, the first two digits give you the day, and the remaining number represents the month.

The start-date for AQUARIUS is 20.1. – 20 January – and the end-date is 18.2. – 18 February.

Pisces: **19 February to 20 March**

Once again, the dates can be simplified into two groups of numbers: **1**, **9**, **2** for the first, and **2**, **0**, **3**, for the second. The obvious image to use this time is not the tank, but the FISH itself.

The newspapers report that a giant shark has been spotted swimming in the sea close to your house. You'd love to chase it, to take photographs of this amazing fish, but no boat is going to be fast enough to catch it up.

You have an idea. Running to workshop, you design yourself the perfect mode of transport – an aeroplane, which you can fly low over the water to photograph the shark.

Unfortunately, though, your very first flight ends in disaster. Before you even arrive at the shoreline, you fly straight into a hollow tree . . .

As before, there are two actions, the second coming only as a result of the first. You DESIGNED – **1** – YOURSELF – **9** – an AEROPLANE – **2**, but, as a result, you FLEW – **2** – into a HOLLOW – **0** – TREE – **3**.

When you think of the FISH, you'll remember the lengths you went to in your pursuit! The simple story gives you two sets of numbers: **1**, **9**, **2** and **2**, **0**, **3**. As always, the first two digits in each group give you the day, and the remaining number confirms the month.

The start-date for PISCES is 19.2. – 19 February – and the end-date 20.3. – 20 March.

Aries: **21 March to 20 April**

The dates are simplified to **2**, **1**, **3** and **2**, **0**, **4**. Aries is the RAM.

You find youself in the middle of a fairytale. A huge RAM

has taken over a village, terrorising the people and forcing them out of their homes. They try to placate the beast by throwing offerings of colourful flowers – but the ram thinks they're starting a fight, and throws back a snooker table!

In this sort of story, the two actions are especially clear. One thing happens, followed by a balanced response. One side THROWS – **2** – COLOURFUL – **1** – FLOWERS – **3**, and the other THROWS – **2** – a SNOOKER – **0** – TABLE – **4**.

The RAM is always the centre of attention, and the two sets of numbers are clear: **2, 1, 3** and **2, 0, 4**.

The start-date for ARIES is 21.3. – 21 March – and the end-date 20.4. – 20 April.

Taurus: **21 April to 20 May**
The dates here become **2, 1, 4** and **2, 0, 5**. Taurus is the BULL.

Spain is traditionally the home of the bull, so picture yourself sitting on an aeroplane waiting to fly to the continent. You soon wish that you'd paid a little more and chosen a better airline; as you watch, the pilot walks down the aisles putting an extra coat of paint on the seats!

Suddenly an argument erupts. The plane's cleaner says that *she* should be the one to paint the seats, and she screams at the pilot to let her do her job. In the end, the only way to decide is for the two workers to play a game of tennis in the aisle, the pilot hitting from the left and the cleaner from the right. The winner will get the paint . . .

The story began when the PILOT – **2** – PAINTED – **1** – the SEATS – **4**. It ended with the PILOT – **2** – playing TENNIS – **0** – with the CLEANER – **5**; the man on the left, the woman on the right. When you think of TAURUS, you'll remember this strange trip to Spain, and have no difficulty returning to the two sets of numbers: **2, 1, 4** and **2, 0, 5**.

The start-date for TAURUS is 21.4. – 21 April – and the end-date 20.5. – 20 May.

Gemini: **21 May to 20 June**
The two sets of numbers are **2, 1, 5** and **2, 0, 6**. Gemini represents the TWINS.

For once, since it's so appropriate, why not keep both **2**s simply as numbers? This allows you to create a doubly balanced story . . .

Imagine watching a television programme about identical twins. Two twin-sisters are brought on – although they haven't seen each other for ten years, they both do exactly the same jobs, and have exactly the same odd hobbies. Both twins design cranes for a living; examples of their work are wheeled into the studio. And they both enjoy juggling violins; the programme ends with a double demonstration of this strange skill!

Both TWINS – **2** – DESIGN – **1** – CRANES – **5** and both TWINS – **2** – JUGGLE – **0** – VIOLINS – **6**! The two sets of numbers are clear: **2, 1, 5** and **2, 0, 6**.

The start-date for GEMINI is 21.5. – 21 May – and the end-date 20.6. – 20 June.

Cancer: **21 June to 21 July**
These dates are simplified to **2, 1, 6** and **2, 1, 7**, and the similarity between the pairs will be of great help when you come to create your story. The symbol for Cancer is the CRAB.

Imagine watching a nature documentary about the crab. The clicking of its claws sounds like castanets, but this musical talent is more than equalled by the crab's ability to move through the water. Perhaps there's a special school somewhere that teaches crabs these two skills!

Sure enough, the programme shows just such a school. It's situated in a foreign country, and the only way for the crabs to get there is by air. You watch with interest as they FLY – **2** – to STUDY – **1** – MUSIC – **6**, and FLY – **2** – to LEARN – **1** – to SWIM – **7** . . .

The programme has shown you a side to crab life you never knew existsed. It has also given you two sets of numbers: **2, 1, 6** and **2, 1, 7**.

The start-date for CANCER is 21.6. – 21 June – and the end-date 21.7. – 21 July.

Leo: **22 July to 21 August**
The dates here translate into the numbers **2, 2, 7** and **2, 1, 8**. Leo is the sign of the LION.

Lions are beautiful creatures to watch, especially in their natural habitat – but it's not a good idea to get too close . . .

Picture a pilot flying his light aircraft over a jungle-covered island, looking down on a whole family of lions – when the engine cuts out and he flies straight into the sea.

Luckily, the plane floats, but there's not much food left on board. It's no use even thinking of swimming ashore: the lions rule the island, and take all the food for themselves. Instead, the pilot consoles himself by taking a cook-book and *reading* about food . . .

The lions are a central force throughout the story. The PILOT – **2** – FLEW – **2** – into the SEA – **7**, and, because of the lions, the PILOT – **2** – was forced to READ – **1** – about FOOD – **8** – rather than eat it! The two sets of numbers are **2, 2, 7** and **2, 1, 8**.

The start-date for LEO is 22.7. – 22 July – and the end-date 21.8. – 21 August.

Virgo: 22 August to 21 September
As always, begin by turning the dates into two sets of numbers: **2, 2, 8** and **2, 1, 9**. The symbol for Virgo is the VIRGIN.

The beautiful young girl in this story is a circus-star's glamorous assistant. She stands against a board while her partner throws knives, missing her by inches every time. He seems a little unsure of himself, though, and after every throw he crosses to his assistant and studies her carefully, only leaving when he's sure she's unhurt.

This process happens again and again. It's easy to see the two actions in the story. The THROWER – **2** – HURLS – **2** – a KNIFE – **8**; then, straight away, the THROWER – **2** – STUDIES – **1** – the GIRL – **9**. The two sets of numbers are **2, 2, 8** and **2, 1, 9**.

The start-date for VIRGO is 22.8. – 22 August – and the end-date 21.9. – 21 September.

Libra: 22 September to 22 October.
These dates are simplified to create another two sets of numbers: **2, 2, 9** and **2, 2, 10**. Libra is the SCALES.

People are terrified of scales – or, to be more precise, terrified of what scales tell them about their weight! Some people will go to great lengths to make themselves lighter . . .

Imagine seeing two such people, a man and a woman, climbing

on to a set of scales outside your local shops. They've both covered themselves with *feathers* – and although this strange technique has made them lighter, it also seems to have affected their personalities.

You discover this when you follow them home, and find that they live in two identical bird-houses, side by side . . .

There's a strange sort of logic to it all. TWO – **2** – FEATHERED – **2** – PEOPLE – **9** – require TWO – **2** – BIRD – **2** – HOUSES – **10**! The two sets of numbers are **2, 2, 9** and **2, 2, 10**.

The start-date for LIBRA is 22.9. – 22 September – and the end-date 22.10. – 22 October.

Scorpio: **23 October to 21 November**

For this sign, the sets of numbers are **2, 3, 10** and **2, 1, 11**. Scorpio is the SCORPION.

You dream that you're being attacked by a huge, fierce scorpion. The only way to beat it back is to throw things at it – and there are only two items nearby. First you THROW – **2** – a WOODEN – **3** – DOOR – **10**, but the scorpion just flicks it away with its giant tail. As a last resort you THROW – **2** – a PAINTER'S – **1** – LADDER – **11**, and manage to catch part of its body between the rungs . . .

Imagine the great effort it takes to hurl each of these items, and picture the scorpion stuck to the spot by the ladder. The two sets of numbers are clear: **2, 3, 10** and **2, 1, 11**.

The start-date for SCORPIO is 23.10. – 23 October – and the end-date 21.11. – 21 November.

Sagittarius: **22 November to 20 December**

Two more sets of numbers – **2, 2, 11** and **2, 0, 12** – and another symbol: the ARCHER.

As always, the trick is to find the most appropriate pictures – and here, the first number **2** in each set can become the archer himself, since section **2** in the number system is based on throwing and flying . . .

You're standing on your local playing-field, watching a budding young archer practising his skills. He's been there for hours, and his supply of arrows is running low – so he chops up an old ladder and uses the rungs instead.

Eventually, these too have been used up – but he's determined to show off his abilities, and starts playing hoopla with passing cars! He uses anything ring-shaped – a hoop, a tyre, an elastic-band – and tries to throw his rings over passing vehicles.

Run back through the events in your mind. There were two main pieces of action. First, the ARCHER – **2** – FIRED – **2** – LADDER-RUNGS – **11**, and later the ARCHER – **2** – RINGED – **0** – passing CARS – **12**. The two sets of numbers are **2, 2, 11** and **2, 0, 12**.

The start-date for SAGITTARIUS is 22.11. – 22 November – and the end-date 20.12. – 20 December.

Capricorn: **21 December to 19 January**

This final pair of dates is simplified to **2, 1, 12** and **1, 9, 1**. Capricorn is the sign of the GOAT.

A farmer decides to turn one of his fields into a race-track. He has the clever idea of using a flock of GOATS to trim down the grass and eat any unsightly weeds. As a way of rewarding them, he lets them stay at the side of the field to watch the action.

Two bright-red sportscars line up to do battle. There's a large media presence, and the newspaper-writers chatter amongst themselves, commenting, amongst other things, on how useful the goats have been . . .

The scene itself is a simple one. TWO – **2** – RED – **1** – CARS – **12** stand ready, and WRITER – **1** – TALKS to – **9** – WRITER **1**. The two sets of numbers are **2, 1, 12** and **1, 9, 1**.

The start-date for CAPRICORN is 21.12. – 21 December – and the end-date 19.1. – 19 January.

By learning these details about the signs of the zodiac, you put into practice so many of the key techniques of *Mindpower*.

You make a decision to use your memory – to approach the material properly so that you only have to learn it once. You turn the details into their simplest form, moulding them to work *with* the memory rather than against it. You change abstract numbers into pictures, and then connect the images together into stories and scenes.

Twelve words and seventy-eight individual digits are *made* memorable. Whenever you think of a star-sign, you're prompted to recall a simple pair of actions or events.

AQUARIUS: Aquarium
   Someone THREW an EMPTY PAINT-TIN, so . . .
   . . . you MADE A NOTE to EAT CHICKEN.
PISCES: Shark
   You DESIGNED YOURSELF a PLANE, but . . .
   . . . FLEW into a HOLLOW TREE.
ARIES: Ram
   People THREW COLOURFUL FLOWERS . . .
   The ram THREW a SNOOKER-TABLE.
TAURUS: Bull/Spain
   The PILOT PAINTED the SEATS . . .
   The PILOT PLAYED TENNIS with the CLEANER.
GEMINI: Twins
   The TWINS DESIGNED CRANES . . .
   The TWINS JUGGLED VIOLINS.
CANCER: Crab
   Crabs FLY to LEARN MUSIC . . .
   Crabs FLY to LEARN to SWIM.
LEO: Lion
   The PILOT FLEW into the SEA . . .
   The PILOT READ about FOOD.
VIRGO: Virgin
   A THROWER HURLED KNIVES . . .
   A THROWER STUDIED the GIRL.
LIBRA: Scales
   TWO FEATHERED PEOPLE require . . .
   . . . TWO BIRD-HOUSES.
SCORPIO: Scorpion
   You THROW a WOODEN DOOR . . .
   You THROW a PAINTER'S LADDER.
SAGITTARIUS: Archer
   The ARCHER FIRES LADDER-RUNGS . . .
   The ARCHER RINGS CARS.
CAPRICORN: Goat
   TWO RED CARS . . .
   WRITER TALKS to WRITER.

To complete the process, spend a few minutes creating a story to remind you of the signs themselves.

Since the first sign, Aquarius, starts in January, the second in February, and so on, being able to remember the list will give you enough information to start defining a particular sign. When someone tells you their birthday, you can move quickly to the general area of the zodiac, then use your more specialised knowledge to confirm the appropriate sign.

As a memorable starting-point, imagine sitting in a gipsy's tent, waiting for your zodiac chart to be compiled. Your eyes wander to a huge AQUARIUM in the corner of the tent, and, looking closer, you see that it's full of expensive FISH. But at that moment a RAM bursts through the wall of the tent, *rams* into the glass, and sends water showering in all directions.

The gipsy is most concerned about her souvenir collection. As the water-level rises, she gathers up her model bulls and matadors, and escapes with all her memorabilia from SPAIN. She leaves the tent by a door on the left – but, to your amazement, she appears again a second later from the *right*! The answer is that this is a different woman, the second sister in a pair of TWINS . . .

She apologises for all the water and asks if you'd like to leave. You're just about to say No, but a sudden pain shoots through your toe. You've been bitten by a huge CRAB – in seconds you've changed your mind, and you wade out of the tent.

The door is blocked by a ferocious LION. His roar sends you flying backwards into the water. A young GIRL sees your plight and pulls you out, then finds out how much water you've swallowed by hauling you up onto some SCALES.

Together, you come up with a plan for escape. She hands you her pet SCORPION, and you throw it at the lion, terrifying the huge animal and making it run away in shock. A loose lion is a terrible threat to the public, so a team of ARCHERS is brought in to slow the beast down.

Unfortunately they're all short-sighted, and again and again they hit harmless GOATS. The goats are hardly affected by the arrows at all; mostly they just pull them out and eat them . . .!

When you can remember the key elements in this story, you know the order of signs in the zodiac: the aquarium

(AQUARIUS), the fish (PISCES), the ram (ARIES), the Spanish souvenirs (TAURUS), the twin gipsies (GEMINI), the painful crab (CANCER), the fierce lion (LEO), the life-saving girl (VIRGO), her scales (LIBRA), her scorpion (SCORPIO), the archers (SAGITTARIUS), and, finally, the goats (CAPRICORN).

To put your knowledge into practice, simply combine all the appropriate techniques.

To work out the star-sign for someone born on 25 June, for example, these would be the mental steps to take.

June is the sixth month – remember the noisy dunes, the sunbathers' radios? ('radio' = **6**). By counting through the story above, you find that the main sign for the sixth month is CANCER (the story's sixth element is the crab).

Your memory-story about the crab tells you the key dates for this sign. Crabs FLY – **2** – to STUDY – **1** – MUSIC – **6**, and FLY – **2** – to LEARN – **1** – to SWIM – **7**. The start-date is 21.6. – June 21st – and the end-date 21.7. – 21 June. Since 25 June falls between the two, the star-sign in this case is indeed CANCER.

On other occasions you'll find that a sign falls outside the 'main' month. You locate the right area of the zodiac, but find that the date in question appears in the sign immediately after or before.

This is the case if you work out the star-sign of someone born on 15 August.

You remember straight away that August is the eighth month (the GUST of COOKERY SMELLS – 'cooking' = **8**).

By counting through the list of star-signs you find that the main sign for the eighth month is VIRGO (the girl who saves your life is the eighth element in the story).

By recalling the story for VIRGO, you can write down the dates when this sign begins and ends.

The girl is having knives thrown at her . . . the THROWER – **2** – HURLS – **2** – KNIVES – **8**, then the THROWER – **2** – STUDIES – **1** – the GIRL – **9**. The start-date is 22.8. – 22 August – and the end-date is 21.9. – 21 September – so the star-sign for August 15th must be the one before VIRGO, the *seventh* on the list: LEO.

With practice, you'll be able to work through the steps in

seconds. A huge amount of knowledge has been taken under your control – and will remain at your fingertips for as long as you need. It proves that any sort of material can be remembered, and that simple memory techniques can be of use at every stage in the learning process.

MEMORY TIME

As well as dates, your number system is also the perfect resource for remembering times.

Once again, the first step is to mould information into the most efficient shape. Times can be written in many different ways: two o'clock . . . two pm . . . fourteen hundred-hours . . . 14.00. The simplest form is the last – 14.00 – and if you treat *every* time in terms of the twenty-four hour clock, you're faced with just four numbers to learn. No 'pm' or 'am', no 'o'clock' – just four digits, ready to be changed into ideas and images and formed into a story.

If you're not already familiar with the twenty-four hour clock, it only takes a moment to learn.

Midnight is treated as 00.00, and every hour after that adds an extra unit – 1 am becoming 01.00, 2 am 02.00, and so on. The time in minutes is written in the same way as always, and appears after the decimal point. 5.30 am is 05.30; 7.46 am is 07.46.

Even after 12 noon – 12.00 – you keep adding units. 1 pm becomes 13.00, 2 pm is 14.00, and so it goes on, until 11 pm: 23.00. After 23.59, it's back to midnight and 00.00 again.

The advantage of this system is that you never need worry about 'am' or 'pm'; 3 am, for example – 03.00 – could never be confused with 3 pm – 15.00. When you start thinking of *all* times in terms of the twenty-four hour clock, you prepare them to be fitted into the basic number system; they all now consist of four digits, two on either side of a decimal point, and they can all be remembered in exactly the same way.

'Six forty-five am' would become 06.45. Perhaps this is the time you have to catch a flight. Imagine sitting on an aeroplane, and looking out of the window to see that a fat singer is about to be loaded in through the cargo-hatch. He sits down on a hook, and waits to be hoisted up . . .

The ROUNDED – **0** – SINGER – **6** – SITS – **4** – on the HOOK – **5**. The time for your flight is 06.45; six forty-five am.

'Eight minutes past five in the evening' would become 17.08. If this was the time of your doctor's appointment, you might picture yourself sitting in the waiting-room. The doctor is behind schedule and you're having to wait for hours. You've read every magazine in the room – even an old yachting-magazine, which was so boring that you rolled it into a ball and ate it . . .

You READ – **1** – the YACHTING-magazine – **7** – before rolling it into a BALL – **0** – and EATING it – **8**. The time of your appointment is 17.08; eight minutes past five in the evening.

If you travel abroad regularly, call relatives overseas or deal with businesses around the world, it's useful to remember 'world times'. This is a perfect example of *Mindpower*; information is moulded into the simplest form possible, then brought to life with pictures and stories. The important point to notice is that the time-zones of most countries and cities can be remembered as just two digits!

Times around the world are measured by comparison with the time in London; Greenwich Mean Time or G.M.T. A time-zone is labelled by whatever time it is *there* when it's twelve noon in London.

Shanghai, for example, is eight hours ahead. At 12.00 G.M.T., the time in Shanghai is 20.00. New York, on the other hand, is five hours *behind*. At 12.00 G.M.T., the time by the Statue of Liberty is 07.00.

Rather than learning 'five hours before' or 'eight after', it's best to concentrate on the first two figures in the 'zone' time. Almost all the zones are whole hours ahead or behind G.M.T., so you can forget about the second pair of numbers. The '.00' can be assumed; the other two numbers give you all the information you need, and your number system lets you memorise them in seconds. In fact, having *two* numbers presents you with enough variety to remember as many 'world times' as you need.

Isolate the two numbers, turn them into a scene, then link your pictures with the time-zone itself.

Printed below are examples of ten 'world times'; the times in ten cities at 12.00 G.M.T. When you've read through the list of

suggestions and visualised the scenes, test yourself from this
original list.

ATHENS:	14.00
BRUSSELS:	13.00
CAPE TOWN:	14.00
CHICAGO:	06.00
HELSINKI:	19.00
JERUSALEM:	14.00
MOSCOW:	15.00
NEW YORK:	07.00
SYDNEY:	22.00
TOKYO:	21.00

Suggestions

Athens: **14.00**

All the information is included in the digits **1** and **4**. Picture all
the ancient, ruined buildings in Athens. Imagine it was your job
to restore them. Where would you start? Perhaps you'd begin
painting the seats in one of the arenas.

PAINT – **1** – the SEATS – **4**. This simple action is all you
need to remember the **1** and **4** and to know that the time in
Athens at 12.00 G.M.T. is 14.00.

Brussels: **13.00**

Here, the digits are **1** and **3**. Sometimes it's easier to link your
story with an object rather than with a particular place. In this
case, Brussels *sprouts* would be a good focal point.

Where might Brussels sprouts grow? On a green plant!
GREEN stands for **1** and PLANT stands for **3**. At 12.00
G.M.T., the time in Brussels must be 13.00.

Cape Town: **14.00**

Super-heroes wear *capes*, so perhaps 'Cape Town' is where
they go to study their super-skills!

Picture Superman – the 'Man of Steel' – sitting at his desk,
STUDYING – **1** – STEEL – **4**; how to bend it, how to see
through it . . . The image gives you the two key digits; the
time in Cape Town at 12.00 G.M.T. is 14.00.

Chicago: **06.00**

If possible, create more than one link between your memory-scene and the city or country in question. Chicago is known as the 'windy city', but it's also the name of a rock group.

Imagine walking down a street in Chicago as the wind blows CDs around your feet. To help warm yourself up, stop for a moment and kick some of the discs along the pavement. As you KICK – **0** – the CDs – **6**, you remind yourself of the two important digits. It's 06.00 in Chicago when it's twelve noon in London.

Helsinki: **19.00**

If a place-name sparks off no images or associations, it's often possible to find a 'hook' within the word itself. Here, the first two syllables could be changed into 'hell sink' – the place where the Devil does his washing-up!

Concentrate on your picture of the Devil. Most striking of all is his colour. The RED – **1** – DEVIL – **9** – prompts you to remember that, in Helsinki, the time at 12.00 G.M.T. is 19.00.

Jerusalem: **14.00**

Two more digits: **1** and **4**. Imagine kneeling in a church in Jerusalem, deep in thought and prayer. You're kneeling in front of a STUDY – **1** – DESK – **4**. At 12.00 G.M.T, the time in Jerusalem is 14.00.

Moscow: **15.00**

Russia is known for its philosophers, as well as for its intellectuals in hiding. Imagine walking around the capital city, and listening to the road-sweepers discussing philosophy and amazing ideas. Everywhere you go there are INTELLECTUAL – **1** – CLEANERS – **5**! It's 15.00 in Moscow when it's twelve noon in London.

New York: **07.00**

From your vantage point on top of the Statue of Liberty you can see that the lip around the torch is a perfect circle of stone. As you watch, this circle starts slipping, tears away from the rest of the statue and crashes down into the sea. Its weight sends a circle of water rising high into the air.

The CIRCLE of stone in the WATER . . . the CIRCLE of WATER itself – both remind you of the all important numbers, 0 and 7. At 12.00 G.M.T, the time in New York is 07.00.

Sydney: **22.00**

The Sydney Opera House and Harbour Bridge are among the finest and most famous structures in the world. Imagine asking the pilot of your Qantas plane to fly as low as possible so that you can take some stunning photographs. He obliges: the PILOT – **2** – GLIDES low – **2** – over the whole harbour. The time in Sydney at 12.00 G.M.T. is 22.00.

Tokyo: **21.00**

As well as moulding your stories around famous buildings, you can make *people* the focal point.

The Japanese are known for putting great pressure on their students to succeed in exams. Picture the typical Tokyo school-girl. Her British counterpart might open one book, but the Japanese girl has so much to do that she holds up *two* – one in each hand. TWO – **2** – BOOKS – **1**, and two digits: the time in Tokyo is 21.00 when Big Ben strikes twelve noon.

Remembering 'world times' helps you to conduct business around the globe, to plan your transatlantic phone-calls – even to pass geography exams.

Once you've created a strong bank of memorable scenes, all you have to do is bring one of them to mind, extract the two central elements – the CIRCLE and the WATER, for example, or the GREEN FLOWER – and you have all the information you need. The images become numbers, and, by adding '.00', you return the material to its original form. If you had to, every time-zone in the world could easily be taken under your control.

A MEMORY TO COUNT ON

As well as helping you to learn specific numbers, the *Mindpower System* can turn numbers into prompts for remembering other information. Just as individual words can simplify a long text, order and pattern it and provide you with a series of 'hooks', so numbers can also form the foundations of memory.

Imagine you had to learn the following shopping list.

APPLES, BREAD, FLOUR, CHEESE, MILK, WASHING-UP LIQUID, CEREAL, WINE, CUCUMBER, POTATOES

An alternative to connecting the words into a story, or placing them in rooms around an imaginary route, is to 'peg' each word to a number. This is especially useful when you need to know the number of each item – to be able to call out the 'fifth', say, or the 'seventh', and to prove your total control over the original list.

You already have a stock of pictures and ideas for each number, 1 to 12, so any list of up to twelve items can be learnt in seconds simply by connecting each item with an appropriate image.

Below are suggestions for remembering the shopping-list. When you've read them, practise pinpointing specific items, remembering the list backwards, or picking out all the odd-numbered words . . .

Suggestion
For any one list, it's best to treat each item in a similar way. You might *place* them all somewhere; you could *do* something odd to them all, or perhaps *give* all the things to memorable people. This helps to avoid confusion, and gives you a clear starting-point each time. Rather than having to consider every possibility for a number, you can go straight to the OBJECTS column, the ACTIONS or DESCRIPTIONS.

With this shopping list, why not concentrate on *actions*? Treat each object in a memorable way – appropriate both to the thing itself in some way, and, most importantly, to the particular number in your system.

1: *Apples*
Take a perfect, shiny, red APPLE, and scratch your initials into its skin with the nib of a pen. Imagine what it would look like, feel like – even sound like. Perhaps you take a whole bag of

apples, and spell out your name by writing a different letter on each one. The key action is WRITING, connecting 'apples' with the number **1**.

As always, add enough imaginative detail to make the picture specific. You have to stress that the fruit here isn't pears or peaches. Why not use your pen to draw a cross on each apple, then use it as a target when you shoot an arrow through it like William Tell!

2: *Bread*
Perhaps you THROW pieces of BREAD (to the BIRDS!). It's a windy day, and you have to use all your strength to throw the crumbs more than a few feet. At the last minute you notice that the 'bread' has turned to *money*, the other sort of 'bread' . . .

3: *Flour*
Walking is one of the main actions in section **3** of the number system. Imagine walking through a huge packet of FLOUR, and treading white, powdery footprints across a newly cleaned carpet. It *used* to have a beautiful *flower*-y print . . .

4: *Cheese*
Imagine your job is to make CHEESE-slices . . . by *sitting* on them to press them into shape! By the end of the day, the seat of your trousers is covered in cheese, and you change them quickly to look presentable for your photograph-*sitting*. Say 'cheese'!

5: *Milk*
You've spilt MILK everywhere, and it has to be *cleaned* up immediately. What do you use? You try a vacuum-cleaner, but the milk leaks out from a hole in the bag. You try sweeping it into a bin, but the milk seeps through the bristles.

In the end you use a mop and bucket – but just as you've finished cleaning the whole floor, a herd of cows stampedes across it . . .

6: *Washing-up Liquid*
By blowing into the nozzle of a WASHING-UP LIQUID bottle you can create your own musical instrument! Imagine the taste

when you accidently suck up some of the soapy liquid. Pour out what's left of it to help you wash the dishes – and turn the saucepans and lids into drums and cymbals by hitting them with spoons . . .

7: *Cereal*
Imagine what it would feel like to *swim* through a huge bowl of breakfast CEREAL – no milk, just the cereal, threatening to submerge you in flakes of corn. You let out a great sigh of relief when a plastic boat rises up from beneath the cereal – a novelty gift, which you quickly learn to sail on the cereal sea . . .

8: *Wine*
Use bottle after bottle of WINE when you're *cooking*. Put red wine in the mashed potatoes, white wine in the soup, and a nice rosé in with the carrots. You'll know the meal is ready when your huge saucepan lets out a *whine* of savoury steam . . .

9: *Cucumber*
Try to reduce the bags under your eyes by applying slices of CUCUMBER. In fact, while you're at it, why not *wear* cucumber all over your body? Cut the pieces to make wonderful clothes in the latest styles. Inspect yourself in a mirror, and check that you look as 'cool as a cucumber'!

10: *Potatoes*
Play a practical joke on the Prime Minister: block his *doorway* with a huge pile of POTATOES! Take a raw tube of potato and squash it into the keyhole. You've *locked* him in – but the policeman standing outside turns out to be an old-fashioned 'Peeler', and he peels all the potatoes, weakening the pile and bringing it crashing to the ground. The Prime Minister orders all the potatoes to be burned – the definitive 'political hot potato . . .!'

A useful last step is to connect all ten stories to a particular place. For the list above, it might be the supermarket you plan to visit; you throw bread to birds sitting on top of the tills, give a musical performance with washing-up liquid bottles in the aisle, and use potatoes to lock a visiting politician into the storeroom.

This step allows you to create many different lists using the same ten or twelve numbers. You could have one for each shop you need to visit; each list would be set *in* the appropriate shop, and each action connected with some specific element of the location.

You might *throw* rolls of WALLPAPER against a particular tiling display in the home-improvement store, and hurl a CAKE into the oven in the BAKERY. Both items are 'number 2' on their respective lists, but the specific connections mean that both remain memorable.

'What did I throw against the tiles in the DIY shop?' *Wallpaper*. 'What did I hurl into the oven in the baker's?' *Cake* . . .

If you need to remember more than twelve items on a single list, the easiest way is to learn them as *groups*. Make each number 'hook' the starting point for a series of connections, and, as far as possible, have the same number of items in each 'group'.

Printed below is another shopping list – this time containing fifteen items, and demonstrating the techniques for creating a numbered list as large as you need. In this case, three items can easily be connected to each of the numbers from one to five.

Read the suggestions, then follow the instructions on how to recall any individual item on the list.

1. CRISPS,   2. ORANGES,   3. BANANAS,
4. BUTTER,   5. TIN-FOIL,   6. TOMATOES,
7. SUGAR,   8. GARLIC,   9. JAM,
10. LETTUCE,   11. SOAP,   12. HAM,
13. SALT,   14. CHOCOLATE,   15. TEA

Suggestions

Group 1: **Crisps, Oranges, Bananas:**
Rather than concentrating on actions, as above, why not go first to the OBJECTS column? Begin each three-part story with an appropriate *thing*.

You're reading a BOOK – **1** – entitled 'A History of CRISPS'!

A differently flavoured crisp has been fixed to every page. Imagine the crunching sound when you close the book. Bits of crisps drop out on to the bright ORANGE carpet, changing its colour to yellowy-brown.

To change it back, you squeeze the juice of an *orange* all over it – and even lay down thin bits of peel. The real test comes when you try to walk on it. You go carefully, determined not to disrupt the peel – but, just when you're almost across, you slip and fall backwards, covering yourself in bits of crisp and orange-peel.

There has to be a reason for your fall – and, sure enough, when you lift back the carpet you see that the underlay is made from BANANA-skins! You might as well make use of them, so you put one skin on each foot – they make a great pair of 'slippers' . . .

You decide to write a book about your new invention.

At the start, and again at the end, the focal point here is BOOK – **1**. The book was full of CRISPS, the carpet was covered with ORANGES, the underlay was made from BANANAS, and your 'slipper' invention was the subject for a BOOK. The three items are connected, in order, to the number **1**.

Group 2: **Butter, Tin-foil, Tomatoes**

This story might begin with an AEROPLANE – a huge jumbo-jet being prepared for take-off. You watch closely to see what jobs have to be done.

The first is to lubricate the wheels and the runway. A team of technicians spreads BUTTER on to each, as well as cutting back the *butter*-cups that have grown on the tarmac.

Unfortunately, the butter is starting to dry up in the sun. Something is required to shield it – so they pull out long strips of TIN-FOIL and lay them on the runway and around the wheels. One of the most vain technicians checks his hairstyle in the reflective surface of the foil.

To his horror, he sees that it's covered in bits of TOMATO! He looks up, and sees that tomatoes are pouring out of an open cargo-door in the plane. He covers his head with his hands to protect himself, and shouts to his supervisor: 'Tom . . .!'

In this example, the plane – **2** – remains at the centre of the whole scene. It was spread with BUTTER, wrapped in

TIN-FOIL, then leaked TOMATOES. The second group of three items is locked in the memory.

Group 3: Sugar, Garlic, Jam

As the object for group 3, look down at your SHOE. White powder is pouring out from the lace-holes and seeping through cracks in the sole. Taste a little on your finger; it's SUGAR. More and more sugar pours out, and soon you find it difficult to walk. You have to prop yourself up with a stick – a 'sugar-cane'!

The trail of sugar is attracting birds and animals – most worryingly of all, a number of bats. In case these are Vampire-bats, you take out a bulb of GARLIC and wear bits of it on a necklace.

As you keep walking, the garlic has two main effects. The bats are kept away, but so are all the people you meet! They rush to escape the smell, squeezing through doorways and narrow roads and causing a huge JAM. This gives you an idea. When you get home, you use all your sugar to make pot after pot of sweet, sticky jam.

Group 4: Lettuce, Soap, Ham

The TABLE – 4 – in your hallway is usually full of *letters*, but today it's covered in *lettuce*-leaves. They've started to go mouldy, and the smell is terrible.

You decide to wash them all with a large bar of SOAP. The job will take hours; you set up a TV set nearby so that you can watch your favourite *soap*-opera.

The acting is really HAM-my. Those actors ought to be asHAMed of themselves! They seem as wooden as your hall table . . .

Group 5: Salt, Chocolate, Tea

Begin this final group with the image of a HOOK – 5. As the punishment for a terrible crime, your frustrating job is to move a huge pile of SALT – using just a tiny hook! You can only balance two or three grains of salt on its edge at once, and the whole task will take years. At least it might teach you not to commit as-*sault* again . . .

If only the hook was bigger, the job would be so much easier.

You have a bar of CHOCOLATE in your pocket, so you melt it in the sun, and mould it into a shovel-shape. When the chocolate is set, you start using this instead. Instead of just a couple of grains, this time each shovel-full is *choc*-a-bloc with salt!

Soon the job is finished, and your reward is the traditional end-of-work cup of TEA. Your punishment is over, and you can start living the good life again. You grab a handful of *tees* and go off to play golf.

When you hit the ball into a bunker, the bad memories come flooding back; the sand has been replaced by fine, powdery *salt*, and the ball is stuck fast – thanks to your terrible *hook*-shot!

As always, the three items have been linked, in order, to the number of their group. Think of 5, and you remember the HOOK, the SALT, the CHOCOLATE and the TEA.

As well as recalling each group of three items – the fourth group, the second group, and so on – it's possible to pinpoint individual items within the list. Whichever number item you want to find, simply divide it by 3. If it divides exactly, then recall the group with the same initial number as your answer; the item you want is the *last* one of the three.

To find item nine, for example, dividing 9 by 3 leaves you with 3 – an exact division. The ninth item must be the final one in 'group' three – JAM.

If the sum doesn't work exactly, you finish with two numbers – the nearest division, and a 'remainder'. The number 13, for example, divides by 3 *four* times, with a remainder of 1; 8 divides by 3 *two* times, with a remainder of 2.

To locate the item, recall the *next* group of three after your answer. If the remainder was 1, the item you're looking for is the first of the three, and a remainder of 2 points to the second. The thirteenth item, for example, is in the fifth group, and, since the remainder was 1, it must be the *first* of the three SALT. The eighth item is in the third group; the remainder was two, so the *second* item of the three is your target: GARLIC.

As often happens, this sounds much more complex than it really is. A few minutes practice will allow you to locate any item in the list in seconds. If you're using groups of four, obviously you *divide* by four rather than three; groups of ten mean that you *divide* by ten. The larger the list, the more useful this 'pinpointing' technique, and as long as the connections are strong and all the rules of *Mindpower* observed, this system can be used to remember as many items as you need.

Test Yourself
The best way to learn the technique is to put it to use.

Printed below are fifteen more items, this time taken from an inventory for a rented house. Create images and reminders, connect them to the numbers – as before, three to each number from one to five – then test your knowledge from the original list.

When you've learned them all, the items are at your disposal. You can read through them all in order, or you can perform a quick calculation to locate any numbered item. The information has been learned perfectly, and *numbers* have helped you to put yourself in control.

1. FRIDGE,   2. TELEVISION,   3. HEATER,
4. BOOKCASE,   5. RUG,   6. TOASTER,
7. BED,   8. WARDROBE,   9. KETTLE,
10. TELEPHONE,   11. BLANKET,
12. RADIO,   13. BIN,   14. BARBECUE,
15. VACUUM-CLEANER

Rather than being difficult and confusing, numbers are *useful*. They can help you remember other information, especially if you need to know it item by item, and can be made into 'hooks' for the memory.

Rather than being separate from everyday life, numbers are everywhere: in dialling codes, in dates, in times . . . Numbers are invaluable parts of an organised lifestyle, and the ability to learn them is of great use.

Rather than being impossible to remember, numbers are, in fact, perfectly suited to the *Mindpower System*. By learning to bring them to life, to mould them into connections, scenes and stories, you can remember *any* number that might be useful for you.

Spend a little time developing a basic number system, practise the techniques and applications, and numbers will never frighten you again.

PART FOUR

MINDPOWER FOR LIFE

Having a powerful memory means having the ability to remember anything you need.

The right approach is crucial; the *Mindpower System* gives you a range of techniques, and then it's up to you to choose the best one for a particular type of information.

Part One explained the basic principles of memory, demonstrating the need to work *with* your mind and to take control of the material you have to learn. It described ways to turn abstract ideas into memorable pictures, to connect them together into stories, and to create your own re-usable memory 'routes'.

Part Two concentrated on words. It outlined ways to manipulate letters and sounds, to bring them to life and to connect them together in pairs, groups, lists. Words were shown to be useful tools in themselves, allowing you to simplify longer texts and to use key words as the memory's 'hooks'.

The same is true for numbers. Part Three demonstrated ways to learn them individually and in lists, as well as showing you how to release their potential and to make them the *foundations* for memory. Just as key words can help you memorise an essay, so key numbers can be used to remember huge lists of items – objects, facts, ideas.

The aim of Part Four is to emphasise the importance of combining all the tools at your disposal. By learning how to approach information, deciding how it needs to be recalled and finding the most efficient ways to learn it, you become confident in your ability to remember *anything*. You can learn essays containing numbers and names; speeches with sales-figures and jokes; plays, codes, poems, recipes. You can combine the systems for numbers and words, mix sequences with lists, stories with routes, words with pictures.

Part Four explains new practical uses for the *Mindpower System*, giving specific techniques and suggestions, but at the same time promoting the most important skill of all: the ability to use your memory for your own personal needs. Mindpower helps you to see every opportunity in your own life of benefiting from memory, and to design, combine, and *use* the most successful techniques.

These techniques are often most useful when they provide a 'stepping-stone' to knowledge. In daily life, information is often presented to you in a very haphazard way – no precise, ordered list or table, but instead a mixture of elements: pictures, words, numbers. Among the mass of material are the key elements that you need to know, and the *Mindpower System* can give you the vital hooks you need to hold on to them – as well as the *time* you need to learn them for good.

When information is haphazard – a name here, a telephone number there, an appointment, a joke – it's important to be prepared. A trusted stock of techniques allows you to use memory to its full potential, and to give yourself as much help as possible with the material you're given.

WHAT'S IN A NAME?

Perhaps the best example of this sort of information – and of the uses of *Mindpower* – is the whole area of names.

Picture the scene: you're at a crowded party or meeting, and the host introduces you to a group of people. 'This is Andy . . . this is Mr Chapman, he's head of the Physics Department . . . that's Mark over there, the guitarist . . . this is Conrad, the one in television . . . and have you met Rebecca Goodman . . .?'

In just a few seconds, you're presented with a mass of varied information: names, jobs, faces. You're busy shaking hands and introducing yourself, and the temptation is to let it all wash over you.

Be honest: how often are you told someone's name, and then forget it within five seconds?

On one hand, you're not *expected* to remember it. The host has rattled through the introductions, jumbling all the information and ideas – and the people themselves will assume that you've forgotten their names anyway.

But on the other hand, how useful it would be to recall all the key points. You could approach people without the embarrassment of not remembering who they are, and you'd know how to contact them if you wanted to see them again.

Perhaps best of all, you could avoid all those terrible moments when you've been talking to someone for a while, and then have to introduce them to somebody else – just as you realise that you can't remember their name . . .

People may not expect you to remember them, but they appreciate it when you do. A good memory for names and faces is a useful social skill, as well as a powerful business tool.

It begins, like so many memory techniques, when you learn to make things easier for yourself. Before the specific steps come into play, there are some basic, practical tips that pave the way for memory.

1: *Hear* the Name

When you forget someone's name after five seconds, it's usually because you haven't heard it in the first place. This is a skill that comes with practice. As you hear a name, make a point of repeating it silently to yourself, ensuring that you *listen* to what you'll have to remember later on.

2: Slow Down the Introduction

As in the 'party' example above, introductions tend to be haphazard and fast. Gone are the days when a guest's name was announced to the room as he or she walked through the door, or the butler brought in a calling-card! Names today seem to be fired at you like bullets from a gun: 'Jonathan, this is Claire, Duncan, Fiona, Graham, Peter . . .'

The trick is to slow them down. If the names are too fast to cope with, simply ask the host to pause a moment. Rather than offending anyone, this approach proves your interest, stressing that you want to know who these people are.

3. Be Interested in Names

If you hear an unusual name, make a point of asking about it – what it means, where it comes from, how it's spelt. As well as giving you valuable time to concentrate on the name, this step presents you with extra material for later stages in the memory process.

If a girl called Leticia told you her name meant 'happiness', for example, or a guest explained that the Richmond family came originally from the Yorkshire Dales, you would immediately have a stock of images to build on. As with all forms of information, the memory takes hold when otherwise empty, abstract words are brought to life.

4. Repeat the Name

You're much more likely to remember a name if you've used it. In every 'first' conversation, make an effort to include the person's name – especially when you say goodbye. As well as impressing *them*, proving that you've been interested enough to remember who they are, it emphasises their name to you, and makes recalling it later much more easy.

You hear most new names in situations where there's little time to think. You're introduced to someone, then immediately you're shaking hands and talking. The trick is to use just a couple of seconds to form a 'hook' that will still be there when you *do* have time for memory.

Later, you can use the short-term hooks to remember the new names, decide which ones you could benefit from knowing, then fix them into your memory for good. In some cases, the initial 'hooks' will be all you need, allowing you to remember for a while names that you can happily forget as soon as the party or meeting is over. But in others, the names need to stay with you for longer. By using the hooks to build on, you can create long-term pictures and connections, fixing the names and faces into your own mental file.

To form the 'hooks', use everything available – associations that come to mind, images suggested. As always, pictures are the key. The aim is to create a connection between the person and their name, and the more visual this connection, the better.

The most effective method is to build up a link in stages. The first time you hear a name, all you have to go on is a pair of words and their owner's appearance. The easiest way to begin is by imagining that it isn't them at all!

When you hear their first name, immediately picture someone else with the *same* name. This can sometimes be done with surnames, too, if you've heard them before; but you should always have a 'substitute' person for a Christian name. It could be another friend, a celebrity, a fictional character – even a member of your own family.

For a second or two, imagine you're talking to this 'substitute', and suggest to yourself why they might be here, why they might have come to this part of the room, why they might be wearing these clothes . . .

As you look at the real person in front of you, notice similarities and differences between them and their namesake. If you met a man called Robin, you might have substituted Robin Hood – so look for bits of green on his clothes. Ask yourself some questions. Would that shirt be good camouflage? Would those shoes last long in Sherwood Forest?

Perhaps you can find strong connections; if not, at least suggestions for ways to *make* them. For a new acquaintance called David, you might substitute the *Biblical* David, complete with slingshot and stones. So, does anything on this David's person look like a weapon? Perhaps that neck-chain could be used to hurl pebbles, or the wire in those glasses straightened out to form a sling?

You meet a lady called Delia, and you think immediately of the cook Delia *Smith*. The white dots on her blouse might be flour stains, and her skirt is the same colour as melted chocolate! Of course, she'll have to tie back that long hair before she starts to work . . .

As you learn more about the real person, you can add new details to the picture. David turns out to be a doctor – very handy for when he's knocked people to the ground with his stones! Delia is really a shop-manager. Imagine the pots and pans strewn around her shop, but think of all the wonderful food she brings to the coffee-break . . .

The more information you learn, the more detailed and accurate your picture becomes. A name is always the foundation; the extra details reinforce it, but also *use* it as the hook on which to hang.

The beauty of this technique is that you can strengthen the memory as time allows. As you talk, the first few connections are made; but later, if this is a name to learn for the future, enough new links can be made to hold on to it for ever.

It makes sense to use the same technique for surnames whenever you can. If you're lucky, the name will already suggest images and ideas.

As far as the memory is concerned, there are six main 'types' of surname.

1. Famous Names

If you met John Clinton or Joan Thatcher, Fred Presley or Susan Monroe, you'd be presented with a clear 'substitute' picture. If the surname is all you have – Mr Eastwood, Mrs Streisand – then the technique is exactly the same as for Christian names. Open up the store of ideas contained in the name, and build up connections between the real person and their substitute.

Imagine Mr Eastwood pulling out his gun. Where does he keep it? In that briefcase? Those boots are ideally suited to horse-riding . . .

The brooch Mrs Streisand is wearing looks a little like a microphone, so perhaps she'll start singing in a moment. If she does, she'll probably give you that handbag to hold. She turns out to be a keen sailor. Maybe the song she'll sing is 'Sailing', or 'On The Good Ship Lollipop' . . .

If, on the other hand, you're presented with a first name as well, the trick is to combine two sets of images. An easy method is to create a 'substitute' person for the first name, and then to see them carrying out the main action suggested by the second, famous name. The more bizarre the combination the better!

Below are five examples of 'party guests' followed by suggestions for possible substitutes and combinations.

SCOTT SHAKESPEARE
ELIZABETH MacDONALD
ARNOLD CHURCHILL
JENNY HOUSTON
ROGER GASCOIGNE

Scott Shakespeare

The first name here, Scott, might suggest the explorer Scott of the Antarctic. As always, look for connections with *this* person's appearance. Perhaps he has snowy white hair, or is wearing a thick winter jumper. The best connections involve links with both facial features and clothes; what he looks like today will help you to form the initial hooks, giving you time later to build stronger connections with his more permanent appearance.

The famous surname here, Shakespeare, suggests an obvious pair of actions: writing and acting. As you continue talking, imagine how you'd feel if he suddenly started speaking in rhyming couplets! He might perform a melodramatic play about his Antarctic experiences, using a sledge and a husky-dog as props . . .

A combined picture like this reminds you of both parts of the name. If you had to remember Scott Shakespeare for a long time, it would be worthwhile adding extra details as you found out more real information about him: his job, his hobbies . . . The importance of the initial 'hooks' is that they allow you to start using the name from memory, as well as giving you the time you need to fix it in your mind.

Elizabeth MacDonald

A good substitute for *Elizabeth* would be Queen Elizabeth. Once again, include as many emotional reactions as possible. After all, you remember the times when you were embarrassed at parties or jubilant in meetings, so it's only sensible to make *use* of emotional responses when you want to remember names.

How would you feel if you were introduced to the Queen? What tell-tale signs are there that this person really *is* the Queen? Perhaps those gold earrings are bits of an old crown. This lady is a dentist by profession, so picture her seating patients on a reclining *throne*, and refusing to fit anything but *gold* fillings!

The surname here, MacDonald, is famous through its link with the fast-food chain. To combine it with your Christian-name picture, why not imagine Queen Elizabeth's reaction to being served cheeseburgers at an official banquet. In her golden dentist's surgery, she might criticise people for having too many sweet milk-shakes, or give children French-fries as a reward for clean teeth. Put the technique into practice as soon as possible. Use Elizabeth's first name in the conversation a few times, then repeat the whole name to yourself when she leaves. The imaginative, visual reminders are an important stepping-stone to *using* the name and developing an instinctive knowledge of it, as well as a handy safety-net for the times when your mind goes blank.

Arnold Churchill

Arnold could become Arnold *Schwarzenegger*. Compare his famous appearance with *this* Arnold, once again looking for differences and similarities. Perhaps he's a teacher – no doubt with a very subdued class! Presumably he lifts weights at break-time. He must have grown that moustache for a new role . . .

The Churchill name suggests cigars and victory-V-signs. Picture Arnold Schwarzenegger leading his schoolchildren on a march around the playground, smoking a cigar and giving the victory sign to waiting photographers. Combine as many elements as possible from the three sources: the 'substitute' first name, the action suggestions of the second, and the *real* details of Arnold Churchill – his appearance, as well as his character and job. Practise recalling his name a few times from the pictures you've drawn, and it can be fixed in your memory for good.

Jenny Houston

The 'substitute' you choose for Jenny might be a good friend or family member with the same name. Would you be pleased to see her at this party? What are the similarities and differences between *that* Jenny and this one? The Jenny you know might be a painter. Look at *this* Jenny's clothes and imagine seeing wet paint all over them. Perhaps that beauty-spot is really a dot of black paint . . .

Whitney Houston is a famous singer and dancer. What sort of dance would *this* Ms. Houston perform, and what song might she sing? 'True Colours?' 'A Whiter Shade of Pale?' Perhaps she performs a medley of Whitney Houston hits, painting a picture to go with each one.

As you add more and more elements and connections, the

images may seem increasingly crowded and jumbled. But they all have a role to play; by using the reminders, putting the techniques into action and saying the name, you'll confirm for yourself the picture's key elements, and turn it into a powerful tool.

Roger Gascoigne

This name suggests a pair of sporting connections. 'Roger' could become Roger *Bannister*, the famous athlete; and 'Gascoigne' transforms into England footballer *Paul* Gascoigne. When you learn that Roger Gascoigne is a potter, you have all the elements you need to create a memorable picture.

Link him to Roger Bannister by imagining him stripped down to his shorts and vest and sprinting round the room. How would the other party-goers respond? Is there anything in his appearance to suggest that he's already a keen runner? Perhaps those shoes are a little heavy, but his bald head is certainly streamlined!

On his run, he starts to kick anything in sight: chairs, tables – even people. As you look at him, think what position he might fill in a football team. Not a goalkeeper, because of the glasses, but he's left-handed and might make a good left-winger . . .

The violence of his running and kicking has left valuable ornaments lying broken on the carpet, but he mends them quickly on his potters wheel. He also makes models of two famous sportsmen . . .

At a party you may only have time to form the most basic links – to visualise the running-vest or to hear Paul Gascoigne's Geordie accent – yet even these can be enough to give your memory the hooks it needs. More detail can be added later, but only if you've taken the vital step of turning an abstract name into a memorable, moving picture.

Imagine you're back at the same party or meeting a year later, and meet three of the same people.

The first man you see has snowy-white hair and a long nose like a ski-jump. You're reminded of the Antarctic, recall that his name is Scott, and feel a larger picture coming back.

He's using a sledge and a dog . . . as props for a Shakespearean play! His melodramatic speech is all about his explorations. This is *Scott Shakespeare*. The seconds you spent at the party a year ago forming connections – along with a few minutes invested in practising the technique later that same evening – have paid off.

Standing next to him is a lady you seem to recognise. You remember comparing her face to . . . the picture on a coin. This lady is called Elizabeth, like the Queen.

Once again, a more detailed picture forms in your mind. A gold filling . . . a throne-like dentist's chair. She must be a dentist by profession – but why, in your picture, is she handing out cheeseburgers? Of course – this is Elizabeth *MacDonald*.

The third familiar person you meet has a bald head, and you remember thinking how streamlined it would be for running. You recall something about his shoes, a picture starts to form of him stripping down to his vest, and soon you can remember all the key points.

First of all he was a runner – *Roger* (Bannister) – and then a footballer (Paul) *Gascoigne*. You even remember to ask him about his pottery . . .

2: Familiar Names

Many of the surnames you hear are the same as those of friends, colleagues and family members. These can be used in the same way as famous names, as long as the pictures they suggest are strong and clear.

When you're faced with a familiar name, decide on a theme to represent it, based on the job or hobby of the person you already know. If you were introduced to a Mr Young, for example, you might think instantly of a friend of yours called Young, and concentrate on his hobby. He's a talented guitarist, so guitar-playing becomes the 'theme', ready to be built into the picture you create for your new acquaintance.

With familiar names, the trick is to make use of associations that already exist. When you've thought of someone else with the same name, highlight the most unusual and memorable aspect of their character.

You're introduced to a Mrs Powell, and you think instantly of a colleague with the same name. Perhaps this colleague has an office job and is quite interested in sport, but neither points would be strong enough for a memorable picture.

But maybe the 'Powell' you know lives in a converted

windmill, drives a unique vintage car, or has the most powerful laugh you've ever heard! *These* are the sorts of images and ideas that let you create distinctive, memorable scenes.

3: Professions and Titles

At one time in history it must have been very easy to remember names. In your village, the man who cooked the bread, and whose family had done so through several generations, was called Baker. The man who provided him with his main ingredients was called Miller, and the wood-working family were the Carpenters. There were obvious connections between a person's profession and his name, and his appearance, tools and work-room provided you with all the clues you'd need.

Times change, but there are still plenty of people with jobs and professions for surnames – Butcher, Cook, Barber – as well as titles: 'Lord', 'Bishop', 'King'. They probably don't wear the appropriate clothes any more, or carry the expected tools – until, that is, you use your imagination.

Below are examples of ways to connect three people with the meanings of their names.

Baker

In the first few seconds after you've heard this name, imagine how you'd feel if your new acquaintance handed you a newly baked loaf of bread! Just a moment's thought like this can be enough to remind you of the name when you come to learn it properly later on.

As you have more time, look for evidence of baking in the person's appearance – flowery-white hair . . . a flat nose, like dough flattened under a rolling-pin . . . wire spectacle-frames that might be used as pastry-cutters . . .

Build up connections with the person's Christian name. If his name is John, you might substitute John Major, and create a picture based on the Prime Minister and parliament. John Baker's hair is fittingly grey . . . he has bright, Conservative-blue eyes . . . he has an earring, a small hoop, which you compare to the handle on the door of Number Ten.

Now you can combine this picture with the baking theme.

Perhaps the earring is really a piece of hardened dough! Imagine an intruder eating through the wholemeal door on

Downing Street. Perhaps John Major tries to win a debate by handing out freshly baked scones . . .

Mix all the images and ideas together; the more 'hooks' you have the better, and the stronger they'll be if they all intertwine. You can be more precise later on, practising and reinforcing the images if you need to know them for the future. For now, the stock of images will be more than enough to see you through the meeting.

Bishop
When you're introduced to Miss Bishop, you instantly imagine a Bishop's mitre dropping down from the ceiling and landing perfectly on her head. Look at her hairstyle: would the mitre fit, or would it tumble to the ground? Look at her face and listen to her voice, and ask yourself whether she suits her name? Perhaps her teeth are crooked, reminding you of the Bishop's *crook*. If she seems small, it may be because she's kneeling . . . Begin with a simple link, then add more and more detail as time allows.

Cooper
It's worth reminding yourself of some of the more unusual 'professional' names. For example, a *chandler* makes candles and ships' supplies, a *farrier* shoes horses, and a *cooper* makes barrels.

Picture Mr Cooper talking to you from inside his barrel, or with bits of curved wood hanging from his glasses, his long nose, a broken tooth . . . Perhaps he's barrel-shaped himself, or wears a bracelet like the metal hoops on a barrel. Combine specific elements of his appearance with the more general barrel-making ideas, and the mixture of pictures will help you remember him when you meet him again.

4: Place-names
This section includes another large percentage of names – those connected with towns, cities and countries. Like job-names, these tend to confuse us today rather than remind us of their owners – until the imagination comes into effect again, and new connections are built.

As always, the key step involves finding a picture to replace an abstract idea. Many place-names will already suggest strong associations for you, and a particular area, building, or even character will come to mind.

Other place-names need to be made specific. Unless you lived there, or had visited often, the town Scarborough, as a surname, might suggest beaches, fishing boats and the sea. These could be the basis for your imagery – Mrs Scarborough might be pictured up to her neck in the cold North Sea, or her starry earrings compared with starfish – but a *definite* reminder of this particular resort would also be required.

Concentrate on some mark, scratch or *scar* on her face. Perhaps something she's wearing is *scar*let; picture her wrapping herself in a *scar*f, or trying to '*scar*per'! Combined with the general imagery, this sort of specific prompt will confirm the precise word you need to recall, and clarify any confusion.

A place-name can be a powerful aid to memory – just as soon as you take it fully under your control.

5: Objects and Animals

Names which are also *things* are among the easiest to remember. The imagery is already there. What you have to do is add definition and clarity, and connect it with the rest of the information: Christian name, face, background. As with place-names, objects need to be specified, so that you never call Mr Stone 'Mr *Brick*', or Mrs Fox 'Mrs *Wolf*'!

Imagine you're at a business reception and you meet Margaret Bull. For her first name you might substitute Margaret *Thatcher*, imagining what effect her sudden appearance might have on the room and thinking about what you would want to say. Perhaps her voice is very different from the lady in front of you; on the other hand, Margaret Bull might have *blue*-framed glasses, and an untidy *thatch* of hair.

Look at her nose: imagine there was a ring through it. What would happen if this woman started snorting, scraping her feet on the floor, then charging around the room and goring the other guests? Check your own clothing for anything red . . .

The snorting and the wild movement are quite general ideas, but the animal in question is made specific by your nervousness about the colour red.

Once again the images are intertwined. In just one scene you combine suggestions about her Christian name, elements of her appearance, ideas about her voice and character, and images specifying her surname.

Enough of the picture can be created as you talk to allow the rest of it to be created later. Even the most basic *Mindpower* techniques are a vital way of buying the time you need.

6: All the Rest!
When a name has no obvious associations or meanings, its appearance and sound need to be worked on until it does.

Bring into play all the techniques described in Part Two – all the ways of bringing words to life and of finding 'hooks' already present. Use puns; pick out individual syllables to make new words; imagine what a name *could* mean, then build up pictures based on your imaginative ideas. As soon as the images emerge, they can be connected with the person in front of you – their first name, their appearance and their character.

Printed below are seven surnames, followed by suggestions of how to give them shape and colour, how to bring them to life.

TREWIN, WEBBER, BATES, GOLDING, LATIMER, PRESTON, CURTIS

Names to be remembered are more likely to be heard than read, so concentrate on their *sound*. Somtimes you may have to resort to manipulating their spelling and construction, but sound and pronunciation always allow you much more room for manoeuvre.

Highlight the main elements of the name, then use these to suggest the images and themes. The beauty of a name is that, by remembering just one key syllable, the whole thing can be helped to fall into place.

Suggestions

Trewin
Sometimes, as you say a word to yourself, new meanings suggest themselves. TREWIN could be split into two words: 'TRUE WIN'.

Imagine arguing with Mr Trewin. He's holding a trophy, and claiming to have won it fairly – a 'true win'. You don't believe him, and the shouting match goes on.

You could connect this with the real Mr Trewin by imagining what sport or game he might be good at, or which one it would be impossible for him to win. Perhaps the gold trophy you *imagine* has the same shine as the gold-framed glasses or gold filling that you can *see*.

Now that the pictures and links are being formed, you can connect them with any other useful information, and build up a memorable scene as you intertwine them with new details and prompts.

When you met this man again, you would see the gold, recall the physical appraisal you made, remember the fierce argument, and return to the name: TREWIN.

Webber

As you take control of names and language, you're able to invent new words. You'll remember them again, just as long as there's some sort of logic to your invention.

Perhaps a WEBBER is someone who makes *webs*. As you shake Ms. Webber's hand, imagine what would happen if your fingers were stuck together with white, sticky strands. Picture her demonstrating her trade, building a web and engulfing the whole room! If you look closely, the corners of her wispy hair have been woven together – they've even trapped a fly . . .

Bates

A name like this shows the importance of concentrating on *sounds*. When you ignore the spelling, Ms. Bates can become Ms. *Baits* – complete with worms wriggling out of her pocket, or even dangling from her nose!

As soon as a memorable theme has been created, links with all the other information are easy to make. The more striking a picture, the faster it will take hold in your memory, and the less work you'll have to do to fix it there for good.

Golding

There are two strong possibilities here. One would be to invent another word – a verb, this time: '*golding*'. You could picture

Mr Golding interrupting the conversation to start panning for gold, or to examine the gold jewellery he's wearing.

The other, still on the theme of gold, is make use of '*gold ingots*'. Imagine talking to him as he climbs out from under a pile of gold blocks, or see him asking the other guests for *their* gold, then melting it all down into ingots. You'll remember that his name isn't 'Mr Goldingots', but your play on words will provide enough of a pointer to his real identity!

Once the new action of 'golding' has become the theme, all the other connections can be made. You would clearly begin by looking for any *real* gold – in his glasses, his clothes, his teeth – and then bring the imagination into play. Perhaps his hair is a golden colour; his nose might be beaked, like a golden eagle.

Hold on to every link, building up the picture as you talk, then spending time strengthening it later on.

Latimer

Whenever you hear a word, try to imagine what it looks like. By seeing the word in your mind, you present yourself with added possibilities. If the sound of a word doesn't suggest anything or spark your imagination, you can look to the name's spelling and construction instead.

Here, the last two syllables give you a real word: TIMER. Perhaps an 'L.A. TIMER' measures the speed of joggers in Los Angeles! Imagine Mr Latimer showing you his new American watch, or timing the pace of famous Hollywood stars as they walk into the room. Look closely at his face; perhaps *he* is a movie star? Who does he look like? What might *his* time be to run around the room?

By recalling and using his name a few times from memory, and by putting these images into practice, you'd stand a good chance of remembering Mr Latimer the next time you met.

Preston

When you meet someone new, a couple of seconds spent thinking up the easiest way to remember their name is an excellent investment.

A simple way to remember Mrs Preston would be to change her name to 'PRESSED ON'! Imagine her shaking your hand and pressing it tightly on to hers. Perhaps she surprises you by pressing you down on to the floor! As you look at her face and clothes, which bits might have been pressed on just for tonight? Are her eyelashes false? What about her hair? Picture yourself reaching over and finding out . . .

Curtis

If necessary, a name can be considered in terms of both spelling and sound.

Imagine Miss Curtis being rude and abrupt – she's the definition of what *'curt'* *is*! 'Curt', the key syllable here, also suggests 'shortness', so notice everything that's 'short' in her appearance; her hair, her nose, her earrings, her skirt . . .

Perhaps her clothes have been made out of old *curt*ains? By backing up the general theme with specific reminders, you'll insure that there's never any confusion. A larger picture can be built up, bringing in her first name, job, hobbies – but the key syllable is always at the centre. When you meet her again, you remember the rudeness, notice again her short hair and even shorter nose, think of the curtains and say, with confidence, 'Miss Curtis, it's good to see you!'

A name may *seem* one of the hardest things to remember but, through *Mindpower*, it can become one of the easiest. Names are full of meanings, associations, places, objects – and even when they appear hard to handle, they can soon be made memorable.

As a summary, printed below are reminders of all the key steps involved in learning a name.

1: *Hear* the name.
   ARTHUR TAYLOR

2: In the next few seconds, concentrate on the first associations that come to mind. For a Christian name, think of someone else with the same name; for a surname, use any hooks already present – places, people, objects, jobs – or manipulate the name until images appear.

ARTHUR: Perhaps *King* Arthur, dressed in armour and seated at his round table.

TAYLOR: A *tailor*.

3: As you talk, build up as many links as possible between the pictures you've created and the person himself. Look at his face in particular, using your imagination to find connections. What is there in this person's appearance to suggest that he *is* a Baker, a Griffin, a Castle, a resident of Hull . . .?

ARTHUR: Imagine him sawing the edges off a nearby table until it's perfectly round. The metal in his spectacles might have been taken from an old suit of armour. He has short arms, so he would have needed a suit specially made. If he wore a crown, the two tufts of his hair would stick out on either side.

TAYLOR: If he was a king *and* a tailor, he could have made his own royal clothes. What might he be wearing under his armour? That chipped tooth might have been caused by holding too many pins in his mouth. Picture him breaking off from conversation to sew up an entire suit of armour and lay it out on the round table . . .

4: When you've connected a person's name with his face, clothes, personality – even position in the room – concentrate on adding extra details. Any new information, such as favourite pastimes, real job or sporting interests can be given its own picture and be linked with the rest. By binding all the pictures together, a single scene will tell you everything you need to know.

Arthur Taylor is a banker. He has to sew up the suit extremely tightly and carefully, to prevent all his coins and notes from pouring out. Imagine him pulling down the visor on his helmet to reveal the dreaded words: 'This Position Closed'!
His favourite pastime is fishing. If he wore his suit of armour when he went to the river, he would keep dry and warm, and could screw his fishing-rod to the metal.

Imagine him clanking noisily as he gets up, and frightening all the fish away. As he stands there talking to you, notice that his hair is as wavy as the water . . .

5: Later, perhaps on the way home from a meeting or the day after a party, practise using all the images you created to recall the new names. Decide which ones you need to know for the future, then spend a few minutes confirming the images in your mind. The *Mindpower* techniques have given you all the time you need to memorise them properly.

Once you know a name, and it exists for you in terms of memorable pictures and scenes, it can become part of a larger memory system. As with the Prime Ministers in Part One, a long list of names – members of a company, say, or representatives on a committee – can be linked together in a story.

If each name had to be given a number, you could connect the images with the key *number*-images from Part Three. In a large company, school or club, members of particular departments could be grouped together in different rooms of a memory 'route', as described in Part One.

Once you know a name, the possibilities are endless. Most people are told a single name, then forget it in seconds. But with a little practice, the *Mindpower System* can be used to hold on to individual names for as long as necessary, to combine them with new pieces of information, and to connect them with other names in ordered files and patterns. Rather than remaining unreliable and embarrassing, the memory can become the most effective and efficient name-file imaginable.

NUMBERS AND WORDS

Combining techniques and systems makes it possible to remember anything. As an example, consider the following information.

Printed below is a series of excerpts from an imaginary list of guidelines. The document they're taken from is about new rules and regulations for teachers. The list, as often happens, is divided into paragraphs and sections, and each separate element has a 'code' – a number and a letter. The ten elements below are all the guidelines that apply to your job.

You've read through the whole document, picked out these ten as being the most important, and summed up each of them in a single word. If you had to be interviewed about the guidelines or give a talk to parents, these headings would remind you of the key areas. And, for reference, you'd need to know the 'codes': '. . . as in paragraph 3c . . . if you'll look at guideline 5d . . .'

SCHOOL GUIDELINES

MAIN AREAS:

Section **1b**: SPORTS	Section **4a**: SCHOOL MEALS
Section **1c**: ARTS	Section **4b**: COMPUTING
Section **3c**: FINANCES	Section **5d**: ASSESSMENTS
Section **3d**: RELIGION	Section **6g**: LANGUAGES
Section **3e**: TRIPS	Section **6l**: SCHOOL BUILDINGS.

Students often have to learn information in a similar way; the facts, and their references within a larger text. Police cadets have to know key points of criminal law, and barristers often need to have specific references to hand. Rather than making things difficult, these mixtures of numbers and letters provide you with clear possibilities for memorable images.

If you've created your own number system, as explained in Part Three, the numbers here present no problem. Each can be changed into one of several pictures, giving them substance, colour and life.

Rather than choosing just *any* images to represent the letters – 'apple' for '**a**', 'boat' for '**b**' – it's important to avoid confusion with your *number* images. It wouldn't be so important with this list, since all the codes here are made up of a single digit and letter – but other lists may involve codes like '**23f**', '**214b**', and it would be easy to confuse a boat-image, say, with number **7** rather than the letter '**b**'. If your picture included an apple, would that represent '**a**' or **8**?

A simple way to avoid this problem is to use images that aren't involved in the number system at all: *animals*. Birds appear in section **2**, and fish in **7**, but *land* animals can be used freely.

In each number-letter pair, make the first 'bit' into either an object, an action or a description from the number system, and turn the second into an animal with the appropriate initial letter. **8d** would split up into **8** – FOOD, EAT or HOT – and '**d**' – perhaps DOG, DINGO or DEER. Your picture could feature a *gravy*-covered deer, someone *eating* a *dingo*, or even a *hot dog*!

Once a striking picture is created, this can be connected with the information from that particular section of the document. By setting all the scenes within an appropriate place – in this case, a school – they can *all* be connected to the original text.

Suggestions

Always use the most obvious animals, and create the most fitting connections. This will allow the memories to work both ways. When you think of a subject, such as sport or catering, you remember the picture that goes with it. And when you see a 'code' – **1b**, **4a** – the appropriate picture, and from that the *code*, springs to mind.

1b: Sports

It's easiest to pick the animal first. For **b** you might choose a BULL – especially useful since it opens up a whole range of images. A powerful image could be created if you turned **1** into RED.

What would happen if you painted a bull bright red? It would go berserk – but it would chase *itself* ! Watch it running around in circles – and think about how to connect this with 'sport'.

The bull chases itself, so the bullfighter is no longer needed. There is no longer any killing, so it's much more of a sport. The crowd still comes to watch and, without bloodshed, the whole affair is more sporting. The matador changes jobs and becomes a footballer instead.

The final step is to set the scene inside the school. Picture the crowds gathering in the sports hall, and see the red bull being led out from a cupboard.

The main image is of a RED – **1** – BULL – **2**. The result of it all is SPORT! **1b** = SPORT.

1c: Art

The obvious animal here is the CAT. In the school art room, imagine setting your class the task of sketching the school cat. Unfortunately they misunderstand you, and start drawing pictures *on* the cat instead, splattering its fur with ink and making it run away in terror . . .

The children DRAW – **1** – the CAT – **c** – in the ART room. **1c** = ART.

3c: Finances
Since you're turning the letters into obvious, familiar animals, it's possible to use the same creatures several times. The number will always be different, so the scene you create will also be unique.

For this section, **3** could become 'sweet-smelling'. Imagine sitting in the school office, investigating the finances. There's hardly any money left. It turns out that most of it has been spent pampering the school cat, buying it the most expensive perfumes. You have no money, but a SWEET-SMELLING – **3** – CAT – **c**! This scene is set amongst all the money, so **3c** = FINANCES.

3d: Religion
Set this scene in the school chapel, and make use of the school DOG. A chapel service is ruined when one of the teachers decides to walk the dog! It's raining outside, so instead of trudging through the puddles, he walks the animal up and down the chapel aisle.

The scene is memorable and clear. He WALKS – **3** – the DOG – **d** – in the CHAPEL. **3d** = RELIGION.

3e: Trips
An ELEPHANT has been hired to take the entire school on a trip around the neighbourhood. It's standing in the foyer, waiting to go – just as soon as someone finds it some big enough shoes . . .

When you've found SHOES – **3** – for the ELEPHANT – **e** – you can go on your TRIP. **3e** = TRIPS.

4a: Catering
You sit down in the school canteen, waiting for your lunch, when something on the chair starts to wriggle! You look down, and see that the whole place is infested with ANTS. Imagine what it

would feel like – and sound like – as all the children run screaming from the room.

You SAT – **4** – on the ANTS – **a** – as you waited for your FOOD. **4a** = CATERING.

4b: Computing
For **b**, use the image of a BULL again, but this time make it a *metal* one.

In the computing room, a robotic steel bull is being made to perform tricks. By typing instructions into a computer, the metal bull can be made to roll on its back or stand on its head. Imagine the creaking noise as its metal joints move back and forth.

Run through the scene to fix it in your mind. In the COMPUTER-room, the performance was being given by a METAL – **4** – BULL – **b**. **4b** = COMPUTING.

5d: Assessments
In one of the classrooms, a large scale assessment is taking place. The children's work is being monitored, and the details recorded by the teacher. The main task being tested today is *dog cleaning*; each child is given a dog, and they have ten minutes to bath and groom it to perfection!

For their ASSESSMENT, the children CLEAN – **5** – DOGS – **d**! **5d** = ASSESSMENTS.

6g: Languages:
To demonstrate the importance of *all* language, the French teacher brings a GORILLA into the classroom. She stresses a comparison: the humans have the power of language, but even a close relative like the gorilla can only play music. She gives the animal a drum, and he beats it enthusiastically, then starts blowing a trumpet. He can make music, but he can't speak.

In the LANGUAGE lesson, the centre of attention was a MUSICAL – **6** – GORILLA – **g**. **6g** = LANGUAGE.

6l: Buildings
For **l**, why not use the king of the animals: the LION. Imagine testing the strength of all your school buildings by pitting them against the roar of ten lions.

You lead the lions from building to building, arrange them into a group, tune them up, then signal with your baton for them to begin. They all roar together, and you act as conductor, keeping them all together and controlling the volume. The walls bulge as the powerful sound grows.

In all the school BUILDINGS you CONDUCT – **6** – the LIONS – **1. 61** = BUILDINGS.

When you've imagined even these simple scenes, the whole list is under your control. You could answer questions about it with ease.

'Do the guidelines cover computing?'

You picture the computing room . . . and see a METAL BULL being controlled by a computer. METAL is **4** . . . BULL is **b**; your answer can be given with confidence.

'Yes, they do. The important section is at **4b** . . .'

The system also works in reverse. For a job interview you might be expected to know the relevant guidelines in detail.

Imagine your interviewer asking: 'Tell us your views about section **3d**'.

The **d** is clearly a DOG – but what about the **3**? One of the main actions in section **3** of the number system is WALK, so can you remember a picture involving walking a dog? The chapel! A teacher ruined the service when he walked the school dog down the aisle.

The subject of guideline **3d** is RELIGION, and you can tell the interviewer all your views about religion in schools.

As with the techniques for learning names, these memory methods are especially useful as stepping-stones, speeding up the whole learning process by giving you hooks and prompts. As you revise a list of points for an interview or exam, you can practise reading out the information from *memory* rather than returning constantly to the printed page. As soon as you start to *use* information from memory, you can repeat it to yourself in odd moments – on walks, in bus-queues – and quickly reach a state of 'instinctive' knowledge.

SPEAKING FROM MEMORY

A list of guidelines like this might form the basis of a talk or presentation. Rather than fumbling with bits of paper, you can step on to the stage confident in the power of your memory. Questions can be answered with clear references, and you can be sure that all the key points will be covered.

Any sort of public speaking can be improved by using the *Mindpower System*. The benefits of being able to talk from memory are immense.

1. Eye-Contact
Rather than looking down at notes, you can maintain eye-contact with your audience, helping to hold their attention and keep their interest alive.

2. Understanding
When you *read* a speech, it's all too easy to speak the words without thinking about what they mean. If you give the talk from memory, on the other hand, you use image-prompts to remind you of all the key points, and are constantly thinking about the meaning and importance of each section of the speech.

3. Naturalness
It's much easier to listen to a speech that sounds natural and alive. By talking from memory, you remember the sections and key points of your speech, and speak *about* them, rather than reading set words on a page.

4. Additions
Since your speech is less rigid, it's possible to change ideas at the last minute, or make additions during the speech itself. You can absorb suggestions from the audience and adapt your speech as you go along, rather than finding yourself stuck with a printed talk that's already out of date!

5. Judging the Time
The system for learning speeches involves the 'routes' described in Part One.

When you're on a familiar walk, you have no problem judging how long it's going to take you to finish. You know when you're half-way, and you can quickly visualise the pathways you still have to travel.

Similarly, when your speech is based on a route, it's easy to judge how far through you are, and how much more there is to go. In an instant you can see the main points still to be raised, and speed up or slow down as necessary.

6. Confidence

For most people, public speaking of any sort is a nerve-racking experience. They fidget with their notes, and fumble with the pages, nervously glancing at their audience from time to time.

By talking from memory, on the other hand, you can be confident that all the information is in your head. You can't loose *these* notes or drop them all over the stage.

You can look at your audience throughout, confident of impressing them not only by *what* you say, but also by the skill and efficiency with which you say it.

The first step is to compose your speech. Rather than writing out every word, write down a list of all the key points, constructing them into the best order and adding new words as ideas arise. Since you're only making notes, it's easy to change the order or delete whole sections as you mould your thoughts into a coherent speech.

Use these key points as a framework. When the bones of the speech have been composed, add references, numbers, quotations, jokes. Any sort of information can be included in the presentation, and it can go in at any time.

The next step is to divide the speech into sections. Ten sections is the ideal number, but it can easily be more or less. Each section should be a 'point' or 'theme'; draw lines on your speech-plan to mark where one ends and the next begins.

Give each section a title. Choose words that will remind you of everything you want to say on this particular theme. If there are any subheadings, write them underneath.

Next, complete the written plan by adding the 'facts' – numbers, dates, references and so on – into the appropriate sections, and giving the whole speech a title.

When these steps have been completed, your plan should look something like this:

EFFICIENCY IN THE WORKPLACE

INTRODUCE MYSELF
FINANCIAL FACTS
- £5,000 spent on PAPER
- £9,000 spent on TELEPHONE CALLS
- £17,000 wasted through ILLNESS

TARGETS
- REDUCE SPENDING by £20,000
- TARGET DATE: 2 November 1996

TRAINING

INCENTIVES
- POSSIBLE PAY-RISES of £3,000

PRACTICAL MEASURES
- NEW PHONE SYSTEM
- CENTRAL STORE for PAPER
- RECYCLING

REST of COMPANY

FURTHER PLANS

ANY QUESTIONS?

This is the plan for an imaginary departmental talk on efficiency, to be given by a consultant. There are nine main sections, some of which include subheadings and specific pieces of information, such as numbers and dates. If he gave a similar talk to other companies or departments, he might keep the same main plan, but change the numbers accordingly.

To commit the plan to memory, use one of your memory 'routes'. The nine sections of this talk will fit comfortably within the ten spaces of the route, and you could even give the 'extra' space to the title. If the talk was longer, you would simply spread it over two or more routes.

Each of the sections has its own room or areas. As an example, imagine you were using the 'house' route described in Part One.

'Efficiency in the workplace': Path

The first 'element' in the plan, the title, is fitted into the first space on the route: the path outside the house. Create a picture to bring the words to life.

Set up a desk in the middle of the path, and lay down a carpet. You've created a workspace, but how could it be made more efficient? You're already saving on lighting bills by sitting outside, but the wind is blowing your papers around and you're wasting time and energy picking them up. By holding them down with stones from the path you can keep them in place.

Continue making alterations to the scene until your workplace is the model of efficiency, open for all to see.

Introduce myself: Front Porch

Since the central concept here is *you*, make the front porch *your* room. Pin up a huge poster of yourself on the door, and write facts about yourself all around the walls.

There's a special safe built into the wall here, containing all your important documents and details.

Financial facts: Hallway

The hallway has the longest piece of carpet in the whole house. Imagine it's been designed to look like a paper till-roll, complete with a long list of printed prices.

The till-roll carpet is split into three clear sections. The first one is covered in bits of paper, blowing around in the draughts from the door. They seem to have spilled out of a vacuum-cleaner that's lying nearby.

Concentrate on the VACUUM-CLEANER – 5. The images in this first section remind you that PAPER has cost '5'. All the figures in this speech are in thousands, so the price here is £5,000.

In the second section sits an old-fashioned telephone. When you lift the receiver, you're put straight through to the OPERA-TOR – 9. This simple combination of images reminds you that PHONE CALLS have cost the company £9,000.

The last of the three sections of carpet is covered in puddles, and a bright red toy boat bobs around in the water. As you look closer you see that the model people onboard look terribly sea-sick. And the movement of the boat even begins to affect *you*!

The theme here is ILLNESS, and the RED – **1** – BOAT – **7** – tells you that the cost to the company has been £**17,000**.

Before moving on, spend a few seconds looking back over this scene. The main image is clear – a long till-roll, full of prices, spreading forwards like a carpet. This section of the speech is about FINANCIAL FACTS, and the rest of the information, the specific details of costs, is contained within the three sections of the carpet.

Targets: Kitchen

The kitchen is full of *shooting*-targets. They're balanced on the cooker, stuck to the fridge, pinned to the walls. You decide to do some target practice, and choose two of them to aim at – one on the left of the room, and one on the right.

You THROW – **2** – a BALL – **0** – at the one on the left, and hit the bullseye. The whole target explodes, sending money showering across the kitchen – as the images suggest, £**20,000**!

When you inspect the target on the right, you see that the bullseye is, in fact, a little door. You throw a pan at it, and it opens . . .

The odd thing is that it doesn't make a sound. It could be that the door is well-oiled. But, on the other hand, perhaps there's something wrong with *you*? You start to worry about your hearing . . .

The key points of this scene give you the figures of a date. You THREW – **2** – a PAN – **8** – at the DOOR – **11**, then WORRIED – **9** – about your HEARING – **6**. The 'TARGET DATE' is 28.11.96. – 28 November 1996. Write this date on the target before moving on.

Training: Utility Area

As expected, this area of the route is full of washing-machines and tumble-dryers. But these appliances are a little out of the ordinary, since they all double up as pieces of *training* equipment. One of the washing-machines has had an exercise-bike nailed to the side. The tumble-dryers have been made into weight-lifting benches. A huge sign on the roof says: TRAINING.

Incentives: Dining-Room

Several people are sitting here, eating their dinner. For each of them, dinner consists of a single carrot, dangling in front of them on a stick. They reach further and further forward as a voice shouts out encouragement, urging them on with a whole range of incentives – the main one seeming to be the promise of new *shoes*. The diners look longingly at the SHOES – **3** – held up for them to see. The real INCENTIVE to be remembered here is £**3,000**.

Practical Measures: Lounge

This is another room that needs to be split up into sub-sections. First, set up the larger theme by fixing rulers, tape-measures and other practical measuring-tools on to the walls and ceiling. Then practise measuring out the area of the room. Lastly, concentrate on the furniture.

The suite here consists of an armchair and a two-seater sofa. When you sit in the armchair, you feel a lump – and find that a tiny telephone, the latest on the market, has slipped behind the cushion.

On the sofa, the very centre of the first seat holds a neat pile of paper, each sheet marked 'Central Stores'.

The other seat is available, but very dirty – covered with tyre-marks, as though someone has cycled across it again and again.

The three parts of the furniture give you the details of the 'practical measures': NEW TELEPHONES . . . CENTRAL STORE for PAPER . . . RE-CYCLING!

Rest of Company: Staircase

Climbing the stairs gives you the best possible vantage point. You can look out over all the activities in the rest of the building. A *company* of dancers is performing on one side, and a theatre *company* is setting up on the other. From where you stand, you have a perfect over-view of it all.

Further Plans: Bathroom

The bathroom is run-down and old-fashioned, but a number of *new plans* have been pinned to the walls. If these are followed, a whole new bathroom will be built. You examine the plans further, and like what you see. This room has a very bright future . . .

Any Questions?: Loft

This last area is the darkest place in the whole house. As you try to feel the way, your mind is full of *questions*: where's the light-switch? Is the floor safe? Which is the way out? The loft is like a dark cell; you could imagine a prisoner being interrogated in here . . .

As with any memory story, run back through the main points in your mind and highlight the key ideas. Walk from room to room; each new area reminds you of a new point in the speech, and any extra information can be found inside. Practise your presentation a few times from memory, and you'll be confident of a perfect performance when the real time comes to stand up and speak.

The first area, the road outside the house, reminds you of the title of the speech. You set up a desk . . . try to improve the efficiency . . . 'The Efficiency of the Workplace' is the theme of your talk.

When you've introduced the speech, pause for a moment to move into area two. There are pictures of *you* everywhere you look, and the wall contains a safe full of all your important details. Taking this as your cue, you introduce yourself to the audience.

Your next mental steps take you into the hallway. Without breaking eye-contact with the audience for a second, you move smoothly to the next topic. The carpet is also a printed till-roll; the theme here is *finances*. As you talk about the company's present financial situation, you back up your words with numbers.

The first section of the carpet is covered with paper, which has spilled out of a *vacuum*-cleaner bag: **5**. PAPER is the key-point; £**5**,000 has been spent on it this year.

In the next section you see a TELEPHONE and, as you hear the *operator's* voice – **9** – you remember that the bill for calls has already topped £**9**,000.

As you look at the final section of carpet, you see a *red boat*: **1**, **7**. The people onboard are looking very ILL, and you point out to your audience that £**17**,000 has been lost this year through illness.

Most audiences use the pauses in a speech to fidget and to lose concentration, but today they're not given a chance. You move cleanly into the kitchen, and on to your next theme: Targets.

As you're describing the need for targets, and the importance of reaching them, you feel the need for some figures. Like someone pressing a computer key, you 'activate' the left-hand target. Money pours out – £**20**,000, since you THREW – **2** – a BALL – **0** – and you tell your audience that company spending needs to be reduced by this amount.

When you activate the other target, you see yourself throwing a pan, watching the door open, then worrying about your hearing. Five numbers are released – **2**, **8**, **11**, **9** and **6** – and you announce that the target date is 28 November 1996.

The utility room is full of training equipment, so *training* is your next theme.

As you explain its importance and outline possible ideas, you glance at the clock. You're almost half-way through your route, so you need to see whether to alter your pace. If you were running drastically overtime, you could decide to give just brief mention to the remaining points, or even miss some of them out – but the firm structure of the route means that you would never lose your way.

The people in the dining-room are being given *incentives*. As you speak on this topic, you remember the shoes – **3** – and tell the audience of the pay-incentives of £**3**,000.

The lounge is full of '*practical measures*'. The items on the furniture remind you of the three key points here: a new phone system, a central paper store, and a scheme for recycling.

On the stairs, you have a wonderful view of the *rest of the company*, and talk about how *this* department compares with schemes happening elsewhere.

The diagrams fixed to the bathroom walls remind you to mention *future plans*, giving the audience all your suggestions and ideas.

Finally, as you grope around in the darkness of the loft and imagine the interrogation scheme, you're prompted to end your speech by asking for questions from the audience. Their *real* question, of course, is – 'How did he do that?'

Your whole speech was given without notes and without breaking eye-contact, yet you spoke with confidence and style, gave an ordered, logical talk, included facts and figures – even finished on time! *Mindpower* can make public speakers of us all.

LEARN YOUR LINES

If you have to learn a part in a play, memory techniques can make the whole process quicker and easier.

This is a good example of the importance of *approach*. By spending time looking at the material you have to learn, and considering the way you'll have to recall it, the very best memory methods can be found.

In a play, there are two main things you have to learn: *your* lines, and the lines before them. If you find images to go with them, and combine them in pairs, each mental scene can be linked into a story, and the whole play taken under your control.

Sometimes you'll speak just a few words; at others, long passages will have to be recalled. But however long a speech is, decide on a few key images that sum it up – either from within the lines themselves, or else pictures of your own creation. For each speech, jot down the images, then put alongside them others to sum up the 'cue line' that comes before.

If your line was, 'Come back tonight; I'll make you a meal and we can talk', the key-images might be NIGHT – perhaps the moon or the stars – and MEAL – complete with smells and tastes. The trick is to pick out words and ideas that prompt you to remember the rest of the line, pointing you in the right direction.

These techniques are designed to speed up the learning process, allowing you to start *using* the lines from memory, practising them without having to look at the script, and quickly reaching the stage where you know them by heart. Eventually you'll forget how you know them, and the images can be left aside. Their importance is as stepping-stones to knowledge.

When you've built up images for your own line, concentrate on the one before it. Look at the last few words – the ones that let you know it's time to speak. Perhaps the character says, 'It's four o'clock already; I have to go'. The key words to choose would be CLOCK and GO. Picture a cuckoo bursting out of the clock, holding a green 'GO'-sign!

The important step now is to link the two sets of images. Do this well, and when you hear the cue, you'll always be prompted to say the right lines of your own.

Imagine the 'GO'-sign bursting from the clock, then being hurled up into the night sky. It knocks against the corner of the *moon*, sending a piece of cheese falling to earth and saving you the trouble of cooking *dinner*! The cue-line is now instantly recognisable, and it points you towards the words that come next.

Look for the *next* cue-line, and do the same. Highlight more images, then link them to the last point in your imaginary story.

Perhaps the next line to listen out for is, 'Can you find a telephone and give me a call?' Going back to the story, you might imagine yourself eating dinner, and finding the cook's mobile telephone inside your pie! Images from your next line would be linked to this . . . and so it would go on, pairs of lines being turned into images and connected in a story.

As you wait for your next line, remind yourself of the story and confirm the key words to watch out for. You'll know your cue when you hear it, and the connections will act as your own personal 'prompt'. If there are lines that always trouble you, look at them in detail and learn them like the quotations in Part Two, manipulating the words until your memory takes hold.

As you practise the play from memory, the imaginary story becomes less and less important. The lines become natural, and *Mindpower*'s job has been done.

REMEMBERING MORSE

A similar process can be used to learn a system such as Morse Code. This is an entire alphabet made up entirely of dots and dashes. As you look at it, printed below, it seems the type of information which really is impossible to learn.

MORSE CODE

A: ·–	N: –·
B: –···	O: –––
C: –·–·	P: ·––·
D: –··	Q: ––·–
E: ·	R: ·–·
F: ··–·	S: ···
G: ––·	T: –
H: ····	U: ··–
I: ··	V: ···–
J: ·–––	W: ·––
K: –·–	X: –··–
L: ·–··	Y: –·––
M: ––	Z: ––··

It may *look* impossible but, in fact, Morse Code can be learned in a few minutes. It takes longer to know the codes instinctively, and to be able to 'translate' both ways; but by committing them to memory, you're able to start using them straight away.

To begin with, the process will be slow. You'll have to think through the memory-links carefully, conjuring up pictures and working out all the dashes and dots. But soon you'll speed up, growing confident with your instinctive knowledge of this complicated code.

The way to learn Morse Code is easy, and splits into two clear parts. The first involves learning 'call-signs'.

Each letter of the alphabet has an official code-word – you'll find that you know a lot of them already. These are used for clarity and accuracy in radio calls, and are all very memorable words.

A good way to remember them is to link them together in a story of their own. All twenty-six call-signs are printed below, followed by suggestions for a memorable tale.

A: ALPHA. Your story might start with 'ALF' Garnett! His latest television programme is just coming to an end.
B: BRAVO. 'Bravo!', cries the audience, delighted with his performance.
C: CHARLIE. The next programme catches your eye; it's a documentary about Prince Charles.

D: DELTA. Charles is shown involved in a poker game. He cries out, complaining that he's been '*dealt a* bad hand . . .!' 'Delta' is also the name of an airline, so perhaps the game is taking place onboard a plane.

E: ECHO. The prince's cry rings around the cabin . . .

F: FOXTROT. When the plane lands, the prince's horse is waiting for him on the runway. He *trots* off in pursuit of a *fox*.

G: GOLF. The hunt bounds over a golf-course, and the prince climbs down for a quick round.

H: HOTEL. It's dark by the time he's finished, and he decides to spend the night in the golf-club's own hotel.

L: INDIA. The theme of the place is 'India'. Indian paintings hang on the wall . . . the restaurant serves nothing but curry . . . the whole building is modelled on the Taj Mahal . . .

J: JULIET. Entertainment is provided for the prince. A play is about to start, and Juliet waits anxiously on the balcony . . .

K: KILO. Unfortunately, the actress playing Juliet is a couple of kilos overweight, and the whole balcony crashes to the ground.

L: LIMA. Prince Charles is told that the nearest Shakespearean performance is in Lima, Peru. He decides to go . . .

M: MIKE. Grabbing the *mic*-rophone on his walkie-talkie, he calls his personal pilot.

N: NOVEMBER. The pilot tells him that it will take until November to fly to Peru, and gives an impressive speech about the perils of the journey.

O: OSCAR. His performance is so good, in fact, that he wins an Oscar!

P: PAPA. In his acceptance speech, he thanks his father: 'Papa!'

Q: QUEBEC. He calls all his family up on stage. There are so many of them that they '*queue back*' all the way to Canada . . .

R: ROMEO. Through the crowd bursts Romeo! It looks as though the Prince might be in luck after all . . .

S: SIERRA. Slightly out of character, Romeo jumps into a *Sierra* car and speeds into the distance. Suddenly, he screeches to a halt. He's heard some music.

T: TANGO. A street-band are playing lively rhythms, and crowds of people are dancing the tango. It turns out to be a dancing competition.

U: UNIFORM. You can only enter if you're wearing a uniform. Some of the men are dressed as policemen – others are sailors or traffic-wardens.

V: VICTOR. The winner of the competition is finally chosen. He lifts his arms in the air, the true victor.

W: WHISKY. His prize is a huge bottle of whisky. He drinks it in one go, and promptly collapses.

X: X-RAY. The man is rushed to hospital for a series of emergency X-rays.

Y: YANKEE. When he regains consciousness, he seems very confused. He sings 'Yankee Doodle Dandy' at the top of his voice, and thinks that *he* is an American.

Z: ZULU. The doctors give up, saying there's nothing more they can do for him. His last hope is a Zulu witch-doctor . . .

Since the list is in alphabetical order, there's a clue for each new word. When Prince Charles' plane lands, the next word begins with F – Foxtrot. What does he do next? The word must begin with G – he plays Golf.

Practise reading through the list from memory, and in just a few minutes you'll know the twenty-six call-signs in full.

These call-signs are useful to know in their own right, but they also become your prompts for learning Morse Code.

The system is simple. Each set of dots and dashes is turned into a word, and that word is connected with the appropriate call-sign. When you want to know the Morse Code for 'T', for example, you remember the call-sign – 'India' – then recall a key-word connected with it. This key-word is broken back down into dashes and dots.

In order to create these twenty-six new words, turn a **dot** into any letter in the *first* half of the alphabet, A – M, and a **dash** into any one from the *second* half: N – Z. By choosing the letters well you can create appropriate words.

Suggestions

A: .–   IT   (Call-sign: ALPHA)
This code demonstrates the system perfectly. The dot becomes a letter from the first half of the alphabet – I – and the dash one from the second half – T.

IT is appropriate for a number of reasons. 'Alpha', is the word for 'one' in the Greek alphabet – a single thing, 'it'. Alf Garnett always points to other people, nationalities, religions: 'It . . . It . . . It.' And the television character A.L.F. – 'Alien Life-Form' – is a non-human, indescribable 'it'!

B: –... SAID (Call-sign: BRAVO)
Four symbols this time, and four more letters – one from the second part of the alphabet, and three from the first.

The call-sign here, 'Bravo', only has meaning when it's *said*. Imagine telling a friend about your wonderful stage-performance – how, after the show, everyone '*said* "Bravo!"'

C: –.–. PINK (Call-sign: CHARLIE)
Perhaps the 'Charlie' you think of is Charlie Brown in the *Peanuts* cartoon-strip. His name may be Brown, but, like all the other characters, his skin is definitely *pink* – a very *deep* shade of pink when he's embarrassed!

D: –.. PAD (Call-sign: DELTA)
Imagine a huge jumbo-jet from Delta airlines touching down on a tiny landing *pad* . . .

E: . E (Call-sign: ECHO)
Since this letter has just one dot, you don't have much choice! By making it into 'E', you can imagine hearing an echo dying away into the distance, until the 'E' is all that's left: 'Echo . . . echo . . . ech . . . ec . . . e'

F: ..–. HARM (Call-sign: FOXTROT)
When the hunting-horses trot after the fox, their aim is to *harm* it . . .

G: ––. SUB (Call-sign: GOLF)
'Subs' – substitutes – are usually only found in football, so it's quite a surprise when one jumps up off the bench to replace an injured *golfer*.

H: .... FEED (Call-sign: HOTEL)
The main aim of a good hotel is to *feed* its guests in style.

I: .. BC (Call-sign: INDIA)
Imagine wandering around the ancient ruins of India. Your guide book tells you that everything here dates back to BC

J: .--- MUST DUST (Call-sign: JULIET)
Her family can't allow it, but, in Shakespeare's play, Juliet *must* marry the man of her choice. To avoid confusion with 'Romeo' – R – perhaps you also think of the young Juliet being forced to do a boring household chore – to DUST.

K: -.- VAT (Call-sign: KILO)
Imagine pouring *kilo* after kilo of flour or sugar into a huge vat. Perhaps you're also charged VAT on each kilo.

L: .-.. COME (Call-sign: LIMA)
The call-sign here, Lima, is the capital of Peru. Maybe the Peruvian tourist-board has just launched a campaign attracting people to 'COME to LIMA!' . . ..

M: -- TV (Call-sign: MIKE)
Most 'mikes' – microphones – you see are being held or worn by people on TV. Also, if you've read *Charlie and the Chocolate Factory*, you'll know that there's a character in the book called 'Mike TV'.

N: -. PG (Call-sign: NOVEMBER)
In cinemas, 'PG' means 'parental guidance'. Imagine these initials being used for one of the most dangerous events of the year: Bonfire Night, NOVEMBER 5.

O: --- WON (Call-sign: OSCAR)
At the Oscar ceremony, every award has to be *won*. There's great excitement every time someone says those famous words: 'And the Oscar has been WON by . . .'

P: .--. JOBS (Call-sign: PAPA)
Picture PAPA doing JOBS around the house . . .

Q: --.- TRIP (Call-sign: QUEBEC)
Imagine taking a TRIP to QUEBEC – maybe even going all the way to Canada just for the day!

R: .–.   DOG   (Call-sign: ROMEO)

Picture a disastrous performance of *Romeo and Juliet*. The tension of the balcony scene is ruined when Juliet hears ROMEO's DOG barking . . .

S: ...   CAB   (Call-sign: SIERRA)

Perhaps you buy a SIERRA car purely to turn it into a taxi-CAB. Imagine fixing up a glass partition, to separate the back seats from the actual *cab*.

T: –   T (T-BONE/T-JUNCTION . . .)   (Call-sign: TANGO)

As with 'E' earlier on, one symbol gives you little choice. Imagine performing your tango in the most dangerous place you can find – the middle of a *T*-JUNCTION! You break off only to munch your way through a *T*-BONE steak . . .

U: ..–   KIT   (Call-sign: UNIFORM)

What better word for UNIFORM than KIT?

V: ...–   GAIN   (Call-sign: VICTOR)

To be a VICTOR you need to GAIN victory. Perhaps you also gain territory, riches, and fame . . .

W: .––   COP   (Call-sign: WHISKY)

In the days of Prohibition, the last person a WHISKY-drinker wanted to see was a COP.

X: –..–   PAIN   (Call-sign: X-RAY)

The doctor takes an X-RAY to find out the reason for your PAIN.

Y: –.––   VAST   (Call-sign: YANKEE)

America, home of the YANKEES, is a VAST country. Imagine setting out to walk from coast to coast . . .

Z: ––..   STAG   (Call-sign: ZULU)

Picture the scene as a group of ZULU-warriors hunts down a magnificent STAG.

When you've read through the suggestions, visualising the new words and confirming the links, you're ready to start using Morse Code.

To change any letter into its coded form, begin by remembering the call-sign. *H*, for example, is HOTEL.

Next, use this prompt to remind you of the key-word. The aim of a hotel is to FEED its guests . . .

Concentrate on this key-word. Turn any of its letters which come from the first half of the alphabet into a **dot**, and any from the second half into a **dash**. In this example, all four letters are from the *first* half, so the word FEED represents four dots. The Morse Code for *H* is: ....

As another example, imagine you wanted to include the letter *X* in your message. The call-sign for *X* is X-RAY . . . this reminds you of the key-word PAIN . . . and the last step is to turn the letters back into dots and dashes.

P is from the last half of the alphabet, hence –

A is from the first half – . – as is *I*: .

N, finally, appears in the second half: –

The Morse Code for *X* is: –..–

As you begin to use the code from memory, your pace and fluency will quickly improve. Soon, you'll be so used to turning letters into symbols that you'll be able to handle the code in reverse, seeing the dots and dashes and recalling the key-words. Eventually, you'll forget the key-words altogether – the code will have become instinctive knowledge, as familiar to you as the alphabet itself.

Without *Mindpower* techniques you could still learn Morse Code, but it would take hours of boring repetition before you could even start to use it. Creating vivid pictures and scenes helps to keep your interest alive, and gives you the stepping-stones you need to move quickly towards fluency. You can also have fun along the way!

THINGS-TO-DO LISTS

The techniques for learning Morse Code demonstrate the importance of organisation. Through an ordered approach, the material is moulded into a logical, memorable form. And, as with the number system, the real work only has to be done once. By investing time in remembering call-signs and key-words, you create a resource for yourself that can be used with ease, whenever the opportunities arise.

The more you use the *Mindpower System*, the more ordered your whole approach will become. At the start of a week, for example, it's possible to make a mental list of important appointments and 'things to do', then *use* this list as the week goes on.

Begin by jotting down on paper the appointments and tasks for the coming week. Deal with the appointments first, by turning each one into a set of numbers.

Every appointment becomes just five numbers: four for the time – 16.30, say, or 09.15 – and then one for the day of the week: 1 for Sunday, 2 for Monday, and so on. For once, you don't have to worry about remembering the date – day, month and year – since the week ahead is made up of just seven days.

Turn each set of numbers into a vivid scene. The number system, explained in Part Three, gives you all the material you need. Choose images that will help you create a link with the *reason* for the appointment.

Spend a few minutes connecting the pictures with the appointments themselves. You might be due to see your accountant at 14.50 on Tuesday, the 3rd day. The numbers – **1, 4, 5, 0** and **3** – could become 'WRITE on the TABLE, then CLEAN the BOWL of FLOWERS'.

Picture yourself sitting in your accountant's office and carrying out these actions. Perhaps you write on the table by accident, then offer to do some cleaning-up to make amends . . .

Each of the week's appointments becomes a combined, interlinked image. When you've finished bringing them all to life, the final step is to link them.

The easiest way to do this is to make use of a memory-route. If your list contains more than ten items, simply move into another route. You could easily create two routes especially for this purpose, using them each week and then mentally cleaning them out before the next.

Concentrate on each appointment in turn, fixing its images into an area on the route. When you've finished, your whole week will be planned out neatly and stored in your mind. To recall your next appointment, simply walk to the next mental space and retrieve all the details.

Printed below is a list of seven appointments for the coming week. Once again, the route used in the suggestions that follow is the 'house', described in detail in Part One.

APPOINTMENTS

10.45, Monday: MEET BANK-MANAGER
12.30, Monday: LUNCH MEETING with TOM
17.30, Tuesday: SQUASH GAME
14.15, Wednesday: MEET BILL at AIRPORT
21.30, Wednesday: COUNCIL MEETING
09.15, Thursday: PRESENTATION to DEPARTMENT
11.20, Friday: PLANNING MEETING

Suggestions

10.45, Monday: Meet Bank-Manager.
The five numbers in this example are: **1, 0, 4, 5** and **2** – the first four for the time, and the fifth for the day, Monday.

Step into the first area on the route – the pathway in front of the house. A purple snooker table has been set up – but, before you and your bank-manager can have a game, you have to clean away a few bird-droppings . . .

Your bank-manager wins, and you owe him even *more* money. He wins the next game, too, and soon you're so poor that you have to give him the snooker table to pay off your debts . . .

The BANK-MANAGER is present to remind you of the reason for this appointment, and the scene itself contains all the details you need. See again the PURPLE – **1** – SNOOKER – **0** – TABLE – **4**, and remember CLEANING-away – **5** – the BIRD-droppings – **2**.

You have to meet your bank-manager at 10.45 on Monday, the second day of the week.

12.30, Monday: Lunch Meeting with Tom.
Here, the numbers are **1, 2, 3, 0** and **2**. The location is the front porch.

This room has been turned into a bird-watchers hide. Imagine sitting in there with Tom, eating your lunch, and watching for activity in a bird box fixed to the window-ledge. You're halfway through the meal when something happens.

A COLOURFUL – **1** – BIRD – **2** – WALKS – **3** – into the EMPTY – **0** – BIRD-BOX –**2**.

You and Tom discuss this beautiful creature as you finish eating

If you hadn't met Tom yet, or found it difficult to picture him, you could include a set of *tom-toms* in the scene, or a *toma*hawk, to remind you of the name. Always be aware of any possibilities for confusion, and add extra images to make the ideas specific.

When you return to this part of the route, you'll remember that you're due to have lunch with Tom at 12.30 on Monday.

17.05, Tuesday: Squash Game.

For this scene you move into the hallway, the third area on the route. Not surprisingly, it's been turned into a long, thin squash-court. You have to be careful not to hit the ball against any of the ornaments on the shelf nearby – or to hurt any of the people walking through!

The game halts again and again as people need to walk past. In one especially long pause, you decide to take out your book and fill the time with some reading. The book is a novel about the sea – *Moby Dick*, perhaps, or *Jaws*. While you read, you juggle absent-mindedly with some newly cleaned shoes from the hall cupboard

You READ – **1** – about the SEA – **7**, and JUGGLED – **0** – the CLEAN – **5** – SHOES – **3**. All of this happened in the hallway squash-court, so your next game of squash is at 17.05 on Tuesday.

14.15. Wednesday: Meet Bill at the Airport.

The next area on the route is the kitchen. Someone has taken a *jumbo-jet* apart; hundreds of bits are spread out on newspapers, and parts of the engine are being cleaned in the sink!

Whoever this mechanic is, he has written notes all over the kitchen table, and there are even a few words scrawled on the chair you cleaned this morning. Make a note of it all, so you can give him the *bill* . . .

The bits of plane remind you about the airport, and the *bill* even confirms the name of the person you're due to meet. The rest of the information is clear to see: someone WROTE – **1** – on the TABLE – **4**, and even WROTE – **1** – on the newly CLEANED – **5** – CHAIR – **4**! Your trip to the airport is at 14.15 on the fourth day, Wednesday.

21.30. Wednesday: Council Meeting.

Your next mental steps take you into the utility area. Here, a large, round table has been set up, and the council meeting has just started. The chairman is having to shout to be heard above the noise of the washing-machine . . .

When it's your turn to speak, you decide to do something special to attract everyone's attention. You THROW – **2** – some COLOURFUL – **1** – FLOWERS – **3** – on to the ROUND – **0** – TABLE **4**.

When you return to this stage of the route, the information is clear. The next council meeting starts at 21.30 on Wednesday.

09.15. Thursday: Presentation to Department.

Move through to the dining-room. Sitting around the table are all your work colleagues, waiting for you to give your talk. A white board has been set up on one side, and you collect your thoughts before starting to speak.

Suddenly, you notice that one of your staff-members is wearing a football shirt! This is hardly appropriate dress for work. He tells you that his other clothes have been ruined by the company dry-cleaner, and he hands you a note from her to explain. It sound like a very poor excuse, and you call in the cleaner herself to find out what's going on . . .

The story began when you saw the FOOTBALL – **0** – SHIRT – **9**, and continued as you were handed a LETTER – **1** – from the CLEANER – **5**, prompting you to call in the CLEANER – **5** – herself. The five numbers here are **0, 9, 1, 5** and **5**, so your next department-presentation is at 09.15 on the fifth day, Thursday.

11.20. Friday: Planning Meeting

The last area of the route you need to use is the seventh stage, the lounge. Another meeting is happening here, so, to set it apart from the others, imagine the walls are covered with complicated plans and projections. You all speak in hushed tones, huddling together as you hatch your plans for the future.

Before you address the meeting, you read through your own plans. When you feel you know them well, you throw them into a hollow kettle-drum lying next to the sofa. It looks like the plans involve some loud music . . .

When you return to this room, simply remember what you did when you were here last. You READ – **1** – your PLANS – **1**, then THREW – **2** – them into a HOLLOW – **0** – KETTLE-DRUM – **6**. The planning meeting is at 11.20 on Friday.

Spend a final few moments looking back through the route. All your plans for the week are now at your fingertips. Every room reminds you of a particular appointment – the event, the time, and the day.

You can easily recall the whole list if need be, or else pinpoint particular items. You can find out what you're doing immediately before or after any appointment and, if need be, add extra details to the scenes.

Perhaps a special guest will be joining you for the planning meeting on Friday. Simply turn his or her name into a picture, and include it amongst all the plans and instruments.

If you think of an important point to raise at the council meeting on Wednesday evening, just turn it into a picture and combine it with the utility-room scene.

Think how useful it would be to have all the week's details at your fingertips. You could set up new appointments without having to check your diary, and make it easier for yourself to use your time efficiently. Most importantly of all, you would never again forget to be in the right place at the right time!

REMEMBERING *ANYTHING*

As well as important appointments, Mindpower techniques can also be used to recall the most mundane details of everyday life.

To remember jobs and errands, ideas and thoughts – all the things that threaten to vanish from your mind almost as quickly as they've appeared – choose a particular place to *fix* them.

Think of a place you pass several times a day. Perhaps it's the door-frame of your house, a chair outside your office, or a cupboard in your shop. Make this a mental 'storehouse' – the place where you 'hang' thoughts, 'things-to-do', scraps of information. Anything that you need to remember can be left here, to be found again when you need it.

Every time you come up with a piece of information to be remembered – *'take that book to the library'*, *'water that plant'*, *'call to see Mrs Smith'* – design an image to represent it. Make it as simple as possible: the library-book . . . your plant, drenched in water . . . even Mrs Smith herself.

The next step is to fix it into position. Spend a few seconds considering the most memorable way to anchor the image to your chosen place.

Perhaps your 'place' is a doorway. The library book could be nailed to the wooden frame – at head height, allowing you to glance at the title as you pass.

Your plant would grow well twined around the *top* of the frame. Picture a trickle of water dripping down from the roots on to the head of someone below . . .

If your 'place' was a cupboard, you might lead Mrs Smith inside . . . and lock her in! Picture her sitting there in the dark, amongst all your other memorable images: a huge tin of cat-food, glued down to the shelf to keep it upright – *'feed the cat'*; a brand-new football, hanging from the ceiling on a string – *'take Billy to his football match'*; a slightly smelly bag of rubbish – *'put the bins out . . .'*

Whenever you walk past the real place – the doorway, the cupboard, the field – make a point of remembering the images you've put there. This helps solve a common problem: 'I didn't remember I even *had* anything to remember . . .!' By checking for reminders each time you walk by, you'll never forget the things you've resolved to do. Simply concentrate on an image, and the ideas behind it will come flooding back.

As well as checking your mental 'storeroom' whenever you walk past the real location, try to get into the habit of returning to it a few times each day in your imagination. The more often you go back, the more natural the whole process will become.

When an image is finished with, simply remove it – sweep it off the shelf . . . cut it down from its string . . . pull out all the nails. Most reminders will only need to stay for a few days at the most, and your memory will soon accustom itself to holding on to the images for just as long as they're required.

Rather than racking your brains, trying desperately to remember what it is that you *should* be doing, you'll always be able to return to a familiar mental 'area', and look around for the reminders you've left.

Give your memory all the help you can, and it will never let you down.

PRACTICE MAKES PERFECT

The mind is like any muscle: the more you use it, the more comfortable it feels. Forget all the myths about memory fading with age. Keep using your mind, exercising it and making it work, and your memory powers will stay alive.

Whenever there's some word or fact 'on the tip of your tongue', keep thinking about it until the memory reappears. Take the positive approach; assume that your memory *will* work, and feel duly proud when it does.

Try to remember your dreams. During the day, if certain images from the dream flash back to you, try to fill in more and more of the gaps, using any associations that come to mind.

Scientists say that we all dream whenever we slip into deep sleep, but how often do you remember your dreamtime adventures? I remember my dreams in detail, long into the day, and perhaps that's only because I assume that I *can* . . .

The more accustomed you are to remembering your dreams, the more skilful you'll be at creating powerfully imaginative stories. Dreams prove that our minds can conjure up images that seem solid and real, and they provide a glimpse of our potential for creating fascinating characters, wonderful scenes and memorable stories.

Mindpower is all about using that potential when we're wide awake, giving new dimensions to even the dullest material. It's about realising that our memories are our most precious resources, capable of being trained to do anything we want and to absorb everything we need.

Use your memory whenever you can. Always be aware of opportunities for benefiting from its power. The more often you use a particular technique, the more natural it will become, and your own confidence will grow.

The *Mindpower System* can be applied to anything. Its principles allow you to take any sort of information under your control, and to feel confident of remembering it for as long as necessary. Instead of telling everyone what a bad memory you've got, start relishing its power.

A good memory helps you to pass exams, giving you a firm foundation on which to build, and allowing you the time and freedom to be creative.

A good memory helps with social skills – remembering names, handling guest-lists, giving speeches.

A good memory helps in business, prompting you to order your time, and making it easy to give talks and presentations with efficiency and style.

A good memory helps you every day – with shopping-lists, addresses, birthdays, 'things-to-do'.

With the *Mindpower System*, a good memory is within *everyone's* reach.